The NATU

FOUNDATIONS FOR

With flowing tail, and flying mane,
Wide nostrils never stretched by pain,
Mouths bloodless to the bit or rein,
And feet that iron never shod,
And flanks unscarred by spur or rod,
A thousand horse, the wild, the free,
Like waves that follow o'er the sea.
        Lord Byron

RAL HORSE

NATURAL HORSEMANSHIP

by Jaime Jackson

illustrated by Larry Lindahl

star ridge publishing

SECOND EDITION
ISBN 0-9658007-0-9 (previously ISBN 0-87358-536-4)
Library of Congress Catalog Card Number 97-62094
Manufactured in the United States of America
Cataloging-in-Publication Data
Jackson, Jaime.
    The natural horse : foundations for natural horsemanship / Jaime Jackson; illustrated by
Larry Lindahl. -- 2nd ed.
    192 p.
    Includes bibliographical references and index.
    ISBN 0-9658007-9 (pbk.) : $24.95
    1. Horses.   2. Wild horses.   3. Hoofs.   4. Horses--Paces, gaits, etc.   5. Horsemanship.   I. Title.
SF285.J28   1997
636.1--dc20   97-62094
                                                                                        CIP

Book design: Larry Lindahl
Typography: Jennifer Swaffar
Printing: Publishers Press
Cover photos © 1992 by Jim Hansen

Permissions have been obtained for use of the following photographs:
Page 3: Wild horses entering corral courtesy U.S. Department of Interior, Bureau of Land Management.
Pages 5, 6, 7: Courtesy U.S. Department of Interior, Bureau of Land Management.
Page 11: *Eohippus*, by H.S. Rice, neg. no. 312630, courtesy Department of Library Services, American
    Museum of Natural History.
Page 23: Helicopter roundup of wild horses near Susanville, California. Photograph by Bill Tarpening,
    courtesy U.S. Department of Interior, Bureau of Land Management.
Page 86: From *Horseshoeing Theory and Hoof Care*, by Leslie Emery, Jim Miller, and Nyles Van Hoosen.
    Courtesy Lea & Febiger.
Page 87: From *A Handbook of Horseshoeing*, by J. A. Dollar. New York: William R. Jenkins, Co., 1898.
Page 92: Half-pass to the right from *The Complete Training of Horse and Rider*, by Alois Podjahsky.
    Courtesy Doubleday, a division of Bantam, Doubleday, Dell Publishing Group, Inc.
Page 117: Courtesy Les Emery.
Page 133: Courtesy the *American Farriers Journal*.
Page 138: Courtesy The American Horse Protection Association, Washington, D.C.
Page 146: Courtesy People for the Ethical Treatment of Animals, Inc., Washington, D.C.
Additional photographs are credited throughout the book. All remaining photographs were taken by the
author.

CONTENTS

FORWARD

THE YEAR 2001 has arrived and nearly 20 years have passed since I first entered wild horse country to lay the foundations of this book. Although slow in coming, *The Natural Horse* has had a definite and positive impact, even though the average horse owner may not yet realize the connection. For example, the "natural trim" — an important cornerstone of hoof care now familiar to many horse owners, and increasingly so in recent years — was unheard of before the first edition of *TNH* was published in 1992. The wild horse hoof described faithfully in this text has defined the very meaning of natural hoof care, and the natural trim. And the animal may yet start a revolution in natural horse care — time will tell. I know my thinking, and horse care practices, have changed. One of these changes has ironically put me at loggerheads with one of the principal hoof management practices advocated in this book! *Horseshoeing.* But rather than delete the entire shoeing segment, and then face the monumental task of re-writing and integrating the alternative to shoeing — "de-shoeing" and "high performance barefootedness" — I elected to leave the main text as it is. But with this caveat: shoeing horses is something I used to do, but no longer practice because I believe it harms the hooves, and because it is entirely unnecessary. Otherwise, the trimming guidelines, the descriptions of the wild horse feet, and the suggestions for boarding horses to maximize hoof health, have not been abandoned and, to this day, I manage my clients' hooves based upon this information.

What then are "de-shoeing" and "high performance barefootedness"? They mean removing the horse's shoes, conditioning the hooves for barefootedness, and then riding the horse without shoes. This may come as a shock to many readers, but it is the true foundation for natural hoof care. The fact is, horses don't need horseshoes at all if we provide them with bona fide natural hoof care. To help horse owners bridge the gap, I've written a new book, *Horse Owners Guide to Natural Hoof Care*, and three learning videos. These and related educational materials and products are discussed in the new Resource section at the end of this book.

With this fourth printing of *TNH*, I am delighted to convey another important piece of information. Many horse owners, possibly in the thousands, have now taken up their own hoof care as a result of the "natural care" revolution. Some farriers — far too few — have joined them, turning their hard worked backs on the centuries' old tradition of blacksmithing for the promise of a better way. Natural hoof care just makes sense, they've discovered, and from their ranks is evolving a new generation of natural hoof care practitioners. I am involved personally with many of these persons, and efforts are underway to form an official organization that promotes the new hoof care order. More on this, hopefully, in the next edition of this book.

So I welcome you to the world and adventure of the natural horse. This book is my story about what I know of it. The natural world of the horse is a spiritual place with much to teach us. It commands our respect. In mysterious ways, the wild ones seem to cross our paths to impart what we go to learn, even when we've failed to frame the relevant questions. Indeed, conjecture is transformed in wild horse country by tangible and palpable truths. How do they take care of their teeth without the vet to float them? How do they control the ubiquitous digestive parasites thought to be harmful to equids? What if colic strikes? Exactly how much wear can their bare hooves endure? Why is there no founder or navicular? Why do they *piaffe*? Do they back? When do they sleep, how do they sleep, where do they sleep? Do they interbreed? What is a herd? When do they die? How do they die? Do they prosper without humans? Do we need them more than they need us? I know of no person who has gone among the wild ones with half an open mind, to return empty handed, without something that has elevated their understanding of the animal. Indeed, I'm drawn to the words of another horseman who went among the last great herds of wild horses on our Great Plains before their extermination along with the buffalo . . .

> It is noticeable that the equine race, in its wild state, has none of the ills of the species domesticated. The sorrows of horse-flesh are the fruits of civilization. By the study and imitation of Nature's methods, we could greatly increase the usefulness of these valuable servants, and remove temptation from the paths of many men who lead blameless lives, except in the single matter of horse-trades. [W.E. Webb. *Buffalo Land: An Authentic Narrative of the Adventures and Misadventures of a Late Scientific and Sporting Party with the Full Descriptions of the Indian As He Is, the Habits of the Buffalo, Wolf, and Wild Horse.* 1872]

ACKNOWLEDGMENTS

AS IN THE first edition of *The Natural Horse*, I thank foremost the wild, free-roaming horse. The wild horse is the central pillar upon which the School of Natural Horsemanship is built, so it is fitting that our tradition pay homage where it is principally due.

My wife Nancy, my partner in life, works closely with me in every detail upon all fronts and this work bears her imprint commensurately. Ironically, she is not a horse enthusiast, has never ridden, and entertains no interest whatsoever in the animal save that it be treated with the same respect and dignity that all of the Creator's life forms deserve. But her intelligence and wisdom match her deep sense of caring and morality, so I'm always at my most attentive edge when she speaks that I may improve my own insights and become a better advocate of natural horsemanship.

Mr. Leslie Emery, principal author of *Horseshoeing Theory and Hoof Care*, will forever be in close confidence. *The Natural Horse* undoubtedly would never have been written had it not been for Les's inspirational work as well as his input both as a horse professional, philosopher, and friend. This book bears his indelible mark.

Others mentioned in the first edition are thanked again here: Carmoreau Hatier, Phil Shurden, Pat Deamer, Karl Mikolka, Bob Peters, Phillip Deer—all influencing your author in diverse ways.

The Natural Horse has passed from beneath the auspices of Northland Publishing to Star Ridge Publishing. Managing Editor Betty Albrecht, who received my unpublished manuscript in 1990, and created a real book from it two years later, passed away from a sudden and tragic bout with cancer shortly after it was released in 1992. Quietly, from this small corner of the present edition, *The Natural Horse* is dedicated to her.

LEARNING FROM THE NATURAL HORSE

Jim Hansen

Introduction

MY WORK AS A FARRIER (horseshoer) began nearly sixteen years ago—first shoeing my own horses and later those of my friends. In time, this activity, not at all by design, culminated in a rather substantial, full-time business in northern California. Over the years, I came to realize that there are as many ways to trim and shoe a horse as there are to ride one. Indeed, in the horse world, shoeing methods are usually linked to the working requirements of the horse; for example, we find racing Thoroughbreds shod one way and draft horses another. But always troubling me was the uncertainty as to what really constituted a naturally shaped hoof and the natural locomotion of the horse. What had nature, through selection of the equine species, intended for the horse's hooves and locomotion? While a few horse-care professionals I met or read about speculated on this subject, I was not able to find a clear description anywhere of natural hoof shape and natural equine locomotion based upon tangible evidence.

Years ago, I heard stories about large numbers of wild horses roaming at liberty in Nevada and elsewhere within the surrounding Great Basin area of the western United States (Figure i-1). Like most people in the horse world, I knew very little about these animals, except what I had heard in the form of rumors, seen on television, or read in the newspapers and Old West stories. Still, the idea came to me one day that perhaps the hooves and locomotive behavior of the wild horse might exemplify the shape characteristics and locomotive style that nature had intended for the modern horse. As a horseman and farrier, I felt especially qualified to examine their hooves, observe their locomotive behavior, and report my findings. Two weeks later, I found myself miles off the nearest maintained road, deep within the high desert rangelands of western Nevada: wild horse country.

My first stay among the wild horses of Nevada lasted less than a week. I learned quickly—from a distance—that these animals, which always seemed to travel about in small groups of four to twelve, were often flighty and not easily approached, at least not close enough to look at their hooves. In most instances, the monarchs, or breeding stallions, were extremely protective and moved quickly to drive their harems beyond my reach. From what I did see, I was impressed by the apparent good health of these animals, including what appeared to be an absence of lameness. In this respect, my observations tended to conflict with the many tall tales I had heard about lame,

FIGURE i-1

Wild horse and burro areas in the West.

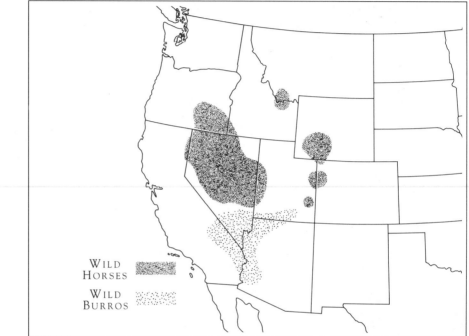

WILD HORSES

WILD BURROS

malnourished, and stunted wild horses with crooked legs, tattered hides, and chipped and disfigured hooves. Peering hour after hour into my binoculars revealed the opposite. The monarchs, for example, were often quite large (in excess of 1,100 pounds) and robust, very well muscled, and sound. The mares, while normally somewhat smaller (700 to 1,100 pounds), were also healthy, sound, muscular, and otherwise well developed.

Constantly on the move, either running at play (or from me) or peacefully meandering along as they grazed, these animals penetrated nearly every gorge and ridge of the vast desert landscape, including the steep, rocky mountain slopes where I literally had to watch my every step. From what I could see, their heavily worn hooves appeared to reflect the abrasiveness of the terrain through which they moved. From a farrier's standpoint, this meant that they bore little or no excess growth anywhere. I also noticed two basic hoof shapes cast everywhere upon the earth, which I suspected then to be front and hind.

Finally, it became clear that I must take the necessary steps to look more closely—and safely—at the hooves of these creatures. Before long, I made arrangements with officials of the Bureau of Land Management (BLM) to conduct a thorough examination of the hooves of over 100 wild, free-roaming horses. At the time, I did not realize the formidable and lengthy task that lay ahead. It would take years of observing wild horses in their natural habitat to begin to understand the complexities of natural hoof shape and the locomotive behavior from which that shape arises.

ENTER THE BLM

For many years, the wild horse has been the center of much controversy, a matter that is probably best understood in its historical context (discussed briefly in chapter 1). Important to this discussion is the BLM's task of removing systematically thousands of wild horses from public lands—a management practice instituted in 1971 that has pleased some and outraged others. Despite the varying feelings toward this practice, I was able to use it as a way to safely carry out my examinations. As newly captured horses were removed from the open range, I was there to examine them. All of these animals came from the Great Basin area, with most coming from Nevada and northern California, where my range observations were to center for the next four years. The actual task of capturing the horses was somewhat complicated and required the strict cooperation of numerous personnel. Following is a short description of the procedure.

To start, an airborne wrangler in a helicopter carefully drove the animals toward a predesignated site. Here, a temporary corral and chute were constructed to receive the horses. Wranglers, hidden from view, waited patiently and silently nearby on horseback. Next, specially trained horses, called traitors by the wranglers, were released just ahead and in the path of

the approaching wild horses. Generally, the traitors would lure the wild horses into the corral where the wranglers, taking up the rear, promptly sealed off the entrance. Last, the horses were driven by the wranglers through loading chutes and into large vans and trailers suitable for transporting livestock. Never to roam in the wild again, the animals were shipped from the rangelands to several of the BLM's permanent, wild horse processing and holding facilities. Unfortunately, some of these facilities are now greatly overcrowded, and the fate of many detained wild horses remains in limbo; too few are adopted into private ownership.[1]

The facility where I measured the hooves of captured horses is known as the Litchfield Corrals, located twenty miles east of Susanville, California. Wild horses and burros captured by officials and wranglers of the BLM are processed here for sale to the public under the government's Adopt-A-Horse Program. The neatly maintained facility consists of several large pasture turnouts, which surround an impressive labyrinth of passageways, chutes, and holding pens. At the heart of this complex network is the central roping pen, where teams of wranglers work together to isolate and restrain individual horses for identification and veterinary care. This is where I examined the animals' hooves.

The manner of processing horses at the Litchfield Corrals has actually changed since the year of my hoof survey (1984). Currently, most horses are driven into a narrow chute, where their movements are restricted just enough to enable the BLM staff to carry out their tasks. This method is thought to be less stressful for the animals. But because the animals are still able to stand on all four legs, they are not sufficiently immobilized to permit a close and safe examination of hooves. Previously, horses were restrained by roping, a technique that made my work feasible.

First, wranglers worked to separate small groups of horses from the main herds in the outer pastures. Driven to the central corral, individual

Young stallion with paint markings pursued by wranglers. Headers and heelers secure horse with ropes, stretched out on ground. I was able to measure, examine, and photograph over 200 sets of wild horse hooves just removed from the outback.

horses were then isolated and pursued by two or three mounted ropers. Coordinating their skills, the wranglers managed to secure each animal's front and hindlegs in pairs. This left the horse stretched out upon the ground between the two roping horses in a relatively immobile state. At this time, the horse was "aged" by dental examination, treated for parasites, branded, gelded if a stallion over a certain age, and otherwise checked for good health by a veterinarian.[2] The weight of the horse was also estimated at this time. Because of the horse's sensitive nature and its predisposition to shock while restrained, the above procedures had to be completed within five to ten minutes, which is exactly how long I had to examine the hooves of each horse. On the average, BLM wranglers were able to process twenty-five to thirty horses in an eight-hour work day.

VALUE OF THE WILD HORSE

For me, this investigation proved to be both humbling and rewarding. The wild horse, whatever we may think of it—pest, romantic spirit of the Old West, or just another horse—is full of valuable information, free for the tak-

ing. I have learned that there is such a thing as natural hoof shape. In addition, there is a natural way in which the horse is meant to move. To this day, I am awed at how such powerful animals can move so quickly and forcefully over difficult terrain and yet experience little or no lameness, while generating what I have come to appreciate as the perfect hoof. Keep in mind that the natural locomotion of the horse, while uniform in terms of the animal's natural gaits (i.e., walk, trot, and canter), is diverse in terms of individual locomotive styles—reflecting not only the great demands of the animal's environment, but also the considerable variations in body/leg conformations that characterize wild horse populations.

TEXT OUTLINE

Chapter 1 traces the origins and history of the wild horse in America, recognizing that the ancestors of these animals were once domesticated by man, becoming wild or feral as a result of escape or abandonment.

Chapter 2 discusses social organization among wild horses, emphasizing the importance of equine families in the horse's natural world. Also discussed is the relationship of natural locomotion to the horse's locomotive behaviors, which are germane to the horse's balanced life in wild horse society. The chapter ends with a brief look at the natural habitat of the wild horse, addressing terrain, climate, and the widely misunderstood home range.

Chapter 3 explores the natural locomotion of the wild horse. In some respects, this is the most important chapter in the book because so little research has been conducted in this vital area. Throughout the horse world, equine locomotion still remains the providence of unsubstantiated opinion—opinion based on the locomotive behavior of domestic horses in specific (and unnatural) situations, such as the racetrack, rodeo ring, and dressage court. So the purpose here is to draw attention to nature's grand plan for the locomotion of the horse, stated in terms that horse enthusiasts everywhere, regardless of use or performance orientation, are likely to understand and identify with.

Results of the hoof examinations of the 100-plus captured horses at the BLM's Litchfield facility are presented in chapter 4. I have tried to focus on the salient features of their hooves, along with those that the majority of horse enthusiasts, farriers, and other equine professionals would probably find most interesting and meaningful in their own work with domestic hors-

es. For example, what is a naturally shaped hoof, and what does it look and feel like? How are front hooves different than hinds? What is the incidence of light colored hooves compared with dark ones? What range of toe angles do we find among naturally shaped front and hind hooves? What constitutes a balanced hoof? The chapter concludes on a slightly enlarged focus: Because the naturally shaped hoof is inseparable from the natural locomotive process that produces it, I offer my observations and ideas about how this shaping process occurs in the wild. In part, I have also done this as a result of my experiences with domestic horses, from whom I have learned that the occurrence of unnaturally shaped hooves results not just from the misguided farrier's rasp or harmful habitat conditions, but also from unsound equestrian practices. As horse enthusiasts, we must try to understand, in the broadest sense, how balanced, naturally shaped hooves are forged and sustained, particularly in relation to the forces of motion.

Chapter 5 attempts to bring the knowledge of the natural horse to the world of the domestic horse. This chapter begins with ideas about the general care of the horse—watering, feeding, pasturing, stabling, controlling parasites, floating the teeth, and breeding practices—and raises questions and doubts about the efficacy and reasoning behind such practices.

In chapter 6, specific suggestions and guidelines are offered to the interested farrier, veterinarian, and horseowners, who might want to apply what we now know about the naturally shaped hoof to their own work. Some may discover that they already shape their horses' hooves "the natural way" and are satisfied. Others, unfortunately, may find the information difficult to incorporate because of the highly specialized working requirements of their horses or because of the limitations of competitive regulations specified by different equestrian organizations. But most will probably find something tangibly useful here, if not immediately, then perhaps in the future.

Chapter 7 includes a conceptual model of natural horsemanship. A paradigm is presented for inexperienced and unsatisfied riders—or any person who feels that the art of horsemanship still eludes them—to contemplate. It is based upon a synthesis of the natural locomotion of the horse and observation and study of the European-based traditions of classical horsemanship—the latter still not well understood in this country.[3] To ignore how these two areas overlap would constitute a grave injustice to the rare talents and insights of many of the world's greatest equestrians, who, down through the centuries, have managed to gain great psychological insight into the horse and, ultimately, to understand and appreciate the very spirit of the natural horse.

Wyoming rancher Bill Francis works cattle with a former wild horse he obtained through the Bureau of Land Management's Adopt-A-Horse program. The horse, named Spider, is a five-year-old gelding.

Jim Hansen

The Wild Horse and Its History

Like many people unfamiliar with the history of America's wild, free-roaming horses, I had always thought that the wild horse was a "mustang," that is, a unique breed of horse. In reality, wild horses are feral horses, the offspring of domestic horses that have been turned loose, or escaped, into the wild. By wild, I mean the animals are not owned privately, and they basically fend for themselves without any care or supervision. Moreover, they live in some of America's most remote and sparsely populated high desert country.

What has particularly interested me about these horses is that, after thousands of years of domestication, they have adapted so successfully to life in the wild. If these horses are really as healthy and as sound as they appear, then there is probably a lot we can learn from them, such as the way their hooves are shaped and the manner in which they shape them. For this reason, I have come to think of them as embodying the spirit of the "natural horse," nature's model of the ideal horse fitted to the rigors of survival without the need for human intervention.

Still, before committing my time and energy to investigating these animals, I felt that I had to know more about them. For example, what kind of horses were they and how did they get out there in the first place? So, before planning a trip into wild horse country, I did a little historical research. What I found is that the wild horse is the product of many different breeds of horses that have been interbred rather haphazardly, over a period of several hundred years. Indeed, since the days of the Spanish conquistadores (ca.

A.D. 1500), America's high desert hinterlands have been serving as a kind of complicated equine melting pot in which you can probably find nearly every trait and sundry characteristic—from jackass to draft horse—extant in domestic horses living today in the United States. Yet, not every wild horse has the same combinations of these many traits, since there is much variation from herd to herd, depending upon specific regions. For this reason, the history of the wild horse cannot be separated from that of its modern domestic counterpart, since, as we shall see, the two animals are really one and the same.

BEGINNINGS

The modern horse, or *Equus caballus*, belongs to the family of animals known as Equidae, which also includes donkeys, zebras, onagers, and all their ancestors dating back to *Eohippus*, the earliest known relation of the

FIGURE 1-1

CLASSIFICATION OF THE HORSE AND RELATED SPECIES OF EQUIDS

Class:	Mammalia
Order:	Perrisodactyla
Family:	Equidae
Genus:	Equus
Species:	*Equus Caballus (domestic and feral)*
	Equus asinus (African ass)
	Equus hemionus (onager~Asian ass)
	Equus Grevyi (Grevy's zebra)
	Equus zebra (mountain zebra)
	[*Equus Przewalski (pure form extinct?)*]

horse. All living Equidae represent a single genus, *Equus*, which has six species, including domestic horses and their wild relatives (one species), asses, domestic and wild (one species), onagers (one species), and zebras (three species). Thus, *Equus caballus* includes only the domestic horse and

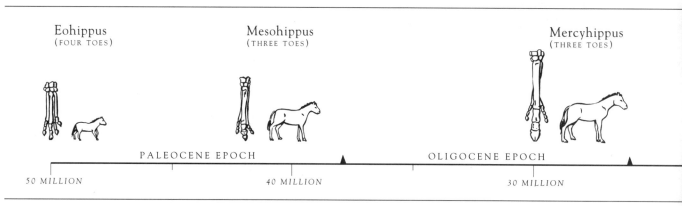

Eohippus
(FOUR TOES)

Mesohippus
(THREE TOES)

Mercyhippus
(THREE TOES)

PALEOCENE EPOCH

OLIGOCENE EPOCH

50 MILLION

40 MILLION

30 MILLION

its wild, free-roaming relatives, both of which are capable of interbreeding and producing fertile offspring (Figure 1-1).[1]

As stated above, the modern horse includes all the various kinds or breeds of horses that have descended from a small, four-toed creature popularly known as *Eohippus*, or the "dawn horse."[2] This rodent-like animal lived in both Europe and North America since the beginning of the Eocene epoch, nearly 60 million years ago (Figure 1-2). *Eohippus* had four separate toes on each front foot and three toes on each hind; each toe ended in a tiny, separate hoof. Scientists believe there was more than one species of *Eohippus* and that they varied considerably in size. The smallest are thought to have been ten inches high at the shoulder and the largest around twenty inches. *Eohippus* had teeth and was distinctly herbivorous, feeding on plants instead of grasses, which may have led to its extinction.

At the time of *Eohippus*, North America, Europe, and Asia were all attached as part of a single supercontinent called Laurasia. Until Laurasia

Eohippus with four separate toes on each front foot

split apart to form the separate continents we know today, many animals, including *Eohippus*, were able to migrate freely between the various land masses. As a result, *Eohippus* lived and evolved in both Europe and North America. After these continents divided, *Eohippus* continued to evolve in North America but, for reasons still unknown, became extinct in Europe.

Over the next 50 million years, *Eohippus* evolved into *Mercyhippus*, an animal about the size of a small pony. Like *Eohippus*, *Mercyhippus* was an herbivore, although its high-crowned teeth allowed it to masticate a greater variety of vegetation than its predecessor.

Somewhere between 6 million years ago and 600,000 B.C., *Mercyhippus* evolved into *Equus caballus*, that is, the modern horse we know today. During this period, *Equus caballus* survived in both North America and Eurasia, but, with the advent of the Ice Age, it disappeared altogether from North America. Sometime after 600,000 B.C., however, *Equus caballus* again emerged in North America, where it flourished (as well as in Eurasia) until approximately 7,000 B.C.

FIGURE 1-2

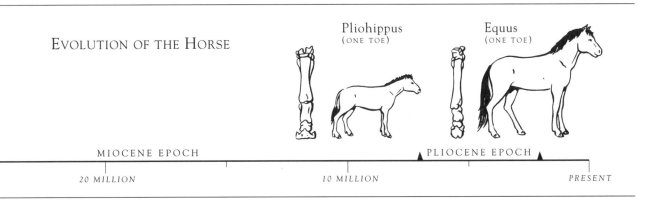

EVOLUTION OF THE HORSE

Pliohippus
(ONE TOE)

Equus
(ONE TOE)

MIOCENE EPOCH

PLIOCENE EPOCH

20 MILLION   10 MILLION   PRESENT

After 7,000 B.C., *Equus caballus*, along with many other large land mammals, including the mammoth, mastodon, and sabertooth tiger, vanished once more from the North American continent. This was not the case, however, in Europe, where the glacial ice sheets retreated under a generally warming climate. Here, *Equus caballus* migrated onto the steppes, or grasslands, of eastern Eurasia and survived.

Tribes of early humans followed these migrations of horses onto the temperate grasslands of Eurasia and, by 5,000 B.C., domesticated the onager (Asian wild ass) and reindeer. The natural evolution of *Equus caballus* was about to be changed forever.

DOMESTICATION OF THE HORSE

Around 4,000 B.C., several wild subspecies of *Equus caballus* evolved in the Eurasian grasslands, including the tarpan, which inhabited areas surrounding the Black and Caspian seas; Przewalski's horse, found in Mongolia and Manchuria; and a third subspecies, described as a Polish forest horse. The

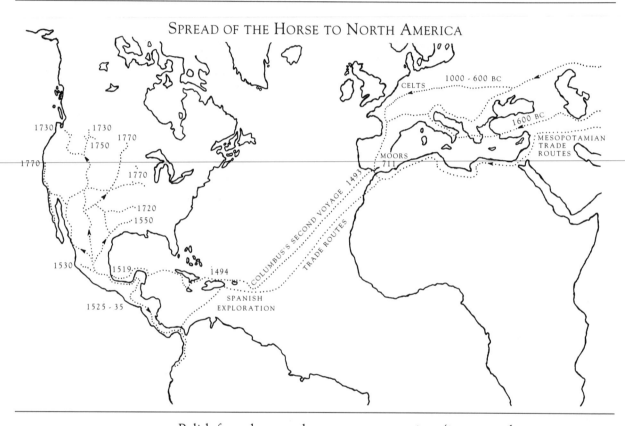

SPREAD OF THE HORSE TO NORTH AMERICA

FIGURE 1-3

Polish forest horse and tarpan are now extinct (interestingly, some scientists believe that the tarpan may have been the first domesticated horse). Przewalski's horse still survives, although it is uncertain if it survives in pure form.[3]

Also around 4,000 B.C., the steppes were invaded by Indo-Europeans from the southeast. These seminomadic people probably domesticated the horse as early as 4,000 B.C. and are believed to have developed the first pull-carts. In time, their horse culture spread north and east, eventually encompassing the sedentary tribes of Mongolia. Around 2,000 B.C., warrior societies from the Asian steppes crossed over the Iranian Plateau with horses and soon conquered the entire Near East. In another thousand years, horses were spread across Africa (in Egypt by the warlike Hyksos), all of Europe, Scandinavia, and Britain (Figure 1-3).

Widespread horse trading flourished among many different groups of people during this time. New, relatively sophisticated breeding practices developed, spawning highly specialized breeds of horses, including many that we know today. How all this happened is not entirely clear, but many theories have been advanced. One, in particular, is that all the light, fast, Mediterranean and Middle Eastern horses arose from an original breeding stock, which we know as the Arabian. Another suggests that all heavier horses—animals large and powerful enough to carry medieval knights in armor—were developed in Spain, Germany, France, and Britain.

In the eighth century A.D., the Moors brought Arabian horses with them from North Africa during their conquest of Spain. These horses were crossed with the much heavier Spanish horses, in particular, the Norse Dun. The offspring—known technically as Jennets—were referred to colloquially as Andalusian horses, after Andalusia, an area in Spain where many were bred. Thought by many to be far superior to either progenitor, the Andalusian horse crystallized Spain's prestigious reputation for having the finest quality horses in the world.

By the fifteenth and sixteenth centuries, Spain had established itself as a major European sea power. Spanish conquistadores were well equipped with guns and Andalusian horses as they set out to explore and claim lands in the New World . Thus, after a 9,000-year absence, the horse once again came to North America.

RISE OF THE WILD HORSE IN NORTH AMERICA

The first wild horses were runaways from early Spanish settlements, which were started over 400 years ago. Christopher Columbus is thought to have introduced the first domesticated horses to the New World; these were procured from Andalusia and were brought to the West Indies during his second voyage in 1493.[4] In 1521, Juan Ponce de Leon introduced the first horses into what is now the United States. These animals were brought from Cuba or Puerto Rico and were landed in Florida. Hernando Cortez took horses with him to Mexico where he conquered the Aztecs in 1519, and Pedro Mendoza introduced the first horses onto the South American pampas, or grasslands, in 1535.

The demand for horses in the New World by the conquistadores became so great that, in addition to exportations from the Old World, breeding farms had to be established by the Spanish in their West Indian colonies of Cuba, Puerto Rico, and Santo Domingo. These farms were stocked with Spain's finest studs and brood mares. Eventually, Spain began to feel the strain of a diminished horse population at home. Ironically, the country was forced not only to impose an embargo on future shipments abroad, but also to import horses from its West Indies' colonies.

By the seventeenth century, Indian tribes of Texas and New Mexico—mainly the Comanches and Apaches—began to obtain horses. Many of these were stolen from Spanish settlements, and, in turn, bartered to other tribes, including the Navajos, Zunis, and Utes. By 1750, intertribal trading ensured that even the Blackfeet nation in Montana and Canada possessed horses. But lacking fences with which to confine their herds, the Indians lost many of their horses. No doubt, these animals joined other runaways from Spanish, American, English, French, and métis settlements.

Eventually, thousands of herds of wild horses spread across the Great Plains. So prolific were these herds that, by the early 1800s, eyewitnesses estimated America's wild horse population at 2 to 5 million.

DECLINE

By the end of the nineteenth century, barbed-wire fencing crisscrossed much of the Great Plains. With open range severely reduced, the number of wild horses in the American West soon began to dwindle. At the same time, the Boer War (1899~1902) in South Africa created a great demand for the horses, as did World War I soon after. Thousands of wild horses were captured and shipped overseas. Over the next twenty years, countless numbers of animals died. Nearly 500,000 horses, mules, and donkeys died in the Boer War alone, and the British were said to have abandoned hundreds of thousands of horses to their deaths in Middle Eastern deserts after World War I—many of these were feral captives from the United States.

During the 1920s, wild horse meat was used commercially for chicken feed as well as pet and even human food. In fact, to maximize feed yields, some farmers crossed draft horses with wild mares to increase the size of the offspring. Southern farmers, faced with declining cotton prices during the Great Depression, turned to wild horses to replace expensive tractors. Ranchers also infused draft and thoroughbred bloodlines (using both mares and stallions) to create larger offspring for use as riding and work stock, as did the U.S. Army Remount Service during World War I by turning out select thoroughbred stallions.

In the midst of the Great Depression, the Taylor Grazing Act of 1934 was passed. This legislation enabled cattle ranchers, federal agencies, and professional horse catchers (called "mustangers"[5]) to remove wild horses from many public grazing lands. Their efforts were somewhat hindered, however, by the release or abandonment of thousands of domestic horses into wild horse populations by bankrupt farmers and ranchers. During the 1930s, approximately 150,000 wild horses still remained on public lands in eleven western states.

After a brief lull during World War II, additional efforts to rid the rangelands of wild horses were initiated. As a result, during the late 1940s and early 1950s, a staggering 100,000 wild horses were removed from Nevada and other western rangelands. Reduced to dangerously low numbers—possibly approaching their extinction threshold in many areas—the survival of America's wild, free-roaming horses looked bleak (Figure 1-4).

WILD, FREE-ROAMING HORSE AND BURRO ACT

Responding to widespread public outcry over the inhumane treatment of wild horses during removal campaigns and an overwhelming general consensus that America's wild horses are an important and integral part of its history and cultural fabric, Congress passed two laws to protect wild horses. Public Law 86-234, also known as the Wild Horse Annie Act—named after Velma Johnson, one of its principal supporters—passed in 1959. It prohibited the capture or destruction of wild horses using inhumane methods. Public Law 92-195, the Wild, Free-Roaming Horse and Burro Act, was passed in

1971; this legislation was by far the more comprehensive of the two laws. It delegated the responsibility for the management and protection of wild horses and burros to the Bureau of Land Management (BLM) under the secretary of the interior and to the National Forest Service under the secretary of agriculture.

THE BLM AND WILD HORSE MANAGEMENT

Because of the passage of the laws previously mentioned, wild horse populations began again to increase in numbers. According to BLM reports, public rangelands soon became overpopulated and overgrazed. In response, but amid controversy, the government began efforts to selectively remove wild horses, on a recurring basis, from various ranges. These removal operations, which are still in effect, were organized in accordance with "Herd

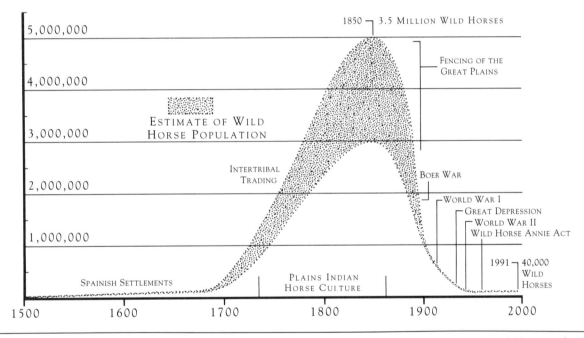

RISE AND DECLINE OF WILD HORSE POPULATION IN NORTH AMERICA

FIGURE 1-4

Management Area Plans," which determine the number of wild horses that can be managed in a particular geographical location.[6] Those horses that must be removed from the rangelands are offered for adoption to qualified individuals through the BLM's Adopt-A-Horse Program. By law, wild horses living on public lands cannot be removed or destroyed for commercial purposes.

The controversy generated by this removal program centers around management. How many horses should be allowed to roam public rangelands? Opinions are extreme, ranging from "as many as the natural biosystems of the high desert can tolerate" to "none at all." Some pro-wild horse advocates claim that wild horses are simply filling eco-niches left vacant after Ice Age climactic changes drove many species into extinction in North America, including wild equids. Opponents argue that these post-Pleistocene niches represent ecologically fragile environments that, from an evolutionary standpoint, lack the necessary types of pre-Pleistocene conditions (including equid predators and compatible flora) that once supported wild equids, camels, and other pre-Ice Age ungulates (hooved animals) now extinct in this hemisphere. Thus, the current existence of wild equids and any other extraneous or "exotic" plants and animals transplanted by humans to western public rangelands contribute to the harmful erosion of those natural ecosystems that have managed to adapt and survive the Ice Age.[7]

However, in between these extreme positions Congress has made clear that a balance must be found in public land use. This affects three areas of usage: grazing of domestic sheep and cattle, as well as other commercial operations (e.g., mining and water resources); public recreation; and wildlife, including wild horses. Finding a balance between these often conflicting interests—especially where livestock–wild horse antagonisms have proven egregious—has been no easy feat for the BLM, which is charged with carrying out Congress's mandate. Accordingly, Congress has directed numerous biologists and ecologists, acting under the auspices of the National Academy of Sciences, to study the various problems and report their findings to the BLM so that the agency can deal with these problems with greater efficacy. It is an extremely complicated undertaking, and researchers are working hard at finding answers—often hampered or halted altogether by insufficient funding. Appendix A includes a bibliography of NAS research reports, as well as a list of organizations concerned with the protec-

THE WILD HORSE~NATURAL HORSE CONNECTION

tion and survival of the wild horse and its high desert homeland.
In spite of the controversy surrounding the wild horse, the animal remains a potentially valuable source of information for interested horse people and equine scientists. From understanding gait to the myriad types of locomotive behavior, we can learn from the wild horse what is natural and best for its species—information that we can only conjecture from horses in captivity.

The belief that the wild horse is nothing more than an equine anomaly or biological aberration of its species, having little or no educational value in relation to the domestic horse, is shortsighted and without foundation. Historical evidence, such as shown in the preceding section, is unequivocal and incontrovertible about the strong interrelationship and consanguinity linking feral and domestic horses. According to a BLM public affairs official, "Calvary mounts, work horses and escaped or abandoned saddle animals have all contributed to the wild horse's lineage. . . . Only a few horses descended from the horses of Spanish blood."[8] Thus, the wild horse— healthy, prolific, and fully capable of surviving on its own—provides us with the perfect window through which to inquire, observe and learn about nature's grand plan for the quintessential natural horse. Be it natural equine socialization, natural locomotion, or natural hoof shape, the paradigm of the natural horse is the *reality* of the wild horse, and in this view, it has great didactic value applicable to all domestic breeds. For example, in areas where draft bloodlines were introduced into wild horse country years ago, such as in some of the herds found in the Painted Desert of Wyoming, we tend to find relatively large feral stock dominating local bands in those areas today. Draft horse enthusiasts might venture to locate these bands to study the influence of selection on the draft breeds released there (e.g., what happens to their hooves?).

Whatever we might find in the outback gene pool as a result of human influence, all feral stock eventually come directly under the forces of natural selection, or, if you will, under the hand of God. What exactly the selection process holds for the future of the feral horse is difficult to foretell, given the unrelenting and diversifying influences perpetrated by people every year (e.g., artificial selection, removal and sterilization campaigns, erosion of natural habitat, greenhouse effect). Nevertheless, I believe that nature, of its own accord—through selection, mutation, isolation—clearly has its own grand plan for the horse in the outback of the New World, propelling it forward toward what it has all along intended the animal to be: *Equus caballus*.

Jim Hansen

2

Social Organization of the Natural Horse

ONE OF THE MOST IMPRESSIVE ASPECTS of equine life in the wild is its orderliness as manifested through the horses' determination to survive. The animals truly have their ways of working things out among themselves in order to eke out an existence in what most horse enthusiasts would consider, at first glance, to be a hopelessly sparse habitat . They accomplish this through unique social units or organizations, called *bands*, which are actually family and extended family groups. There are several interesting variations.

THE HAREM BAND

Most horse families are composed of a single dominant stallion, the *monarch*, and a closely guarded *harem* of females with whom he bonds and breeds. These mares normally include a dominant female, the *matriarch*, or lead mare, who is often the monarch's favorite, plus a varying number (usually less than six) of subdominant females who are acquiescent in certain ways to the matriarch.

The matriarch is extremely independent and moves confidently about the home range ahead of the others. No one, not even the monarch, seeks to contest this self-proclaimed role of point guard—at least when the normal, fluid movements of the group are not thrust into chaos by some threat from outside. By her independent nature, she seems to arouse the herd instinct in others around her. Other members of her family, either too insecure to forge their own paths for others to follow, or simply too exhausted from unrelenting challenges to the matriarch, elect simply to follow along behind. Indeed, if stallion rivalry is the principal force that sustains the divisions between contiguous bands, it is the lead mare's sense of inner-directedness—where she "wills" the group to go—that determines which followers the stallion shall have to acquire or separate.

Depending on the time of year, harem mares may be in foal and have young at their sides. On the average, these polygamous family units usually range in size from approximately a half-dozen to a dozen or more individuals. Families larger than this are rare, at least in the nucleated, or one-band, sense of the harem family. Extended families—more than one harem band roaming as a single herd—in horse society, however, are not uncommon, but claims by some observers that as many as fifty to a hundred members exist per nuclear family do not take into account the natural divisions of equine life in the wild.

Family structure or organization of the harem band is probably best understood when looking at the unique interrelationships that characterize all natural horse societies in the outback. A thorough description of these interrelationships lies outside the scope of this book, but a few of the more interesting and uniform patterns of intraband socialization will be discussed here.

The horse's world is perfuse with interesting social alliances amid a general hierarchy in which every individual relates, alternately, from a position of dominance and subdominance, depending on who is relating to whom and in what activity the band is currently engaged. In the words of BLM wild horse expert Fred Wyatt, wild horse society is replete with "privates, lieutenants, and colonels," all of whom are interspersed according to well-defined coalitions or alliances.

For example, within the harem band, the lead mare may head the pecking order, with others following suit down the line, but she may also have an alliance with another mare, with whom she shares some mutual affection. This ally, acting as her lieutenant, may perceive the others jealously, as a threat to her relationship, and, accordingly, might act defensively (e.g., bite, kick, show her teeth) if another ventures too close to her consociate. In response, other female members of the group will typically respond in fashion, either individually, or in their own alliances if enough remaining mares are available to do so.

This downward "pecking," in which the relative position of "sergeant" to "private" is tempered, or even reversed in some instances, by alliances, is at times humorous to watch. I once sat to one side with a monarch, watching and shaking my head as his entire band of females (their young scurrying anxiously beneath their feet), in response to some agitation, fell hopelessly into a nasty, pathetic morass of quarrelsome back-and-forth bickering: squealing, head-shaking, nipping, biting, kicking, amid general flatulence, all arriving at no visible good end. This behavior only aroused the impatience of the monarch, who, to quell the disturbance and bring about peace, came stampeding in, driving the entire band into a headlong gallop and frenzy across the desert plain. But, in their strange ways, all was soon forgotten and forgiven in the exhilaration of the run, which left me a half-mile in the dust, and old alliances were not long in reforming so that life could resume its former sense of peaceful coexistence.

IMPACT OF STALLION RIVALRY ON THE HAREM BAND

To complicate matters of social organization in the harem band, alliances are routinely subject to modification as new members are introduced to the family by the monarch, or current members depart or are "captured" by other contending, acquisitive stallions roaming about in the area. For example, during the breeding season there is much competition for "unsettled" estrous females among the concupiscent stallions. This occurs normally during the spring and summer months, but can happen at any time of the year. At this time, both harem loyalties and family size fluctuate readily (sometimes wildly) according to one monarch's ability to hold unsettled females while fending off equally restive, acquisitive males. Obviously, this is an interesting time to observe wild horse behavior.

But most of this libidinous activity is short-lived and doomed to a characteristic entropy in the outback. Like the rhythmic ebb and flow of the ocean, sexual tension in the outback experiences its own crescendo and wane, and once all the females have been settled, life soon gives way to a much calmer pace—in fact, comparatively inert on the most bone-chilling of winter days. For sexual energy, following consummation, evaporates into thin air, at least temporarily, and is no longer available to motivate or drive band behavior.

THE CODEPENDENT, SATELLITE HAREM BAND

Socialization, is seldom confined to the vicissitudes of one harem band's struggle to survive in the outback. Typically, it is also shaded and colored by the influences of other bands roaming in the immediate vicinity. Some of these bands could be called codependent, satellite harem bands because the monarchs heading them appear willing to take orders directly from a more dominant, principal monarch of an adjacent band—at least when the entire herd assembly is threatened from outside. What in one moment appears to be a loosely connected array of bands wandering about, suddenly becomes, in another moment of threat, a tightly federated, well-organized aggregate with everyone stationed in position as needed. After witnessing and photographing such mergence of contiguous harem bands, I can testify to the decisiveness with which the principal monarch forges his alliance with other subdominant monarchs. Included in the rearrangement is a whole new hierarchy, which is closely monitored by this head monarch. Once the threat abates, however, the bands disengage in quiet, orderly fashion and life goes on as before, side-by-side, according to the herd's system of simultaneous or decentralized hierarchies and sundry alliances.

THE BACHELOR BAND

At least one other type of band is affiliated with the principal monarch band. This is the well-known bachelor band of wild horse society. As its name suggests, it is composed exclusively of subdominant, or acquiescent, stallions. These males have their own system of organization, which resembles that of the harem mares; that is, it is hierarchical and composed of alliances.

Bachelor bands are formed from the exiled male offspring of various harem bands roaming in the general vicinity. Exiled females are captured by contending stallions and do not form all-female bands—although one observer I spoke with insists that he witnessed one such band in northern Nevada. These young males may spend a lifetime following after a principal monarch band for whom they feel some special affinity. Often, though not always, they are waiting for the opportunity to forge their own harem bands. The latter occurs when they are finally daring or aggressive enough to capture—through stealth or battle—available estrous females. However, this may never happen, and it is not uncommon to find old bachelors swept up in these all-male bands, along with contiguous harem families, during BLM removal campaigns. Some of these bachelors, out of homophile tendencies or passive temperament, just seem to prefer the company of other males. In more than one instance, I have noted that such males never exhibit any contentious behavior toward the monarch when the breeding season is at hand. Whatever the case may be, members of the bachelor band, like the subdominant monarch, also take their cues from the principal monarch to alter their satellite position as a band unit in times of threat or danger.

One interesting herd, described by a BLM wild horse management specialist, was composed of an old monarch, his longtime favorite mare, and, off to the side, a bachelor band composed of one old subdominant stallion. The three roamed together as a herd unit, the old mare leading the way, the old monarch protecting the rear, and the old bachelor maintaining his usual distance to the side, as he always had before when the herd was much larger.

HERD EXOGAMY

Since bachelor bands are normally formed by young males derived from different harem bands in the area, their participation in the herd's socialization through stallion competition is an important component of what can be called the exogamy or clan affiliation of wild horse society. In other words, the bachelor bands provide breeding opportunities between horses not normally a part of the same, immediate social unit. In this way, they are nature's safeguard against excessive inbreeding.

Monarchs also contribute to the herd's exogamy by willfully expelling their young—male and sometimes female—from the family unit during the breeding season. This occurs specifically when the offspring are sufficiently procreant, approximately ages one to two years, and when stallion competition is at its zenith.

Incest appears also to be suppressed by individual male and female preferences for the opposite sex, or sexual selection, which might include such characteristics as coat color, temperament, and conformation (even impressive body postures). When those traits are not available within the immediate group, members may elect to leave to seek new partners. This can be seen in instances in which monarchs defend certain estrous females to the exclusion of others and also in the willingness of some females, for example, daughters, to abandon one monarch in preference for another, one more suitable to their liking.

At least one equine researcher has alleged to have observed miscarriages occurring in harems where the monarch was expelled by a rival stallion. According to Burger, these miscarriages were induced by forced intromission perpetrated by the takeover stallion—tantamount to equine rape—and occurred in roughly 4 percent of the populations they sampled.[1] In my observations, however, I have never seen this happen, nor have I read about it anywhere else, and BLM wild horse management specialists have denied such occurrences.

This tendency among wild horses to breed outside the immediate group causes concern regarding current BLM herd-reduction campaigns that often ignore the nuances of exogamy in feral horse society by implementing the

following practices: (1) the indiscriminate removal of horses without regard to sex ratios or band affiliations in order to satisfy politically acceptable numbers of horses for herd management sectors; (2) The castration of captured males solely upon age criteria by BLM vets and wranglers. (There have also been a number of misguided university professors roaming the outback sterilizing or trying to sterilize—called chemosterilization—both male and female wild horses in the name of population control.[2]); and (3) to the extent that artificial breeding is intentionally implemented, the reintroduction of "exemplary" stallions to improve the local gene pool according to current notions of "correct" equine anatomical configuration, but which may have little survival value in the outback gene pool. All of these practices are not natural and contribute to the erosion of exogamy in wild horse society.

HERDS

In addition to interband satellite family associations (harem and codependant harem and bachelor bands) found commonly in wild horse society, there are a number of other interesting herd combinations (Figure 2-1).

There may be as few as one such satellite group traveling alone, or, in contrast, numerous satellite groups made up of hundreds of horses, roaming as a single herd in the same home range. In some instances, a herd may include just one harem band. Each of these, however, constitutes a herd, yet all have different systems of group cooperation or affiliation. The word affiliation is defined here as horses traveling together as a herd unit for the sake of mutual protection. More specifically, though, there are those bands that are clan-affiliated and travel together, and those that are exogamous but who do not, as a rule, travel as a single clan affiliated herd unit.

FIGURE 2-1　　A water hole, for example, may be the only thing that two or more satellite herd families share in common, but beyond this, avoidance—and

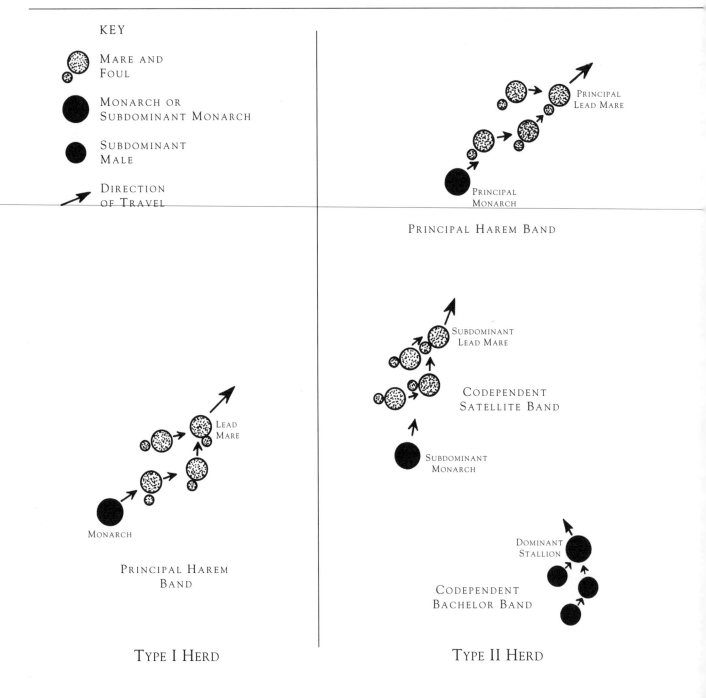

KEY

MARE AND FOUL

MONARCH OR SUBDOMINANT MONARCH

SUBDOMINANT MALE

DIRECTION OF TRAVEL

PRINCIPAL LEAD MARE

PRINCIPAL MONARCH

PRINCIPAL HAREM BAND

LEAD MARE

MONARCH

PRINCIPAL HAREM BAND

TYPE I HERD

SUBDOMINANT LEAD MARE

CODEPENDENT SATELLITE BAND

SUBDOMINANT MONARCH

DOMINANT STALLION

CODEPENDENT BACHELOR BAND

TYPE II HERD

not alliance—between them is the shared understanding. This type of behavior may take place in the more rugged mountain valleys, where one herd is often separated from other herds by entire ridges or gulches. Aside from fleeting eye contact across a distance, or daily stop-offs at any of the ubiquitous stud piles found in a shared home range, there is little direct contact or indirect communication, and alliance is seldom indicated, nor would it be practical in such difficult-to-negotiate terrain. Instead, the bands seem to maintain a regulated spacing as they rotate across the shared areas of the rangeland.

Isolated nuclear families also roam these rugged mountain ranges. In one such rangeland, I observed about twenty herds. Many of these were

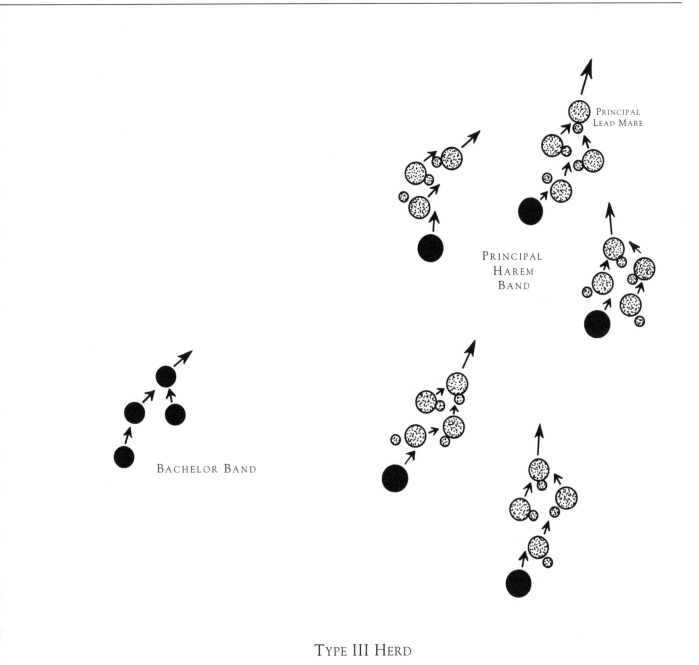

PRINCIPAL
LEAD MARE

PRINCIPAL
HAREM
BAND

BACHELOR BAND

TYPE III HERD

nuclear families with no visible contiguous satellites. Some just had bachelor bands attached and some had both satellite harem and bachelor bands. It was apparent that the entire group of horses was not a single herd because there was no affiliation between them; rather, it comprised approximately twenty independent herds of roughly three different types.

In contrast, on one alluvial plain in eastern Oregon, numerous bands have been sighted roaming together as a single, vast herd of hundreds of horses. According to the BLM wild horse management specialist who described this herd, affiliation was indicated because the horses fled as one body when threatened from without.

In considering these herd combinations, it is best to remain cautious and flexible in drawing conclusions about interband organization in the wild. Stallion rivalry and the terrain, among many other factors, appear to contribute directly to the vicissitudes of herd affiliation and band alliance from region to region.

Herds on the Move

Movement of a herd across the home range is an interesting phenomenon to witness. As described earlier in the chapter, the lead mare of the harem band directs the movements of the other members of her immediate family. However, because one harem band is usually affiliated with one or more other harem and bachelor bands, she also guides their movements across the home range as well. If affiliation of numerous bands (e.g., thirty or more horses) is present, the choreography is impressive to watch.

I have stood, and walked, on many occasions, at the center of such an assembly on the move, accepted (more or less) as part of the group, and have come to appreciate the power of unity as exemplified by these animals. There is great peace and order among these horses as they travel along in a single body to new feeding grounds within the home range. Everyone has his or her accepted and respected place in the herd's hierarchy (including me, when I joined them as a "third satellite" affiliate).

In summary, the basic social unit of equine life in the wild is the band—the horse "family." Each horse, from birth to death, embraces and is embraced by the group, and within this social context, the wild horse is able to act out to its fullest what it means to be a highly motivated and instinctual animal.

Wild Horse Country

Before beginning the discussion of the natural locomotion of the horse in the next chapter, a few more words about the environment and the home range of the wild horse are essential.

Public Lands

U.S. public lands inhabited by wild horses are administered by the BLM and U.S. Forest Service; they include parts of Arizona, California, Colorado, Idaho, Montana, Nevada, New Mexico, Utah, and Wyoming. The largest concentrations are located in Nevada (close to 30,000), Wyoming (almost 5,000), and Oregon (approximately 3,000). Much of this land is extremely rugged and inaccessible, and there are relatively few human visitors or inhabitants. However, in recent years, herd management programs, limited forage, drought, fences, and other barriers, have begun to check the migrations and proliferation of many wild horse populations.

The terrain in wild horse country is as diverse as the wildlife that often roams across it. The horses, whose hooves I examined at the Litchfield Corrals, were removed from high desert locations (woodland-brush biome) in northern California, Nevada, and eastern Oregon. Much of this land is similar. Typically, there are mountains (5,000 to 10,000 feet), small buttes (mesas), gently rolling hills, and broad alluvial plains. Rocks and boulders are scattered everywhere. The plains, where natural, are normally a mixture of firm soil and soft sand, interspersed with small volcanic rocks and a myriad of plant life and grasses.

On the craggy slopes and summits of the mountains and mesas grow considerable varieties of wild grasses, small trees, and other vegetation. And wherever plant life abounds, so does the wild horse—as witnessed by its dung. On many occasions, I have observed wild horses climbing stepwise from rock to rock in search of food.

With regard to food, the animals here do quite well most of the time. Winters can be tough on the animals, forcing them to the edges of towns to seek food, but food shortages are the exception rather than the rule in wild horse country, as their increasing numbers in many locations show.

Stories of wild horses starving in the outback, when true, can usually be attributed to the encroachments of civilization (fencing, housing developments), which often halt winter migrations from the highlands to new pasturage in the lower elevations. However, it is not the policy of the BLM to let any of these animals starve to death in the outback. On more than one occasion, the agency has airlifted hay to some bands stranded without winter graze, and in one recent case, it captured and transported wild horses converging upon a Reno, Nevada, neighborhood to new rangelands.

THE HOME RANGE

Home range can be defined as any area where a band, or assembly of related bands, happens to take up residence in order to exact its survival needs. The size and shape of the home range is not fixed, as though an invisible fence were in place. Rather, its boundaries are fluid and subject to change according to the survival requirements of the group. I have seen one group of horses range ten or more miles from east to west in one day during one season. In another season, the same group may not move beyond a mile's radius of the center of the same rangeland.

Although range boundaries are flexible, wild horses definitely show a preference for living in specific locations. For example, BLM officials report the great difficulty their helicopter pilots have in rounding up bands that cannot be driven from their home range first. Ostensibly, the animals' sense of confidence and ability to elude their captors is undermined by their feelings of disorientation, alienation, and vulnerability experienced upon moving into unfamiliar or less familiar territory. I have witnessed the same anxiety in bands forced to abandon their preferred migration route in order to circumvent some threat; they will go around the obstacle, if possible, rather than just flee in any direction. Thus, it appears that the wild horse identifies strongly with a particular region of the rangeland available to it.

A stereotypical view of the wild horse is that of an aimless wanderer. Consistent observation shows evidence to the contrary. The movements of wild horses within the home range, like the migrations of geese, deer, and antelope, tend to follow fairly regulated, rhythmic patterns. These patterns appear to be governed by the cycles of nature: the changing seasons, the fruition of some edible forage, the expanding or shrinking of water holes, or the inner clockwork of some circadian rhythm. How the horse links into these cycles is what appears to determine the relative size and shape of the home range.

For example, on more than one rangeland, I have been able to set my watch for a particular time, at a particular location, and be reasonably certain that a particular band or herd would pass by me within fifteen minutes on any given day. Such is the regularity with which these animals usually, though not always, govern their movements.

Wild horses, however, cannot be held to a clock. On the contrary, band migrations are much too subject to the vicissitudes of herd socialization, let alone the cycles of nature, to permit such predictable behavior. The point is that wild horses, to the extent that nature permits or compels, are creatures extremely fond of daily routine and peaceful social order, and the home range, its boundaries ever subject to change, is merely a suitable location—carved out of the environment by the animals in response to nature's rhythmic forces—where these routines and social affairs can be conducted.

On the range, horses live in concert with other grazers, such as deer, antelope, and domestic cattle and sheep, as well as other wild horses who choose to occupy the same home territory. Territorial behavior is exhibited by the presence of "stud piles"—fairly large piles of dung, some as high as two to three feet—excreted by various bands occupying the same rangeland. These piles are stacked everywhere, but appear to be placed purposely, and are used as markers of some kind as the horses move along. They do not seem to serve as "boundary" markers, since, as has been suggested before, the boundaries of the home range are more closely related to the availability of forage than any sense of possessiveness of the land. Dominance reminders may be more accurate since the monarchs—aided by their matriarchs—cannot resist using them. Certainly, such piles must alert the astute monarchs to the movements of other males in the area, for we know with certainty that their home ranges can overlap or intersect each other's at any one of these given locations.

CLIMATE

Weather conditions in wild horse country are normally moderate to severe, depending on the season, altitude, and if a storm system is coming through. For example, temperatures in Nevada rangelands typically vary from the low 40s (degrees Fahrenheit) to the midteens in winter, although extremes well below zero were not unheard of in years past, especially at high elevations. In contrast, temperatures during the summer months normally range from highs in the 90s to lows in the 50s, with highs soaring well above 100 degrees.

Annual precipitation levels in high desert rangelands are relatively low, probably averaging less than eight inches per year.[3] When rain does occur, especially during tempestuous thunderstorms, the alluvial valleys often turn to mud, making navigation by vehicle practically impossible. But such conditions never last long, especially in the warm seasons, when the intense desert sun soon restores the earth to its characteristic dry, firm consistency.

In the winter, when ground conditions sometimes stay soft for long periods, the horses must face less than optimum dry conditions for footage. But in many areas, nature bridges this gap by providing a carpetlike flora that reticulates with the volcanic rocks strewn everywhere. In effect, the horses have a rock-lined, plant mat to walk about on in many places; otherwise, the animals sink to their fetlocks or knees in the desert gumbo. Although ground conditions vary widely at every elevation—one area may be incredibly rocky and the adjacent land relatively free from rocks—cold temperatures generally keep the moist ground rigid at most elevations, providing excellent footage for the animals. Where the sun does warm the earth, however, winter snow tends to melt quickly, and the moist gumbo reverts quickly to its normal, firm consistency.

Understandably, the highest peaks of the high desert biome are normally avoided by the horses during winter, although cold and snow do not appear to bother them should they range temporarily through such habitat. There is simply more accessible forage to eat in the lowlands and midlands than there is up above. So all the grazers in high desert country, including the domestic stock of local ranchers who lease BLM land in the summer (who grow hay on their own lands in the summer to feed their stock during the winter), move, or try to move, down the mountain when winter approaches.

With this perspective on the wild horse's social organization, natural habitat, and range requirements in mind, let us now look at how the natural horse, as exemplified by the wild, free-roaming horse, moves.

Jeff Foott

3

Movement of the Natural Horse

ONE OF THE MOST intriguing aspects of the wild, free-roaming horse is the sound, well-balanced manner in which it moves. Whether fleeing from real or imagined threats, or engaging in some social activity, the wild horse knows how to move with athletic grace and precision. Surprisingly, because of rough conditions that can exist in the wild, there is little or no lameness.

In this chapter, I discuss my observations of the natural locomotive process among wild, free-roaming horses. As a horseman, I have tried to relate what I have observed to what I know about horsemanship. For example, when I describe how the natural horse carries its weight upon the hindquarters, I find it helpful to relate these observations to equestrian practices and written works with which many horse enthusiasts may already be familiar. There is much in current thought and models of understanding, particularly from the classical school of horsemanship, that is harmonious with the natural locomotion of the horse. I have also attempted to differentiate between what is natural and normal locomotion for the wild horse and what is imbalanced and abnormal, because in the natural world of the horse, there is normal balanced locomotion, which we see most of the time, and abnormal imbalanced locomotion, which we see only now and then.

Defined in its simplest terms, *natural equine locomotion* is the horse moving in accordance with the way nature intended for it to move. In the outback, the basic elements of the natural gaits—the hereditary locomotive archetype of *Equus caballus*—results from specific behaviors that are routine and uniform across wild horse society.

EXTRAORDINARY VERSUS ORDINARY LOCOMOTIVE BEHAVIOR

A horse's existence in the outback is characterized by two distinct modes of locomotive or behavioral intensity. One can be described as ordinary because it stems from ordinary behaviors, such as watering, grazing, relaxing, and mutual grooming, which takes place most of the time. In terms of the individual horse, it is characterized by a state of general calmness. Communally, it carries over into the group's social dynamic as a general sense of tranquility. Typically, this general calmness takes place when the horse family meanders slowly along behind its matriarch, nibbling at this or that, or during the dreamy, sleep-mope-sleep quiescence of an afternoon nap, when there is an endless shifting of body weight. Locomotion, whether in place or forward seeking, is characterized by a relaxed and easy pace, devoid of any sense of urgency. The body, accordingly, is relatively "uncollected."

The other locomotive intensity, fueled by such extraordinary behaviors as fighting, fleeing, and mating, is anything but ordinary. It is characterized by zing, animation, and vibrant personality. Each horse, from foal to monarch is "on toe" and ready for action: ears to-and-fro at radar, nostrils distended and blowing, powerful flexion at every joint, tail and neck elevated and arched triumphantly, and eyes fully open and alert. (Actually, not all horses may be at attention, for I have seen monarchs fully engaged in the nastiest of combat, while their insouciant mares have stood by, showing no apparent interest in what is going on.) Now there is tremendous potential for movement, if not brisk, rarefied, lighter-than-air movement itself, and bodies are at near or full "collection," because matters at hand are suddenly extraordinary.

Note that "collection"—essentially a natural centering or balancing process of great importance to all natural riders and their mounts—is associated with extraordinary as opposed to ordinary locomotive behaviors. This distinction is an important one for equestrians to make: We must not expect our own horses to collect themselves for us in the absence of an elicited, extraordinary behavioral impulse. In my opinion, the vast majority of all locomotion-based lameness suffered by domestic horses today stems directly from the inability of horse enthusiasts to make this distinction, particularly when they climb into the saddle for the first time. The result is that horses are often forced, at great risk to their bodies, to perform extraordinary tasks without the benefits of naturally collected bodies.

The natural horse, by means of the lifelong process of negotiating a rugged environment and responding to the vicissitudes of wild horse society, prepares for the extraordinary behaviors that must be executed in order to survive. The natural rider, educated in the ways and nuances of the horse's natural world, is cognizant of this and knows that the realm of ordinary behaviors cannot possibly begin to meet the requirements of his or her equestrian goals. Instead, through the powers of intuition, patience, and keen ability to observe, the natural rider learns to evoke the behavioral impulses that underlie the natural extraordinary behaviors because he or she knows that these types of behavioral impulses will, in turn, precipitate the natural locomotive process that will fulfill his or her equestrian goals without harming the horse. The natural rider does this, in part, by transforming his or her own thinking and body posturing toward that of his or her horse. In doing so, a meeting of minds, bodies, and spirits will result—because the natural horse, by virtue of its own nature, stands ready to do the same. The process is explained in more detail in chapter 7.

CAUSES OF NATURAL LOCOMOTION

As we can see, then, it is simplistic to define the locomotive process as "this is how the horse moves" without stressing the causality of every basic movement (e.g., the trot in place arises from the need to rear and fight or to communicate with an ally quickly while head to tail). Depending on the reason or cause, the horse will tend to move in a particular way (first trot in place, then rear). Already we have seen that the animal moves its body in accordance with a full range of behaviors (see Table 3-1), all of which are ignited by its natural instincts to survive. But it also moves as a result of influences stemming from its environment, such as climate, available forage, and predators.

Consequently, we should try to understand the mechanics of the locomotive process within the context of the behaviors that produce it so uniformly across wild horse society. This will give us a clear idea of the density, or frequency, with which certain movements can be expected to occur naturally, and whether or not specific movements are even natural. From an equestrian standpoint, causality can help us to determine the reasonableness of our own equestrian goals, that is, the physical demands made upon the domestic horse, in relation to the horse's own natural world.

The diagram below illustrates a holistic dimension of the relationships that bind together the various parts of the natural horse's life. The horse's natural instincts elicit a series of behavioral impulses in response to the ani-

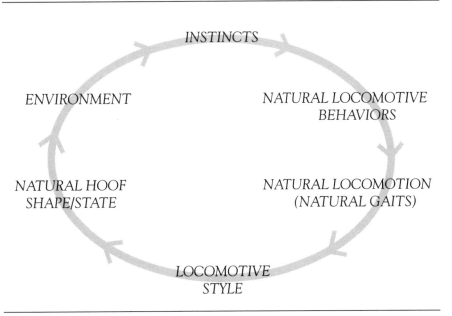

mal's survival needs. These surface as specific locomotive behaviors manifested through patterns of family, extended family, and herd socialization. At the same time, the behaviors are filtered through a wide range of body (conformation) and temperament (personality) types. Thus, while the behaviors

Table 3-1

Natural Locomotive Behaviors of the Horse

Behavior	Description	Level
Agonistic	Alert, alarm, and flight; aggression; stallion inter-actions; influence of rank order on daily activity	Extraordinary
Comfort	Self-indulgent (sunning, shelter-seeking, licking, nibbling, scratching, rubbing, rolling, shaking and skin twitching, tail switching); mutual interactions (mutual grooming and symbiotic relationship with birds)	Ordinary
Communicative	Visual expressions, acoustical expressions, squeal, nickers, whinny, groan, blow, snort, snore, other sounds, tactile interactions, chemical exchanges	Ordinary Extraordinary
Coprophagous	Consumption of dung	Unusual
Dominance	Pecking order and alliances	Extraordinary
Eliminative	Urinating and defecating	Ordinary
Ingestive	Feeding, drinking, nursing	Ordinary
Investigative	Curiostiy	Ordinary Extraordinary
Ontogeny	Perinatal and postnatal	Ordinary Extraordinary
Play	Solitary, foal-mother, sibling, younger-older	Extraordinary
Reproductive	Sexual (male), sexual (female), and maternal	Extraordinary
Resting	Standing and recumbency	Ordinary
Sleep	Recumbency	Ordinary
Social Group	Herd and band structure, migratory, roles	Ordinary Extraordinary
Social Pair Bonding	Mare-foal, foal-mare, peer, heterosexual, paternal, interspecies	Ordinary Extraordinary
Territorial	Home range and territoriality (stud piles)	Ordinary

give rise to natural locomotion, or a highly uniform locomotory process common to all wild (and domestic) horses, they also inspire an infinite array of diverse, genetically desirable locomotive styles.

Forged as a direct consequence of the natural locomotive process are naturally shaped hooves. This represents two highly uniform hoof configurations, front and hind, which, like the uniform locomotive process itself, are archetypal, but are replete with endless minor variations of shape that stem from, or correspond directly to, variations in locomotive style. The hooves, braced by the environment, are shaped and balanced by the compressionary locomotive forces applied to them through the horse's body and legs. Thus, the hooves of the natural horse are like little mirrors that reflect back upon the animal's entire locomotive experience. In this way, they are visible, tangible repositories of knowledge about wild horse society.

Before discussing the more abstract realm of the locomotive process to see how legs and neck stretch and muscles cooperate elastically, we need to take a closer look at the natural habitat of the horse and its suitability for the natural locomotive process.

IMPORTANCE OF HABITAT

Although the natural habitat of the wild horse is rugged, vibrant and alive, it is, for the most part, still and stationary. As such, it is a passive player in the natural locomotive process. Nature, in its infinite wisdom, has created a physical environment that best fits the horse, but to use it effectively for its survival, the horse must be able to move upon it as nature intended. Most locomotive-related problems afflicting domestic horses, including unnaturally shaped hooves, do not arise principally from the work of the farrier or necessarily from the physical limitations of the animal's confinement. Rather, they result, primarily, from how the horse is ridden and exercised and, secondarily, from the type of terrain or management care the animal is given. Once the locomotive experience is brought into line with what nature intended, these sorts of problems confounding the horse (and rider) will tend to diminish demonstrably; however, left unaligned, though accompanied by other desirable changes in the environment (more natural hoof care, feed, terrain), the same problems would diminish only marginally.

Nature has provided a landscape so much more rugged and abrasive than anything in the domestic horse's world, that it is hard to imagine a domestic horse negotiating it without serious injury. Remember, however, that the wild horse is not a superhorse, but is only a feral horse, a lucky domestic horse (or the offspring of one) who "got away." In some respects, the outback may be a tough place in which to make it, but it is ideal for the horse—all horses. In this way, nature draws out of the horse all of its instincts to adapt and survive. This process of bringing instincts "to bear" is what begins to turn the animal into a real athlete, in comparison to its often neurotic, epicurean, domestic counterpart who must somehow weather the high-cholesterol equine "Life of Riley" foisted upon it by so many horse owners. My advice to horse owners interested in developing the natural horse in their own horses is some rather unconventional changes in barnyard management:

First, tear down the stalls and fences and let the horses run about and mingle. Let them argue and fight—horses love to fight—but they like even more to work things out. Contour the pasture to get rid of all the flat spots. Then spread rocks of all sizes and shapes across the up-and-down pasture— and if the horse does not have to put its nose on the ground during the first day to see where it is going, then keep tossing truckloads around until it does. Next, abandon the use of the feed mangers and feed the horses on the ground. Do not worry about them getting worms; in fact, stop using paste wormers altogether. Pull the watering contraptions down off the wall and kick the water troughs over, and then water the horses at ground level so they will use their big, strong necks; make sure they have to stand in the mud if they want to drink. Pull off the horseshoes—especially the fashion- able ones with the "bars," and ride the horse barefooted until it is lean and muscular. If you want the hooves to be really tough when you are through, stop washing them in soap and water every day, stop painting them with "blackout," and throw away the hoof dressings. See chapter 5 for more details on the natural care of the horse.

The difference between feral and domestic horses lies not in their respective musculoskeletal frameworks or even in their hooves; these are essentially the same. Nor does it stem from their mental capacities; both animals are equally intelligent. Nor can it be attributed to the lay of the land, for the modifications made by people, particularly in rugged ranch country are negligible. The difference lies in *how* the horses are able to use what nature naturally endowed them with—their minds and bodies. "Respond to my rhythms," speaks Nature, "and I will help you to become what you are intended to be."

How true this is, especially of the wild horse, who, unlike its domestic counterpart sectioned off just over the ridge, is truly integrated with its nat- ural environment. For lack of better words, it listens closely to nature's rhythms. Then, using its instincts, acts upon them.

THE NATURAL GAIT COMPLEX

The rest of this chapter explores the natural gait complex of the horse. This is a rather elaborate term I have coined to describe the natural gaits and those elements of the locomotive process that make the gaits what they are, specifically: footfall sequences, leads, stride and stride extension, rhythm, tempo, cadence, and suspension. Also discussed are my observa- tions of collection—perhaps the most important phenomenon that occurs in the natural locomotion of the horse—up and down transitions, and how the horse turns.

To aid the reader in understanding the details of the horse's natural locomotion, I have drawn upon the works of some of the world's great equestrians in order to help put into words what I have observed in wild horse society.

NATURAL GAITS

A *gait* is a manner of walking, stepping, or running—in short, how some- thing travels along. The wild horse travels naturally at the walk (Old English: *wealcan*, "to roll or toss"), trot (Germanic: *trotten*, "to tread"), and *canter* (short for Canterbury, England, "to ride at a pace like that of

TABLE 3-2

NATURAL GAITS OF THE HORSE AND THEIR UNUSUAL VARIATIONS

Variations	Walk	Trot	Canter
Normal	Ordinary, relaxed, and uncollected with medium stride extension	Ordinary, relaxed, and uncollected with medium-length stride and medium suspension	Ordinary, relaxed, and uncollected with medium-length stride and medium suspension
Gathered	Extraordinary and collected with maximum stride extension	Extraordinary and collected with very little stride extension or suspension	Extraordinary and collected with very little stride extension or suspension
Extended	Extraordinary and collected with maximum stride extension	Extraordinary and collected with maxium stride extension and increased suspension	Extraordinary and collected with maxium stride extension and increased suspension

Unusual Variations	Walk	Trot	Canter
Movement In Place	Not seen	High-cadenced trot approximately in place with little or no extension and shortest suspension phase of all trots	Not seen
Exaggerated Suspension Phase	Not seen	High-cadenced trot with medium stride extension and maxium suspension phase of all trots	Not seen
Retrogressive Movements	Not seen	Not seen	Not seen
Turns and Lateral Movement	Performed at all forms of walk	Performed at all forms of trot	Performed at all forms of canter
Jumps, Hops, and Rears	Initiates upward transition to trot	Continues upward transition to canter	All jumps performed at canter after trot and walk first excuted

Canterbury pilgrims"). These gaits are summarized in Table 3-2. Some readers may wonder why Table 3-2 does not include the pace, four-beat gallop, rack, running-walk, and other well-known gaits alleged to be executed naturally by domestic horses of their own volition. These gaits do not appear to be natural to the horse; I have never seen them exhibited by wild horses in their natural societies in the outback. I suspect that they arise artificially in domestic horses either as a result of selective breeding (e.g., the pace), or directly from locomotive imbalance (e.g., four-beat gallop) induced by faulty equestrian practices and mechanically obstructive shoeing. So, in accordance with my observations, I have designated the horse's three natural gaits as the walk, trot, and canter.

At the same time that a particular gait is executed, every horse exhibits an individual locomotive style or variation of it, which may differ considerably from one horse to the next. These styles mirror individual conformations and temperaments, contributing greatly to the richness and diversity of natural equine locomotion. In fact, there are unlimited variations of locomotive style among wild horses, each a reflection of the uniqueness of each horse (Figure 3-1).

Footfall sequence is the particular order in which the horse moves its hooves (and legs), depending on the gait in which it is traveling. Figure 3-2 illustrates the footfall sequences for the walk, trot, and canter. The completion of one cycle, or pattern, of a particular footfall sequence by all four limbs is called a *stride* in any of the three gaits. Thus, notwithstanding irregularities stemming from temporary imbalance, the horse naturally exhibits three basic strides or stride patterns: one for the walk, a second for the trot, and a third for the canter.

FIGURE 3-1

Wild horse at trot in suspension (4th) phase

Jim Hansen

The regular recurrence of a given time interval between one footfall and the next is referred to as the stride's *rhythm*. Stride rhythms tend to be constant. The time intervals between each footfall within a single stride tend to be of equal duration, even though a gait's tempo or the horse's rate of travel may slow down or speed up. For example, the count or "hoofbeat" at the walk is as follows:

$$\overset{*}{1} - 2 - 3 - 4, \quad \overset{*}{1} - 2 - 3 - 4, \quad \overset{*}{1} - 2, \text{ etc.}$$
(* = first footfall of stride)

The time interval between each hoofbeat is identical within each stride:

$$1 \overset{t_1}{\rule{1cm}{0.4pt}} 2 \overset{t_2}{\rule{1cm}{0.4pt}} 3 \overset{t_3}{\rule{1cm}{0.4pt}} 4$$
(t = time interval between each footfall and $t_1 = t_2 = t_3$)

Tempo represents the beat of a gait, that is, the time interval between strides. It is something we can hear and count as we listen to the horse move; thus, tempo is an indicator of a rhythm's speed—not how fast the horse is moving, but how quickly it is moving its legs. For example, the count at the canter is the following:

$$\overset{*}{1} - 2 - 3, \quad \overset{*}{1} - 2 - 3, \quad \overset{*}{1} - 2 - 3, \text{ etc.}$$
(* = first beat of stride)

The tempo is the time interval between the first beat (*) of one stride and the first beat of the next stride. The shorter these time intervals, the quicker the gait's tempo and the faster the horse is moving its legs. Conversely, the longer the intervals, the slower the tempo, and the slower the legs are moving.

Speed, in contrast to tempo, is the ratio of the distance traveled by the horse *per* the time it takes for this travel to take place:

$$\text{Speed} = \frac{\text{distance}}{\text{unit of time}}$$

Among wild horses, changes in speed are not always accompanied by corresponding or commensurate changes in tempo, particularly during extraordinary locomotive behavior. The reason is that the horse prefers to change the length of its strides—as opposed to moving its legs faster—in order to move faster or slower. It does this by altering its cadence, that is, the relative position or height of its limbs, with each step. As the horse elevates its cadence, it steps higher but not as far forward; conversely, as it lowers it cadence, it steps farther forward although not as high.

Changes in cadence may also affect the suspension phases of the trot and canter gaits. *Suspension* refers to those brief moments when all four legs of the horse are in flight and have no contact with the ground. Wild horses frequently manipulate their suspension phases during extraordinary behavior (see Table 3-2), especially at the trot. For example, by reducing the suspension time and shortening their strides, they can trot in place, such as before fighting; by lengthening the suspension time and moderating their stride lengths, they can give the appearance of floating in air as they prance along—called the *passage* (French: "a passing") by dressage trainers—while at play or before making a hasty escape.

LEADS

Each gait has two sets of footfall sequences per stride. These correspond to the horse's leads. A *lead* is a well-defined left or right body posture or orientation assumed by the horse during the execution of a stride. A lead is characterized by a propelling hindleg that leads or initiates the footfall sequence, an opposing foreleg that directs or advances the movement of the stride, and usually a a left or right longitudinal bend through the body consistent with the direction in which the horse is turning.

Technically speaking, the lead is named for the propelling hindleg that is always the first footfall (hoof beat) of every stride, so the hind leg always initiates the gait-stride. Thus, as can be seen in Figure 3-2C, the leading leg for the horse traveling at the canter on its left lead is the left hindleg (frame 1). (Compare this illustration with the footfall sequence in Figure 3-3.) Diagonally opposite the leading hindleg is the advancing foreleg—in this case, the right foreleg, which can be seen clearly in frame 4 in Figure 3-2C.

FIGURE 3-2 A.
WALK

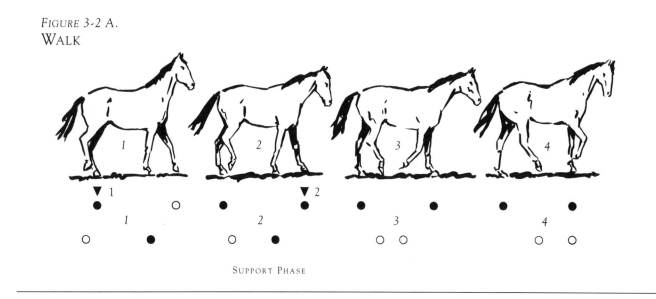

SUPPORT PHASE

FIGURE 3-2 B.
TROT

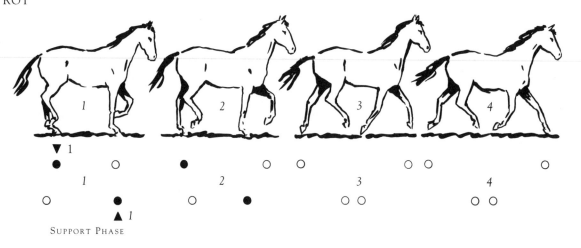

SUPPORT PHASE

FIGURE 3-2 C.
CANTER

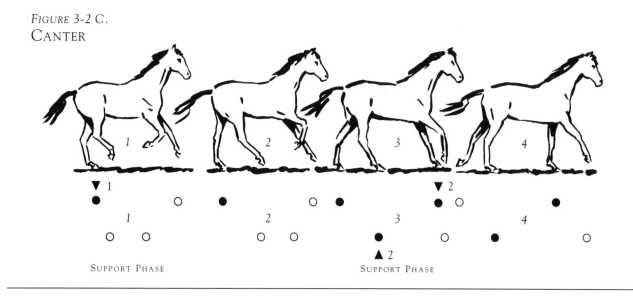

SUPPORT PHASE   SUPPORT PHASE

BEAT / FOOTBALL: ▲

HOOF IN CONTACT
WITH GROUND: ●

HOOF AIRBORNE: ○

SUPPORT PHASE   SUPPORT PHASE

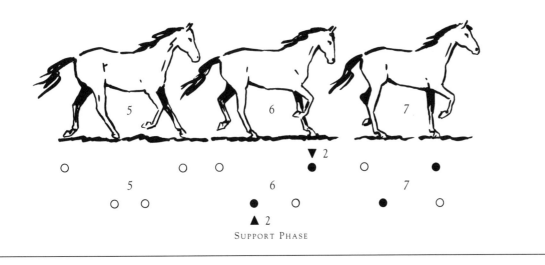

SUPPORT PHASE

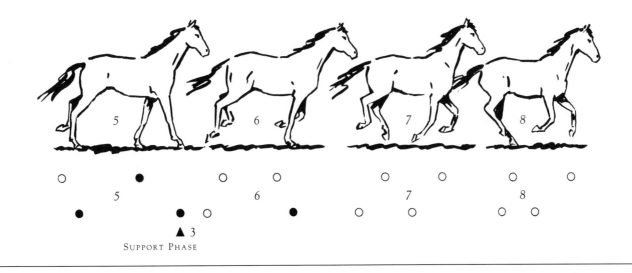

SUPPORT PHASE

Unfortunately, it is commonly, but mistakenly, held by many horsemen and horsewomen that leads are initiated by the advancing foreleg, not by its opposing hindleg. This has probably come about because the front leg is so obvious (e.g., frames 2, 3, and 4 in Figure 3-2C) as it advances conspicuously before the moving animal, especially at the canter. The assumption is a false one and has resulted in a misconception that the horse leads from the front rather than pushes off from behind, particularly when the horse departs from a halt. Smythe notes the following in his description of the horse moving from a standstill:

> It can move a forelimb upon which its weight is resting only by adopting a special attitude or by making some kind of movement which momentarily raises the weight from a forefoot and liberates the joints so that they can move freely.
>
> The adult horse effects this forelimb freedom by a variety of means, all directed towards shifting the centre of gravity backwards. The weight which originally fell upon the forefoot is now in great part transferred to the [leading] hindfoot, or feet as the case may be. The actual degree of movement necessary to effect this weight transfer is very slight and not at all obvious.[1]

Thus, a more accurate portrayal is that the leading hindleg thrusts, or lifts and pushes, the body up and forward, while the opposing front leg simply follows along in advance.

The direction into which the horse bends its body longitudinally, that is, how it arcs its back from head to tail along the spine, also appears to follow from the horse's lead. Thus, the horse cantering on its right lead in Figure 3-3, will, as a rule, tend to bend or arc its body to the left, away from the leading right hindleg. The opposing left foreleg merely points the way to

FIGURE 3-3

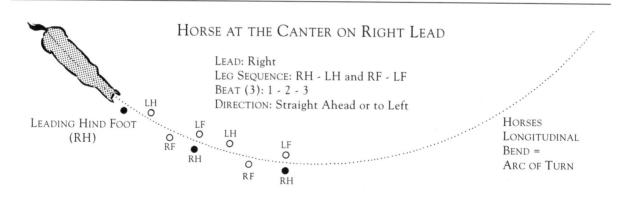

HORSE AT THE CANTER ON RIGHT LEAD

LEAD: Right
LEG SEQUENCE: RH - LH and RF - LF
BEAT (3): 1 - 2 - 3
DIRECTION: Straight Ahead or to Left

LEADING HIND FOOT
(RH)

LH

LF
RF
LH
RH
LF
RF
RH

HORSES
LONGITUDINAL
BEND =
ARC OF TURN

advance the movement and, in so doing, establishes the longitudinal bend of the torso. The wider the turn, the less bend there is through the body; conversely, the sharper the turn, the more bend. But this is not to say that a naturally moving horse is locked into a rigid left or right longitudinal bend through its body because it is moving in a particular lead or direction. On the contrary, wild horses will, if necessary, alternate their bends repeatedly, even from stride to stride—and with great fluidity—while maintaining the same lead, gait-stride, and direction of travel.

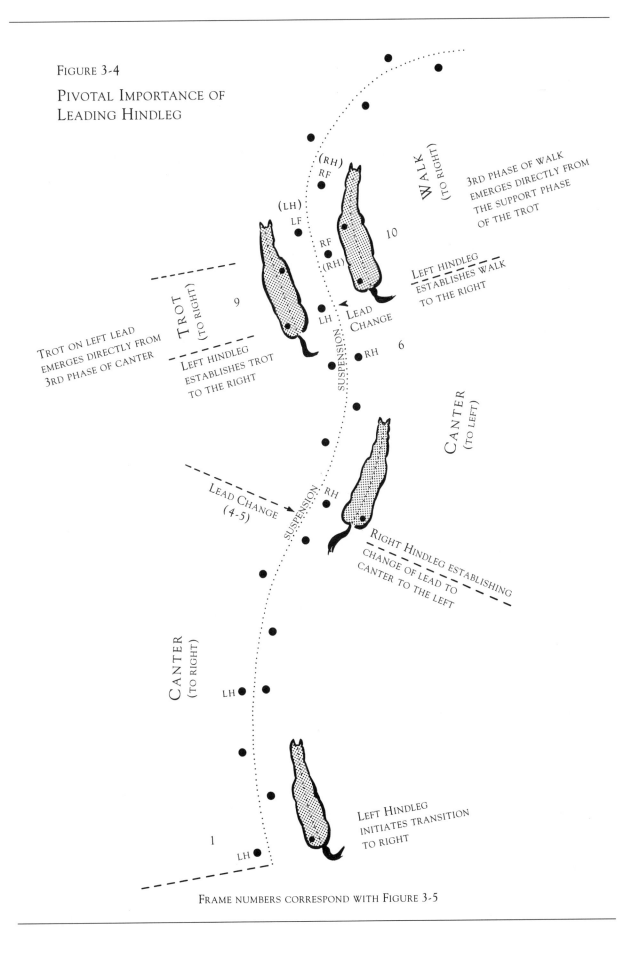

FIGURE 3-4

PIVOTAL IMPORTANCE OF
LEADING HINDLEG

(RH)
RF

(LH)
LF

WALK
(TO RIGHT)

3RD PHASE OF WALK
EMERGES DIRECTLY FROM
THE SUPPORT PHASE
OF THE TROT

RF
(RH)

10

TROT
(TO RIGHT)

9

LEFT HINDLEG
ESTABLISHES WALK
TO THE RIGHT

TROT ON LEFT LEAD
EMERGES DIRECTLY FROM
3RD PHASE OF CANTER

LEFT HINDLEG
ESTABLISHES TROT
TO THE RIGHT

LH
LEAD
CHANGE

SUSPENSION

RH

6

CANTER
(TO LEFT)

LEAD CHANGE
(4-5)

SUSPENSION

RH

RIGHT HINDLEG ESTABLISHING
CHANGE OF LEAD TO
CANTER TO THE LEFT

CANTER
(TO RIGHT)

LH

LEFT HINDLEG
INITIATES TRANSITION
TO RIGHT

1

LH

FRAME NUMBERS CORRESPOND WITH FIGURE 3-5

43

IMPORTANCE OF LEADING HINDLEG TO NATURAL LOCOMOTION OF THE HORSE

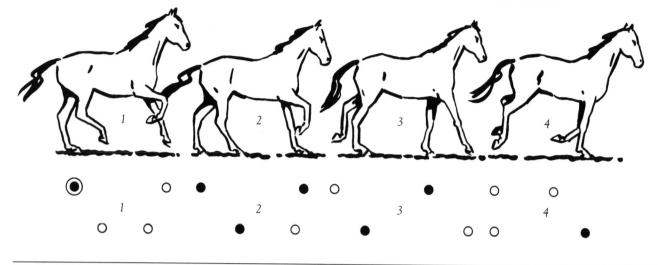

FIGURE 3-5

The leading or initiating hindleg is pivotal in many ways to the natural locomotion of the horse. Not only does it mark the first step, or footfall, of a stride as described above, but it is the leg upon which the horse initiates changes in lead, direction of travel, body extension or contraction, gait, tempo, speed, and collection. These are illustrated in Figure 3-4 as a horse executes a series of transitions from (1) the canter on the left lead while moving to the right, to (2) the canter on the right lead while moving to the left, and (3) while coming to a trot and walk, both on the left lead.

In frames 1 through 4 of Figure 3-5, the horse is cantering to the right, consistent with its leading left hindleg. At the same time, the horse's body has formed a slight but continuous arc from head to tail, consistent with the radius of its turn (Figure 3-6).

In frame 5, the horse shifts into a right lead posture, its body actually bending to the left at this time. In the next moment, frame 6, the right hindleg advances ahead of the leading left hindleg and makes contact with the ground, thereby initiating the new right lead. From this point on, the horse continues to canter onward to the left, frames 7 and 8, in its right lead. In frame 9, anticipating that it must now slow down rather dramatically in preparation for the walk, the horse collects itself extensively through "passive semiflexion of its muscular ring" and, subsequently, contracts, or

FIGURE 3-6

Horse turning at maximum longitudinal bend. In the wild, horses commonly execute turns as small as twenty feet in diameter, such as foals running around their mothers. Arcs less than this diameter normally erupt into brilliant turns on the spot.

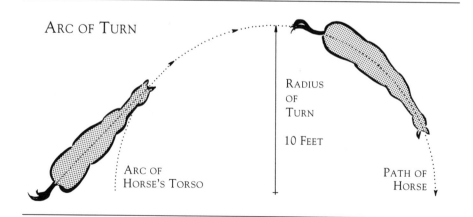

ARC OF TURN

RADIUS
OF
TURN

10 FEET

ARC OF
HORSE'S TORSO

PATH OF
HORSE

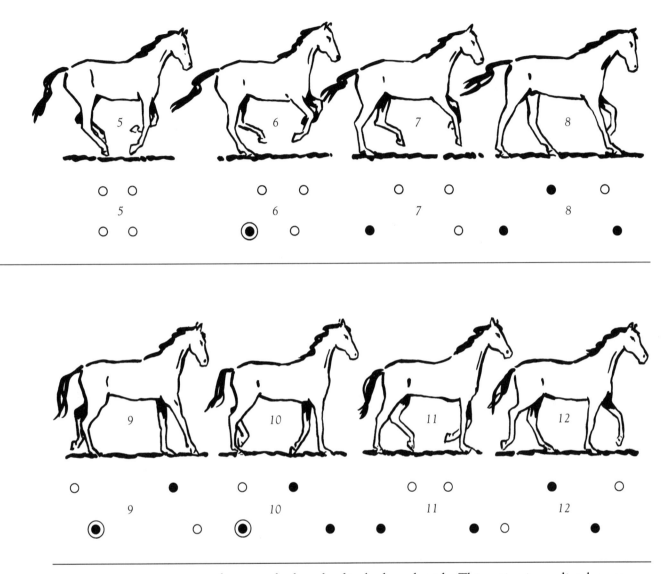

shortens, the length of its body and stride. This action immediately puts the deeply bent left hindleg more directly beneath the descending body weight and, as a result, puts the horse's center of gravity more directly over the haunches in preparation for the final transitions yet to come. Note that in frame 9, the horse has actually entered the first phase of the trot on its left lead (compare with frame 1 in Figure 3-2B). Continuing in this left lead stride pattern, frames 10 through 12, the horse immediately makes the transition to the walk.

COLLECTION

Collection represents a distinct change in the temperament, poise, body posture, and locomotive style of the horse from the ordinary to the extraordinary. As explained earlier, it results from specific behavioral impulses, such as the urge to fight, play, or escape (see Table 3-1). Basically, collection serves to improve dramatically the animal's sense of balance, athletic capability, and overall performance. For example, we see collected behavior in the aggressive posturings of the monarch who defends his harem of mares against rival stallions, or in the young foal who encircles its mother expressively while in play.

During collection, a transference of body weight occurs from the forehand—weight that is normally supported by the horse's forelegs—onto the hindquarters. This redistribution of body mass and weight balances the horse so that it is able to modify its natural gaits to various ends.

For example, to increase or decrease the rate of speed at which it is traveling, a horse will first collect itself, that is, transfer weight from the forehand to the hindquarters, and then extend or shorten the length of

FIGURE 3-7   its strides. In this way, it will be able to go faster or slower, yet maintain

VALUE OF COLLECTION IN RELATION TO STRIDE EXTENSION, ACCELERATION, AND SPEED

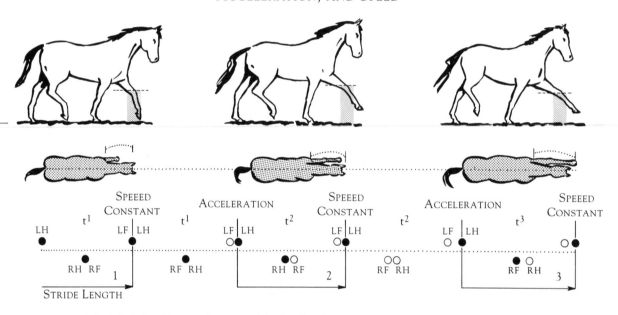

RHYTHM: 1-2, 1-2, 1-2   TEMPO: Constant ($t^1=t^2=t^3$)   RELATIVE STRIDE LENGTHS: 3>2>1
RELATIVE CADENCE: 1>2>3   SPEED: $\dfrac{\text{Stride Length}}{t}$ ACCELERATION: > Δ Speed (increase in rate of speed)

the natural rhythm and tempo of its gait. Figure 3-7 illustrates how this relationship of collection to gait modification might occur at the trot.

At the far left (frame 1), the horse, having already collected itself, exhibits a relatively high cadence (i.e., it steps higher than when not collected) but executes very little stride extension as it trots slowly along. Next, as the animal begins to accelerate (frame 2), its cadence lowers slightly to facilitate stride extension, which also has the effect of sustaining the gait's natural rhythm and tempo. Finally, the animal combines maximum stride extension with a reduced cadence to attain full speed (frame 3). Again the rhythm and tempo remain unchanged, even though the horse is traveling much faster (Figure 3-8).

This corollary between manipulation of stride extension and cadence—amid constant tempo and rhythm—resulting in changes in speed, has been an important focus among many of the world's finest riders and trainers. In

The Complete Training of Horse and Rider, Podhajsky wrote, "The difference between the various tempos—the ordinary trot, the collected trot, the extended trot—does not lie in the acceleration or the reduction of the pace, but exclusively in the lengthening of the stride or the elevation of the steps while maintaining the rhythm."[2]

FIGURE 3-8

Monarch, head and neck arched, is ready for war— collected and exhibiting superb stride extension at the trot. Note rocky, pebbly ground.

Jim Hansen

The principle of collection is universal, as are the fundamentals of natural locomotion, to athletic excellence, whether animal or human. Think of Abebe Bikila of Kenya, who won the grueling marathon in the 1960 Olympics, running barefooted over Rome's cobblestone streets, and more recently in 1988 the remarkable Joyner sisters' sprint triumphs in Korea. What all have in common is *poise* and *rhythm* as individuals relax and "collect" themselves, extend their strides, and increase their speeds to the levels that only years of training can facilitate.

In order to gain some practical experience and insight into the meaning of collection, let's try the sequence shown in Figure 3-7. To start, try walking in place at a slow, comfortable tempo and even rhythm. Count the beat of your rhythm every time your left (or right) foot strikes the ground:

    (beat)   (beat)
    left — right, left — right, etc.

The beat, or tempo, of your walk should reoccur at even intervals. Now collect yourself by marching in place, as though you were a drum major or majorette in a parade. You will need to increase your cadence, that is, step higher and swing your arms more. *And keep the beat of your rhythm the same.* At this point, you should find that you are having to move your arms and legs more vigorously in order to sustain the same tempo.

Next, march forward in this well-collected posture and maintain the same beat: one-two, one-two. To step forward, however, while maintaining the same tempo, you will notice that your cadence must be diminished first, so step lower. Now, keeping your tempo and rhythm constant, really extend the length of your stride forward as far as you can without moving your legs faster or falling on your face (or back). Now, you should find yourself moving forward faster (speed, not tempo) although your legs will be moving at essentially the same rate or tempo. If you are in good shape, like an athlete or a wild horse, these transitions will be vigorous, smooth, and *relaxed*, not in the least bit forced.

In order to understand this concept of relaxation, think of the gymnast who is perfecting the "planche," a stationary move on the still rings in which the body is held parallel to the ground by the arms, which are themselves held straight outward and down slightly from each side of the body like a soaring eagle. In this remarkably difficult and collected position, the gymnast learns to breathe deeply and completely relax—even smiling for the judges on occassion—holding the position for three to five seconds at a time. This exemplifies the very polar nature of collection: The body is athletically prepared to do the very most while it is completely energized and relaxed at the same time.

Back to our walking example. In the absence of collection, you would have little choice but to move your legs faster, and faster, and still faster. As a result, you would be less and less relaxed in order to accelerate and maintain the same level of speed as if you were collected. This would mean also having to do more work.

Consider the case of two horses running the same distance as represented by the graph in Figure 3-9. As you can see, Horse A, which runs without the benefits of collection, exhibits few or no periods of stride extension; consequently, it must execute more steps per minute (i.e., increase its tempo) in order to travel the same distance as Horse B. In contrast, Horse B collects—becomes poised and transfers weight from the forehand to the hindquarters—and extends the lengths of its strides. The result is that it is able to execute fewer steps and exert less work energy than Horse A in the same space-time framework. Curve A, thus, might characterize the locomotive style of an imbalanced, unsound, or unathletic horse, while curve B, in contrast, exemplifies the type of athletic prowess seen commonly among healthy, sound, and well-collected wild horses.

Unquestionably, wild horses *do* move unnaturally from time to time—

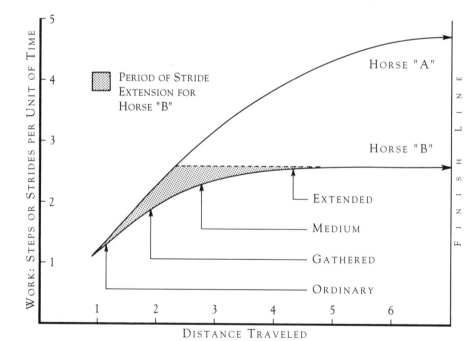

FIGURE 3-9

IMPACT OF STRIDE EXTENSION ON HORSES RACING

that is, imbalanced, uncollected, out of gait and on the forehand, but this is to be expected in the temporary awkwardness of a battle, in play, or during the casualness of grazing. As a rule, though, athletic grace, balance, and—during extraordinary behavior—collection, are normal and necessary ingredients in the alchemy of natural equine locomotion in the wild, where survival is always at stake.

Down through the centuries, collection has been the subject of much concern among the world's greatest horsemen and -women. Many have written extensively about it, realizing its fundamental and integral importance in balanced training and riding. Most have warned that horseback riding under extraordinary circumstances, such as on the racetrack, in the rodeo ring, or on endurance rides, *in the absence of collection*, may very well be the leading, if not primary, cause of imbalance and lameness among domestic horses. Xenophon, an ancient Greek general, described the essential characteristics of collection over 2,400 years ago:

> If you desire to handle a good war-horse so as to make his action the more magnificent and striking, you must refrain from pulling at his mouth with the bit as well as from spurring and whipping him. Most people think that this is the way to make him look fine; but they only produce an effect exactly contrary to what they desire—they positively blind their horses by jerking the mouth up instead of letting them look forward, and by spurring and striking scare them into disorder and danger. This is the way horses behave that are fretted by their riders into ugly and ungraceful action; but if you teach your horse to go with a light hand on the bit, and yet to hold his head well up and to arch his neck, you will be making him do just what the animal himself glories and delights in. A proof that he really delights in it is that when a horse is turned loose and runs off to join other horses, and especially towards mares, then he holds his head up as high as he can, arches his neck in the most spirited style, lifts his legs with free actions, and raises his tail. So when he is induced by a man to assume all the airs and graces which he puts on of himself when he is showing off voluntarily, the result is a horse that likes to be ridden, that presents a magnificent sight, that looks alert, that is the observed of all observers.[3]

Xenophon's colorful image of the collected horse underscores the type of motivated locomotive behavior that can be seen among wild, free-roaming horses. Indeed, it is motivated behavior that creates the posture and state of poise that characterize the substance of collection. As Xenophon duly notes, collection is not something that can be forced upon the horse. It is a process in which the horse engages willfully due to specific behavioral stimuli. And, once more, unless we are able to recognize and understand the types of motivated behavior that underlie the image, we cannot hope realistically to understand the essence of the natural locomotive process nor, for that matter, the mind of the horse.

Unfortunately, in the domestic horse world, I find little concern for or understanding of the horse's true natural state. The result of this neglect is that many equestrians have no real idea of what constitutes natural equine behavior, and collection-based behavior, in particular. As a farrier, I have

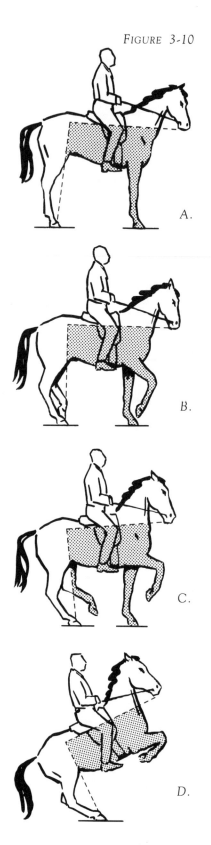

FIGURE 3-10

A.

B.

C.

D.

seen time and again how easily riders will confuse a troubled horse that is excited and frantic with one that is equally excited but collected. Indeed, a frantic horse can exhibit elements of collection because it is natural for it to try to collect itself when subjected to extraordinary mental and physical demands, regardless of how unreasonable the demands are.

With collection, a horse is in a state of mental and physical relaxation—poise, in other words—coupled with locomotive balance. In contrast, the frantic horse appears anxious and unrelaxed, its muscles are tense and do not work together effectively, and invariably, the animal will be imbalanced as its natural gait complex collapses into locomotive disarray. More often than not, the animal's lack of poise can be traced to an ambience of fear, force, and violence, which stems from dishonest communication on the part of its uninformed rider.

Faced with identical situations, such as a race, the frantic horse and poised horse are likely to yield two entirely different sets of results. The forced and imbalanced, frantic horse, unable to think clearly, will often sacrifice its own well-being for its rider in order to win a race at any cost, even if it means going lame or performing while unsound. Emery, Miller, and Van Hoosen, in their invaluable text on horseshoeing, relate a tragic example: "The horse was racing down the stretch toward the finish line. As he passed the grandstand, he tore his hoof completely off below the fetlock and hurled it over the fence. Worst of all, he continued to run on the stump."[4]

This sad propensity for self-destruction surfaces in frantic domestic horses that are coerced by dishonest riders to perform beyond the limits of their natural abilities. In reality, these animals turn to self-endangerment in order to escape the threat or reality of punishment, such as an insensitive rider's brutal and unrelenting whippings and spurrings at the finish of a race (what a great reward for a horse after it has run its heart out, probably at an unnatural gallop, without the benefits of collection, while too young, legal-ly *and* illegally full of chemicals, with other horses it does not know, and under a rider whom it has never met before).

In contrast, the poised, well-balanced, and collected horse will, if allowed or encouraged, maintain its athletic grace and sense of self-preservation at all costs, even if it means losing a race or contest. In the wild, proud and intimidating monarchs battle over estrous mares, conceding defeat only when too exhausted to sustain their collected states. Apparently, nature has seen fit to invoke the importance of stamina, grace of movement, and poise throughout wild horse society in lieu of violence with the purpose of maiming another or injuring oneself. The vanquished and exhausted, but not usually injured, can simply quit and try again another time when rested, whatever its cause. Clearly, this behavior underlies an entirely different frame of mind than that seen in the frantic horse.

What, then, in specific terms, are the mental and physical characteristics of natural collection-based behavior in natural horses?

IMPULSION: UNIFICATION OF MIND AND BODY
With the onset of collection, the motivated and balanced horse stimulates its muscles into a state of high energy or readiness to go to work. As stated earlier, it does this in response to behavioral impulses, such as the instincts

to breed, escape, or fight. Knowledgeable equestrians refer to this mentally and physically energized state as *impulsion*. It is important to note that without impulsion, collection is not possible.

Understanding the difference between natural impulsion and forced locomotive behavior is one way to grasp the mental state of horses moving naturally with impulsion. As an example, Figure 3-10 illustrates a horse and rider moving progressively from a relaxed, uncollected state (frame A) to a highly collected and energized state (frame D), bursting with impulsion (and relaxation) and culminating in what dressage experts call a *levade* (French: "a lifting"). Both horse and rider are composed and fully in control of themselves. The rider understands the natural locomotive progression that leads to the lift (in part, a well-collected trot approximately in place) and, through natural aids, cues the horse to concentrate its energies in the hindquarters to facilitate it, much as wild horses do when fighting, breeding, or playing (Figure 3-11).

FIGURE 3-11

Powerful musculatures of monarchs at work during stallion rivalry near water hole in Red Desert of Wyoming.

Jeff Foott

Figure 3-12, in contrast, depicts another horse and rider merely rearing. There is no collection or poise and the situation is shaky, dangerous, and recalls the frantic horse discussed earlier. The problem here is that there has been no preparation via the natural gait complex, and the frantic horse, understandably, can really only attempt to escape the thrashing or pulling action of the bit by rearing backwards, instead of lifting itself upon its hindquarters.

FIGURE 3-12

Western style rider and mount push test of endurance to limit as horse, clearly overwrought, rebels by rearing.

The difference between the frantic and collected horse lies in the absence of impulsion in the former. The frantic horse acts unnaturally from fear, force, and violence, for it is confused and realizes that it has no means of escape or ventilation through honest communication. It is merely a whipped slave. The collected horse, acting from a state of impulsion, is not forced, for it is a motivated and willing participant because its natural rider has aligned his or her equestrian goals with the animal's natural behavioral impulses.

PHYSICAL STATE:
COLLECTION AS A "CLOSED MUSCULAR RING"

In his scholarly but abstruse work, Waldemar Suenig, the late German author and distinguished horseman, describes collection as an expression of a "closed muscular ring," which "pulsates" rhythmically within the balanced, naturally motivated horse:

> The regular engagement of the hindquarters is produced by muscular pulsations that are elicited by the controls via the central nervous system, and in turn they produce pulsation of the extensor and flexor muscles that extend along the spinal column through the neck, returning along the belly to the pelvis. These wavelike movements will be shorter or longer depending upon the framework, that is, the degree of collection.[5]

The muscles Suenig speaks of form (roughly) a ring of contiguous muscles that span the entire length of the horse's body. The numerous muscles involved serve to link and move the animal's appendicular (legs) and axial (torso) skeletal framework, coordinating the movements of every part of the horse. Thus, when the horse is collected and balanced—and energized with

SUENIG'S RING

FIGURE 3-13

Key muscle groups according to Suenig that form a "muscle ring" and help to explain collection.

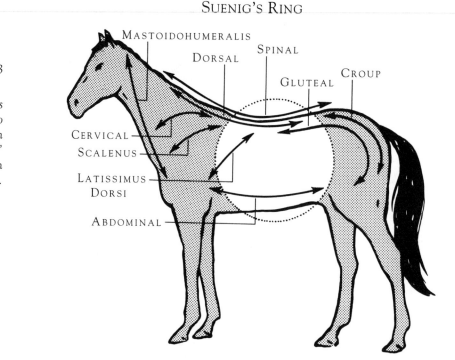

impulsion—the muscles in its neck, back, hindquarters, legs, and abdomen work together sychronously and efficiently to unite the "fore" and "aft" of the horse. Although Suenig's understanding of equine anatomy was limited by the knowledge available in his day and, therefore, may conflict somewhat in terminology and other specifics with more contemporary horse anatomy books, his interpretation of how the various muscles interconnect and work together to foster balanced locomotion is worth thinking about. So, using

Figure 3-13 as a map of the horse's anatomy, let's follow Suenig's description of the muscle ring and see how it facilitates collection in the horse:

Some of the most important muscles involved are the *croup* (ischia) muscles linked to those of the back and reaching down to the stifle and hock joints; the *gluteal* muscles located around the hip joints, which also track down to the stifle; the long *dorsal* muscles, whose action reaches from the dock of the tail to the occipital bone in the horse's head; the *latissimus dorsi* muscles that branch off from them and control the movements of the forelegs; the *cervical* muscles starting at the front thoracic vertebrae (the withers) and connecting them with the cervical vertebrae; and the *spinal* muscles, which transmit the forward pull of the cervical muscles upon the spinous processes to the vertebrae and act as a strong elastic suspensory band to prevent the back from sagging and to produce the free, elevated, and supple carriage of the tail when they function correctly. The *mastoidohumeralis* muscles, which connect the head, the neck, and the humerus, are equally important, because they are necessary for the smooth cooperation of the forehand and the hindquarters. Then there are the *scalenus* muscles, which attach the ribs to the base of the neck, and lastly, the *abdominal* muscles which run along the belly and sides of the horse's body as a sort of truss, affecting respiration and acting as the bottom half of the muscular ring, in combination with the dorsal and scalenus muscles, to establish the connection between the forehand and the hindquarters.[6]

In order to understand better how the parts work together, see Table 3-3 below, which has been broken down into four main groups of muscles:

TABLE 3-3

FOUR MUSCLE GROUPS AND ELEMENTS OF COLLECTION

Muscles Activated	Element of Collection
Pelvic, hip, and thigh	Flexion of hindquarters —provides thrust and main propulsory forces in response to brain impulses
Back and abdominal	Rhythmic contraction and expansion of back and abdomen —unites hindquarters with forehand
Neck	Elevation of neck and flexion of head at axis vertebrae —balances the forehand while hindquarters provide thrust
Shoulder and chest	Elevation of forehand and increased freedom of movement of the forelegs —responds to actions of hindquarters through muscles of back and abdomen by elevating entire forehand, thus, giving greater freedom of movement to front legs; shoulder provides minor thrust and propulsion

FIGURE 3-14

Figure 3-14 shows a well-collected horse trotting approximately in place, called the *piaffe* (French: "a pawing") by some equestrians. Note that this is a movement seen commonly among wild horses exhibiting extraordinary locomotive behavior. It is a type of setup move used in preparation for

ELEMENTS OF COLLECTION

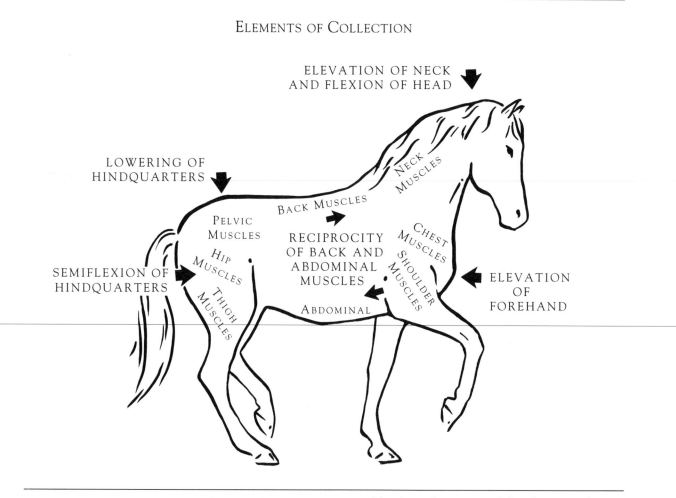

ELEVATION OF NECK
AND FLEXION OF HEAD

LOWERING OF
HINDQUARTERS

NECK MUSCLES

BACK MUSCLES

PELVIC MUSCLES

RECIPROCITY
OF BACK AND
ABDOMINAL
MUSCLES

CHEST MUSCLES

HIP MUSCLES

SHOULDER MUSCLES

SEMIFLEXION OF
HINDQUARTERS

THIGH MUSCLES

ABDOMINAL

ELEVATION
OF
FOREHAND

rearing, jumping, or turning quickly. As such, it exemplifies the type of contiguity and interplay between the muscles of Suenig's ring that are so necessary to balanced locomotion.

In the following sections, the elements of collection (see Table 3-3) are examined more closely.

FLEXION OF THE HINDQUARTERS

The most powerful group of muscles in the horse's body are those that compose the hindquarters, or "haunches." According to many equestrian authorities, the process of collection originates and, for the most part, is sustained here. The muscles of the hindquarters envelop the animal's pelvis, hips, and thighs. They are particularly important during collection because they engage the three major joints of the hindquarters—the hip, stifle, and hock—in what I term "active" and "passive semiflexion."

The word semiflexion is used because the three major joints of the hindquarters (hip, stifle, and hock) are anatomically configured to remain in a *partial* state of flexion at all times (Figure 3-15). Just like our own hip joints, which normally are not fully extended (leg drawn completely to the

CONFORMATION OF SEMIFLEXOR JOINTS OF FRONT AND HIND LEGS

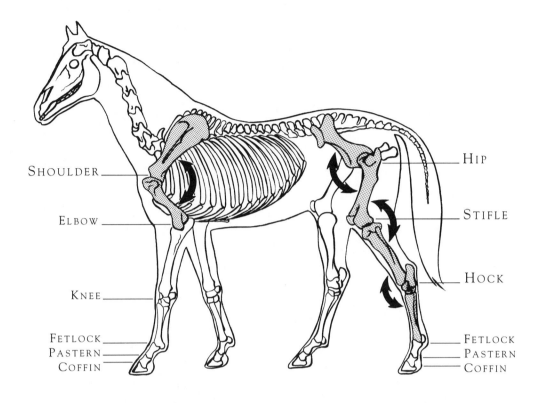

SHOULDER

ELBOW

KNEE

FETLOCK
PASTERN
COFFIN

HIP

STIFLE

HOCK

FETLOCK
PASTERN
COFFIN

FIGURE 3-15

rear) nor totally flexed (leg drawn completely to the front) as we walk along. In other words, they are not designed to hyperextend like the bracing joints of the horse's lower leg (fetlock, pastern) or the human knee. In contrast to the hindlegs, which have three semiflexor joints, the horse's front leg has only one such joint—the shoulder, which provides only minor thrust and propulsion in the forward half of the horse (Table 3-4). The elbow and knee joints of the front leg, which correspond to the hind leg's stifle and hock, are configured to hyperextend and, therefore, can only serve to support the propulsory actions of the shoulder.

TABLE 3-4

At any rate, the semiflexors are primarily involved with propulsion during the natural locomotive process, expanding throughout the leg's support

MAJOR JOINTS OF THE FRONT AND HIND LEGS

FRONT LEG			HIND LEG		
Bracer	*Semiflexor*	*Action of Joint**	*Bracer*	*Semiflexor*	*Action of Joint**
—	Shoulder	Expanding	—	Hip	Expanding
Elbow	—	Closing	—	Stifle	Expanding
Knee	—	Closing	—	Hock	Expanding
Fetlock	—	Closing	Fetlock	—	Closing
Pastern	—	Closing	Pastern	—	Closing
Coffin	—	Closing	Coffin	—	Closing

*Primary configuration of joint during leg's propulsory phase

phase, while the bracers close tight, or hyperextend, and remain stationary until flexed and lifted from the ground by the upward momentum of the horse's body (see frame 6 in Figure 3-16). I use the qualifiers active and

COURBETTE

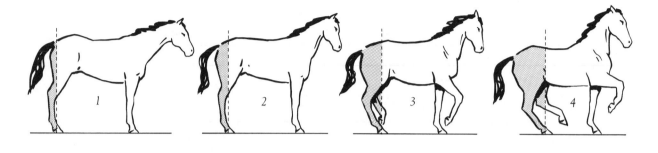

FIGURE 3-16

Jump on the hind legs (courbette). Extraordinary behavior (play, fighting, breeding) among stallions will yield this exciting jump. Note that shaded areas denote extent that body weight has shifted over the hindquarters.

passive to differentiate the more common and ordinary or active semiflexions one sees in the daily lives of wild horses from the less-common and extraordinary passive semiflexions, which only surface occasionally in response to specific behavioral impulses.

Active semiflexion refers to the normal, natural bending (i.e., opening and closing, or extending and flexing) action of the three major joints of the hindquarters. Active semiflexion occurs when the horse is moving in the absence of, or at low levels of, collection. *Passive semiflexion* refers to the additional, increased bending required of the joints when they are "loaded" with weight from the forehand during higher levels of collection.

Consider once more the examples in Figures 3-10 and 3-12. The three major joints of the hindquarters in the horse executing the levade (Figure 3-10) form much smaller angles with each other than in the rearing horse (Figure 3-12). The angles formed between the joints are also more equal in the levade than the rear. Podhajsky noted this important difference in his training of Lipizzaner stallions at the famed Spanish Riding School of Vienna:

> The correct bend of the hind legs must be brought about by
> all three joints being bent equally and to the same degree. If
> the hocks only are bent, as is often the case [in poorly trained
> domestic horses], the bend will be of little value and the horse
> will be prematurely worn out as in all likelihood it will lead
> to spavins or thorough-pins.[7]

The deep bending of these joints has the additional effect of distorting the normal posture of the horse when viewed in profile. "One finds," wrote Museler, in *Riding Logic*, "that the horse shortens its profile from rear to front, with the hind legs working more actively under the centre of gravity and the quarters lowered. A natural corollary to the lowering of the quarters is that the forehand, bearing less weight, is raised."[8]

Actually, it is because of its athletic development that the horse performing the levade in Figure 3-10 is able to bend deeply upon its powerful hindquarters while fully relaxed and poised without risking injury to itself or its rider. The same is true of the wild horse in Figure 3-11. Also, the piaffing

horse in Figure 3-14 is bent equally deep through its hindquarters. Each of these animals, all of which are highly collected and deeply semiflexed, is able to exploit fully the powerful muscles of its hindlegs—unlike the rearing horse in Figure 3-12, whose center of gravity is displaced so far to the rear as to compromise the safety of both horse and rider.

In much the same way that the well-collected horse is able to bend deeply through its hindquarters, it is also able to expand the three major joints to an extraordinary degree. In fact, whether flexed completely or extended fully, both joint configurations of the hindquarters still represent states of passive semiflexion. Both extremes are demonstrated by a horse jumping, called the *courbette* (French: "to jump") by some dressage trainers, which is illustrated in Figure 3-16. In this complex series of movements, the hindquarters bend deeply as the horse squats in a levade in preparation for thrusting its body upward (frame 5). They also open to or near their maximum extent in the next moment (frame 6), consistent with the degree of the animal's high level of athletic development. I have seen monarchs execute as many as five or six deep-bending/max-expanding hops in a row while chasing after elusive estrous mares not quite ready for intromission. I have also observed battling stallions sitting on their hindquarters, then suddenly springing into the air at each other like rockets.

RHYTHMIC CONTRACTION AND EXPANSION OF BACK AND ABDOMEN

Linking the hindquarters to the horse's forehand (forearm, chest, neck, and head) are the muscles of the back and abdomen. As the hindquarters engage in passive semiflexion, the muscles of the back also undergo extraordinary contraction (and expansion) in order to aid in the elevation of the horse's forehand. At the same time, their action is supported by the reciprocal expansive and contractive actions of the abdominal muscles. These give-and-take, rubberbandlike actions between the muscles of the back, abdominal, and hindquarters are complex and require much added effort from the horse. But it is all necessary if the horse is to load weight from the forehand upon its powerful haunches.

FIGURE 3-17

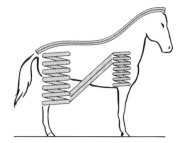

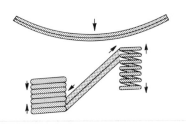

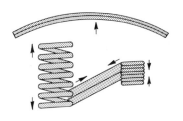

The degree of passive semiflexion required by the three major joints of the hindquarters to facilitate the transfer of body weight upon them from the forehand during collection is what determines the degree of muscle reciprocity that must take place through the back and abdomen. Thus, we can expect greater expansive and contractive actions to occur between these muscles in more concentrated, short-striding, collected movements (e.g., the trot in place) than in extended, long-striding, collected movements (e.g., the extended trot). But, in either case, it is the back and abdomen that must support the rearward transfer of body weight onto the hindquarters, via, to repeat Suenig once more, "pulsations of the extensor and flexor muscles that extend along the spinal column through the neck, returning along the belly to the pelvis."

Given the above, it comes as no surprise that the muscles stretching across the back and abdomen of the wild and athletic horse are often well developed and conspicuous. In fact, they are clear indicators that a horse is an athlete and has been moving naturally. As Suenig wrote, "In well-trained horses, the cervical muscles [are] as hard as marble."[9] Xenophon comments, "A double-back is easier to sit upon and stronger."[10] (The saddle was still in its infancy in Xenophon's day and most Greeks still rode bareback. The expression "double-back" refers to the cervical muscles Suenig describes that emerge along each side of the horse's spine.) In horses that are "poor," or unathletic, these same muscles will fail to protrude, and the spine may rise above them. Riding such horses may border on animal abuse.

With its sturdy back and long, elastic, powerful abdominal muscles, the athletic natural horse can be seen as an elastic system of springs and coils. Figure 3-17 illustrates this concept. The back of the horse is represented as a fairly rigid automobile leaf spring that flexes only slightly upwards and downwards. The hindquarters, represented as a massive coil spring, are linked elastically to the thorax (chest) by the abdominal muscles, represented here as wide elastic bands. The forehand, represented as a small coil spring atop a crutch, braces the forehand of the horse.

With the entire assembly in operation (Figure 3-17), the elastics represent the abdominal muscles stretching, or expanding, as the coil of the hindquarters contracts in preparation for opening and, later, propelling the horse up and forward. The crutchlike forelegs, meanwhile, brace to support the entire torso. At the same time, the rigid leaf spring (double-back) bends slightly downward to receive the thrust of the hindquarters. When finally the horse thrusts itself forward, the massive coil (hindquarters) opens, the leafspring (spine) bends upward, the crutch (forearm) lifts up and reaches forward for new ground, and the elastic bands (abdominals) contract to help bring the coil forward for the next thrust. Peter Goody, in his standard atlas of equine anatomy, echoes a similar idea, noting that the spine of the horse is a relatively rigid structure driven along by the powerful hindquarters:

> The spine consists of a string of incompressible bony vertebrae united by cartilaginous intervertebral discs which are slightly compressible. The vertebral column (spine) forms the main longitudinal girder of the body, providing strength for weight suspension and furnishing a relatively incompressible bony

column through which the propelling forces from the hindlimbs can be transmitted to the trunk.[11]

ELEVATION OF THE NECK AND FLEXION OF HEAD

A corollary of the reciprocal action between the back and abdominal muscles is the elevating of the horse's neck and simultaneous flexing of the head (Figure 3-18). As Xenophon wrote, "The neck should not be thrown out

FIGURE 3-18

How the horse elevates and flexes its head and neck. Flexion (nodding) of head occurs at atlas vertebra (1st cervical joint). Rotation of head occurs at axis vertebra (2nd cervical joint). The neck arches along the entire corridor of cervical vertebrae, of which there are seven; at the same time, the neck is able to bend laterally. These movements are made possible by the greatly reduced spinal processes (protusion) emanating from the central vertebral body.

ELEVATION/FLEXION OF HEAD/NECK

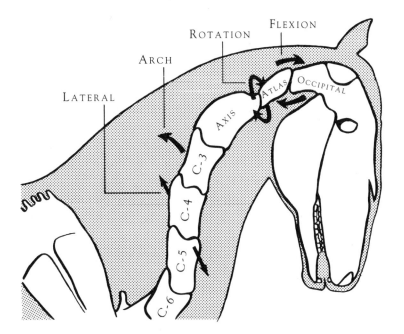

from the chest like a boar's, but, like a cock's, should rise straight up to the poll."[12] During collection, the elevated neck helps to balance the horse as the hindquarters are lowered to support and thrust body weight from the forehand. In fact, the neck raises in direct proportion to the degree of passive semiflexion, or bending, of the hindquarters. The more the horse semiflexes passively (bends or expands) the three major joints of the hindquarters, the higher the neck is raised by the back and abdominal muscles to counteract the rearward transfer of body weight. This balancing action has the simultaneous effect of elevating the forelegs and making their movements much freer. As Podhajsky explains:

> The connection between raising the head and neck and collection has been one of the most misinterpreted notions of equestrian art. . . . To improve the balance of the horse it is necessary to raise the head and neck. This can be achieved only with the increase of correct collection. The position of the head must be maintained while the forehand is carried higher by the lowering of the hindquarters. This will make the horse appear higher in front, his movements will be freer, and the hindquarters will be lowered by the bending of the three joints [hip, stifle, and hock].[13]

Recognizing that the raising of the neck and elevating of the forehand naturally accompany the passive semiflexion of the hindquarters during collection, Podhajsky goes on to warn riders that they should "never try to achieve it by forcing the head up with the reins."[14]

At the same time the neck is raised, the horse also nods or flexes its head at the *atlas vertebra* (first cervical vertebra) behind the poll, which has the effect of lowering it (Figure 3-18). In this raised, "cock's-head" configuration, the horse's vision and sense of balance are stabilized because the head is rendered relatively immobile, in contrast to the more accentuated movements occurring elsewhere in its body (e.g., the legs). Among well-balanced and collected wild horses, the relative position of the head and neck, relative to the horse's torso, changes very little within the locus of a single stride. The relative position of the neck and the amount of flexion of the head will vary, however, with the amount of stride extension. As Podhajsky points out, it will be "greater [in the shortened paces] than in the extended paces."[15] In other words, the relative position of the head and neck, with respect to the torso, appears to change very little, although in relation to the legs and, to a much lesser extent, the ground, it changes considerably.

Looking at the horse's body from the vantage point of the ground, the rhythmic up-and-down motion of the head and neck follows that of the body, which, in turn, responds to the actions of the legs; the gait, its tempo and rhythm; and so on down the line. The unevenness of the terrain upon which the animal is traveling also has impact upon this movement. Collection, however, tends to smooth out the potentially violent oscillations that would otherwise spiral upward to the head. In this context, I think of a black stallion I observed one day in Nevada near Lake Lehontan. Trotting and cantering gracefully but quickly up the side of a hill and over what was extremely rocky and uneven ground, the animal's head and neck scarcely moved in its elevated position relative to the torso. I also think of the countless numbers of horsemen and horsewomen who unfortunately see a fast trot as their equestrian nemesis. Think of the beatings that horses' backs must endure from riders' rears each year before the "post" or canter are resorted to—with or without the rider's consent. Sadly, most of this agony and jackhammering will remain inevitable until collection, cadence, and stride extension are better understood and practiced by the horse-using community.

ELEVATION OF FOREHAND AND INCREASED FREEDOM OF MOVEMENT OF THE FORELEGS

The final link in the horse's closed muscular ring is the musculature of the shoulders and thorax (chest). During collection, these muscles respond to the reciprocal actions of the back and abdomen as they help transfer and load body weight upon the hindquarters. Two important things happen to the forehand as a result of this.

First, the neck and head, chest, shoulder, and front legs become more elevated due to the reciprocal tugging and pulling of the back and abdominal muscles—themselves being acted upon by the powerful muscles of the hindquarters. To visualize this, think of the horse executing the levade in Figure 3-10 or the horse trotting in place in Figure 3-14. Note that the front part of the horse, including the legs, simply becomes more elevated as the hindlegs bend and the hindquarters lower.

Second, and as a consequence of the elevating action described above, the front legs are freed considerably from having to support body weight, resulting in much less restriction. They can extend farther (stride extension), higher (cadence), and quicker (tempo) without all the cumbersome body weight above to load them down. They also can become instruments of sorts, not unlike the horse's prehensile lips: witness the adept monarch who uses them as swords in battle, as means of grasping or holding for support during breeding, when pawing in frustration, or when digging for food and water.

The amount of weight that the hindquarters are compelled to support when weight is loaded on them, and the weight that the forelegs are otherwise compelled to support in the absence of collection, is probably much less than many equestrians think. For those who doubt this, consider R. H. Smythe's observations:

> Being an herbivorous animal with a voluminous intestine, the horse normally carries a large part of its body weight behind its midline. although the chest capacity is of necessity large, the lungs within it are collapsible, inflatable and very sponge-like, and accordingly light in weight. The thorax itself, supported by thoracic vertebrae and comparatively light ribs, would be completely outweighed by the abdomen were it not for the help provided in maintaining balance by the presence of a long neck supporting a weighty head at its distal extremity. The abdomen is at all times loaded with partly digested vegetable matter, weighing seldom less than half a hundredweight and often a great deal more.[16]

On the other hand, when we add a rider to the horse's back, the transfer of weight to the hindquarters would appear critical, especially during extraordinary working conditions (racing, jumping) because such an addition immediately shifts the horse's center of gravity forward toward the forehand and away from the hindquarters, the animal's normal repository of body weight during collection. This explains why proponents of classical or natural horsemanship warn us again and again of the dangers of riding horses without collection and "on the forehand," at least when we are asking our horses to work hard for us.

UPWARD AND DOWNWARD TRANSITIONS

Another fascinating dimension of the horse's three natural gaits is how the animal integrates them in what I have termed *upward* and *downward transitions*. Before studying the movements of the wild horse, I thought a horse could move naturally from the walk directly to the canter without executing the intermediate trot, or, conversely, move directly from the canter into the walk without trotting first. By the same token, I thought the horse could move directly from the halt to either the trot or canter without walking, and vice-versa. What I found, however, is that the wild horse always moves sequentially from one gait to the next, including the halt when appropriate.

Specifically, upward transitions followed the sequence halt to walk,

walk to trot, trot to canter, while downward transitions followed the same sequence in reverse: canter to trot, trot to walk, walk to halt. For example, a horse might move from the walk to the canter, but only after trotting first; it might move from the canter to the walk, but only after trotting and walking first in sequence.

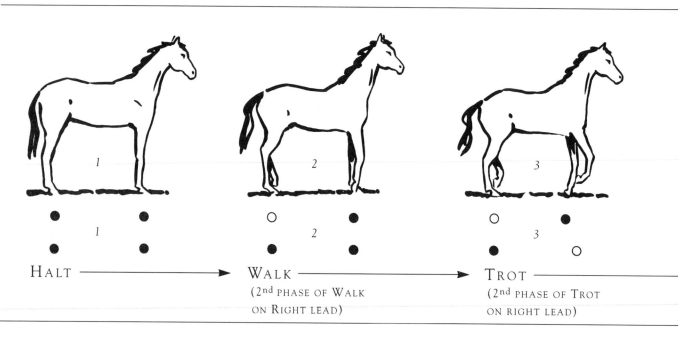

HALT ⟶ WALK ⟶ TROT ⟶
(2nd phase of Walk   (2nd phase of Trot
on Right lead)   on right lead)

FIGURE 3-19

The upward transition of halt canter includes the intermediary gaits of the walk and trot. This is apparent from an analysis of the gaits' footfall sequences. The downward transition from canter to halt is the same progression in reverse.

Even in well-collected, quickly executed movements, such as might occur in a fast get-away, the natural upward and downward transitions of the horse's three natural gaits, including the halt, are still executed. For a long time, it was difficult to see this. What I found was that the execution of a complete upward transition, from the halt to the canter, by a highly collected and deeply semiflexed horse can be carried out with such smoothness, precision, and fluidity, that the transition appears to be invisible.

Yet, as illustrated in Figure 3-19, the movement includes at least one support phase of each of the intermediate gaits (the walk and trot). Predictably, if the same movement were exhibited with less collection and at a slower speed, more elements of the intermediate gaits would begin to unfold until, at a very slow and/or uncollected tempo, the horse would simply start walking for one or more strides, then trot for awhile, and finally canter. The same progression appears to hold true for downward transitions.

TURNING ON THE SPOT

In turning abruptly on the spot, a move recognized by many equestrians as the "turn on the hindquarters," wild horses do not seem to "pivot" on their hindlegs (and hooves), such as we see often among domestic horses required to spin by their riders for various reasons. Instead, they turn around by bending their bodies into the direction of the turn, while thrusting laterally with the leading hindleg. Moreover, they do this while maintaining the same gait-stride (walk, trot, or canter) throughout the turn. This latter observation appears to corroborate an important tenet of the classical school of riding, explained in the following passage by Podhajsky:

The turn on the haunches is wrong if the inside hind leg *pivots* [my italics] without leaving the ground, or is only raised once or twice during the turn, thus losing the rhythm of the pace. It is a greater fault to pivot than it is for the hind legs to perform a small circle in the correct rhythm.

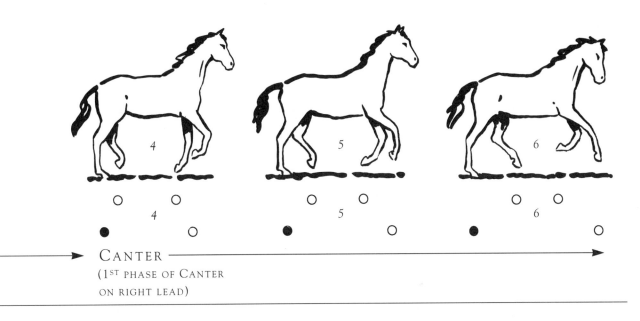

CANTER
(1ST PHASE OF CANTER
ON RIGHT LEAD)

Those who maintain that the inside leg should pivot without leaving the ground are reminded that in equestrian art the horse must either be in the rhythm of the movement or at the halt. If he is in motion, the hind legs must conform to the movement of the forelegs in the pace that nature has given to the horse.[17]

Some turns can occur so quickly, and with such razor-sharp precision, that the animal seems to be rotating or spinning around on a hidden turntable. Figure 3-20 illustrates how the turn on the hindquarters might occur at the canter by a wild horse. In this example, the horse executes a 260-degree turn to the right. Anticipating the impending turn, the horse, moving at a fairly strong pace on its left lead while advancing to the right (frame 1), collects itself to reduce its speed (frame 2). Notice the rearward shift of the animal's center of gravity as it elevates its cadence, which is necessary to maintain the canter stride pattern at a constant tempo and even rhythm. In the next moment (frame 3), the horse commences to turn on the spot by means of longitudinal bends in its body posture and pronounced lateral thrusts with the leading left hindleg, all of which occur in the direction of the turn. Without the longitudinal bending, the horse would tend to fall out of the turn due to the centrifugal forces, and without the lateral thrusts by the leading left hindleg, it would probably have to pivot around on the hind hooves and risk straining the suspensory ligaments of its hindlegs. Still maintaining its bend to the right, the horse finally completes a three-quarters, or 260-degree, turn. It then extends its stride and canters off in a new direction (frame 4).

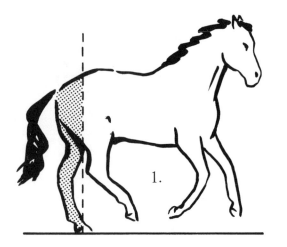

Note in frame 3 that each figure or outline of the horse corresponds to the execution of one complete stride. Thus, in this example, the horse completes five strides at the canter before departing from the turn. Impressive and rapid spins of 360 degrees, or more, are not uncommon among wild horses, especially by the little ones who, when not sleeping or nursing, are running and playing around their mothers, testing and developing their locomotive skills.

Dressage trainers refer to the turn on the hindquarters as the *pirouette* (French: "a whirl") and their descriptions of it, such as Richard Watjen's below, correspond to my observations of the movement among wild horses:

The Pirouette is the turn on the haunches in five to six strides at a collected canter. The horse, with its hocks well engaged, does the turn with its hindlegs completing the smallest possible circle, almost on one spot, and with the forelegs describing a wider circle round the hindlegs. The correct cadence and proper sequence of the strides must be maintained.[18]

FIGURE 3-20

Execution of turn at canter on hind quarters in left lead.

5th STRIDE

4th STRIDE

3rd STRIDE

2nd STRIDE

1st STRIDE

END OF TURN 260°

3.

SUMMARY

In this chapter, I have described the fundamental elements of the natural locomotive process. From this foundation, there are many locomotive variations. For example, nearly everything the horse does forward, it can also do diagonally, that is, sideways and forward at the same time. And it does marvelous things in the air, too.

I feel fortunate that I have come to know both the domestic horse world and the natural horse environment. This vantage point is somewhat of a double edged sword, however. It allows me to appreciate with awe and wonder the capabilities of the horse, but it also makes me aware of how little this is appreciated and comprehended in the domestic world.

This lack of appreciation of fundamentals of natural movement is

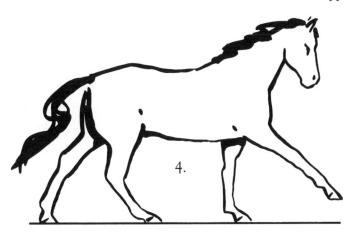

4.

apparent in the competitive spirit of horsemanship in the world today. The pressure is on horse and rider to win, using the horse and its locomotive behaviors as tools to this end. Questions that need to be asked are: Does the locomotive experience arise from the rider's sense of intimidation at failing as well as the desire to excel above others? Or does it stem from the vision of the natural locomotive impulse that spawns all movement and drives the horse forward earnestly with impulsion, not force? There are no glorious medals shining brightly in the mind of the natural horse. These questions should be asked not only by those in the competive ring and on the race track, but also by those private owners who keep horses in community stables, on ranches, and in their own backyards.

The challenge for us is to know and understand the natural horse experience and allow our horses to think and act according to the principles of their natural world. In this way, we can still meet our equestrian goals, but in the process develop wholesome, honest, relationships with our mounts.

Jim Hansen

4

The Natural Horse and Its Hooves

THIS CHAPTER is devoted to the description of the natural hoof and is intended to guide farriers interested in the natural hoof shape. My observations are based on the 107 wild horses I examined at the Litchfield Corrals in northern California. These horses, according to BLM officials, wranglers, and veterinarians whom I interviewed and worked with, are representative of the many thousands of wild horses typically found in the Great Basin area. The horses that I examined at Litchfield had not been in captivity more than a day or two, at most, when I initiated my work, so their hooves are representative of the type of hoof found on any Great Basin wild horse living under the conditions that were described in chapter 2.

Of particular interest to me was the consensus among BLM veterinarians and others familiar with wild horse populations that less than 5 percent of the horses coming through the BLM processing facilities suffer from lameness or poor health. Apparently, what little that does occur can often be attributed to injuries incurred either during roundups or at the processing center itself. On occasion, wild horses have been known to get caught in range fence lines and storm drains.

WHAT ARE NATURALLY SHAPED HOOVES?

The natural hoof, like natural locomotion, is what nature has intended for the hooves of the modern horse. The naturally shaped hoof found among wild horses in the outback is nothing less than a structural masterpiece; it

FIGURE 4-1

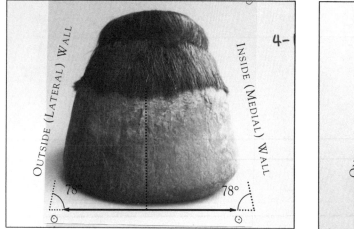

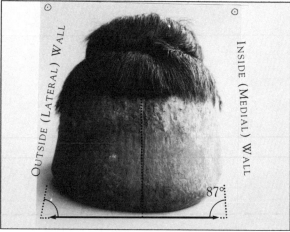

FRONT
ANTERIOR VIEW OF LEFT HOOF

HIND
ANTERIOR VIEW OF RIGHT HOOF

-front hooves are slightly wider than hind

-median and lateral wall angles are higher in hind than front

-median will tend to be higher angled than lateral wall in hind hooves; these
    angles tend to be the same in front

-median line tends to be vertical with a flat bearing surface supporting the hoof

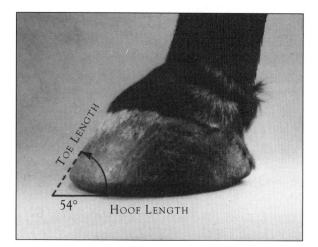

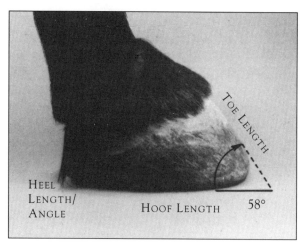

FRONT
LATERAL VIEW OF LEFT HOOF

HIND
LATERAL VIEW OF RIGHT HOOF

-front and hind hooves tend to have the same toe length (about 3.0 inches)

-front hoof length tends to be slightly longer than hind hoof length

-heel length and heel angle tend to be the same for front and hind hooves

-bearing surface (front and hind) tend to sit flush upon a flat support surface

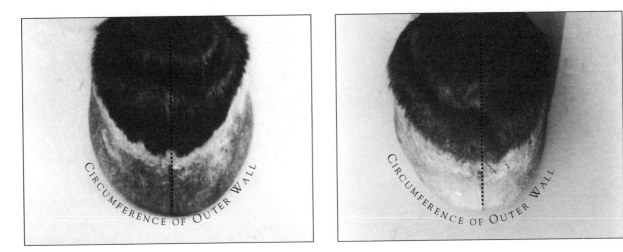

FRONT
SUPERIOR VIEW OF RIGHT HOOF

HIND
SUPERIOR VIEW OF RIGHT HOOF

-front hooves tend to be rounder than hind hooves

-circumference of front hooves tends to be greater than hind hooves

-median line of front hooves tends to divide the profile into two equal and
symmetrically shaped sides

-median line of hind hooves tends to divide the profile into two unequal and
asymmetrically shaped sides

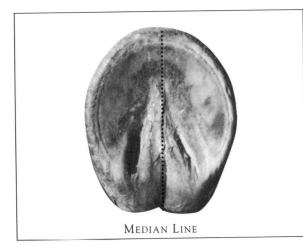

MEDIAN LINE

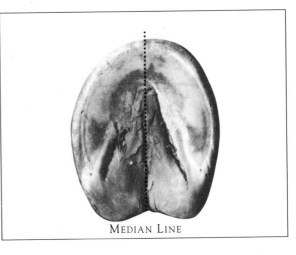

MEDIAN LINE

FRONT
VOLAR VIEW OF RIGHT HOOF

HIND
VOLAR VIEW OF RIGHT HOOF

-front hooves tend to be rounder than hind hooves

-circumference of front hooves tends to be greater than hind hooves

-median lines of both front and hind hooves tend to divide their respective
profiles into two equal and symmetrically shaped halves

has no rival among domesticated horses anywhere. In fact, until I stepped foot into wild horse country, I had never seen anything quite like it in all my years as a shoer. Nature has designed it with perfection in mind, not ego or unsubstantiated opinion.

The natural hoof is alive, just like our own hands. In fact, it breathes just like the skin of our hand, and it has a visible pulse to see and feel. The blood that travels into, through, and out of the hoof is the life blood that comes from the horse's heart, nourishing the hoof like it does every other part of the horse's body. The horse's life and its hooves are shaped together, integrated by the same locomotive forces of nature. The hooves are like tiny mirrors that reflect the vicissitudes of nature, for horse and hooves move together through the natural world as partners.

FRONT AND HIND HOOF SHAPES

The natural hoof is uniform in terms of its fundamental front and hind shapes throughout wild horse society, but it is also uniquely endowed with endless subtle variations in angle, size, and color that set the hooves of one horse off from those of the next.

FIGURE 4-2

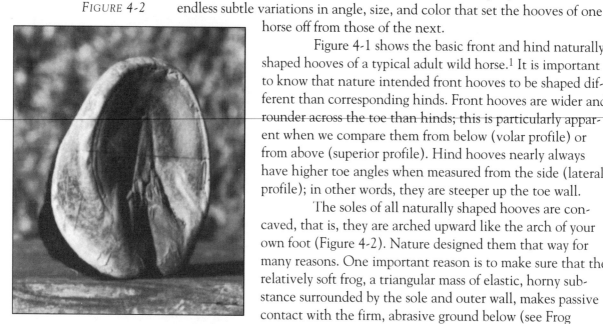

Figure 4-1 shows the basic front and hind naturally shaped hooves of a typical adult wild horse.[1] It is important to know that nature intended front hooves to be shaped different than corresponding hinds. Front hooves are wider and rounder across the toe than hinds; this is particularly apparent when we compare them from below (volar profile) or from above (superior profile). Hind hooves nearly always have higher toe angles when measured from the side (lateral profile); in other words, they are steeper up the toe wall.

The soles of all naturally shaped hooves are concaved, that is, they are arched upward like the arch of your own foot (Figure 4-2). Nature designed them that way for many reasons. One important reason is to make sure that the relatively soft frog, a triangular mass of elastic, horny substance surrounded by the sole and outer wall, makes passive contact with the firm, abrasive ground below (see Frog Passivity, p. 78). A corollary of this arched structuring of the sole, in relation to a passive frog, is that nature has been able to minimize the relative length of the heels. Significantly, heel length, measured from the hairline down to the ground, is constant in all naturally shaped hooves, front or hind. In fact, I did not measure a single heel (measured from the back or posterior profile) that exceeded half a centimeter in length. This, of course, makes sense in the wild: long heels, like long toes, are breeding grounds for breakage in the harsh, rugged environment of the outback.

Oblique view of bottom (volar) of naturally shaped right front hoof, revealing concave character of sole.

HOOF SIZES

A broad range of hoof sizes were noted among the captured wild horses at the Litchfield Corrals. The results of the measurements relating to hoof size are summarized in Table 4-1. Averages and ranges are included for a few of the dozen or so measurement categories sampled.

Hind hooves, on the average, are slightly smaller than front hooves. This is obvious when we contrast the shapes of their bottoms (volar), as seen in Figure 4-1. The main difference in size stems from relative widths of both hooves when measured across toes and quarters—fronts were generally wider and rounder. Interestingly, heel widths, that is, the distance across

HOOF MEASUREMENTS FOR LITCHFIELD SAMPLE

TABLE 4-1

Hoof Dimension [1]	Average Size (inches) [2]		Range of Sizes (inches) [2,3]	
	Front	Hind	Front	Hind
Toe Length	3	3	2 5/8 - 3 1/2	2 5/8 - 3 1/2
Hoof Length	5 1/4	5	4 1/2 - 6	4 1/2 - 5 3/4
Hoof Width	5	4 3/4	4 - 5 3/4	4 - 5 1/2

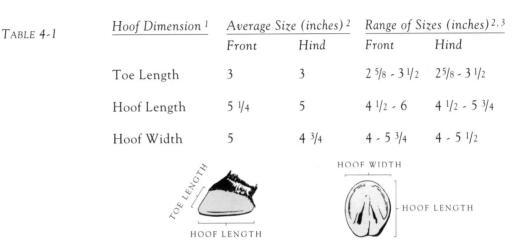

[1] Left or right hoof   [2] Adult horses only (5+ years)   [3] Based on normal distribution (-2/+2 SD)

the inside (medial) and outside (lateral) heel buttresses, were, on the average, the same.

Another important discovery was that toe length, on the average, changed very little as a general trend across all the hooves sampled (factoring out younger horses, of course). Over 99 percent of the hooves varied by less than five-eighths of an inch toe length. None measured over three and one-half inches long. Even the biggest monarchs had short toes like these.

In contrast to these Spartan toe lengths, the bottoms of the hooves examined varied widely in size. Some were as big as salad plates, approaching seven inches wide; others were less than half that size.

IMPACT OF AGE ON HOOF SIZE

FIGURE 4-3

INCREASE IN HOOF SIZE

TOE-ANGLE CONSTANT

ADULTHOOD THRESHOLD

AGE IN YEARS

Not surprisingly, overall hoof size increased directly with a horse's age until about age five. At that time, averages for the various measurement categories sampled appeared to level off. This suggests that, at about this age, horses probably attain adulthood, and hoof growth due to maturation peaks (Figure 4-3). Generally, toe angle remained constant from one age group to the next.

HOOF WALL TEXTURE, CONSISTENCY, AND COLOR

What does a naturally shaped hoof feel like? Imagine holding a small, lightweight, shiny, varnished wooden ball used in croquet. Now tap it with your knuckles or fingertips, listening to the crack and feeling the light vibrations within.

The hoof wall and the entire hoof capsule are dry as a bone in summer, and most of the rest of the year too. The surface has a dull, matte finish, not unlike the patina of fine grain leather. During wet spells, the wall's "hard-as-plastic" surface (e.g., like plexiglass) and matte finish convert to a dullish, slightly softer, hard rubber finish (e.g., like the white thermoplastic, Sanalite).

Figure 4-4 illustrates the distribution of hoof colors sampled at Litchfield. Basically, I found three hoof color schemes among wild, free-roaming horses: light-colored hooves, perfused mainly with yellow pigmentation; striated and mottled hooves, colored as indicated with various combinations of yellow and black pigmentation; and dark-colored hooves, perfused mainly or entirely with black pigmentation. Most hooves, as shown in Figure 4-4, were of the dark-pigmentation version, followed by mixed, and then by light.

FIGURE 4-4

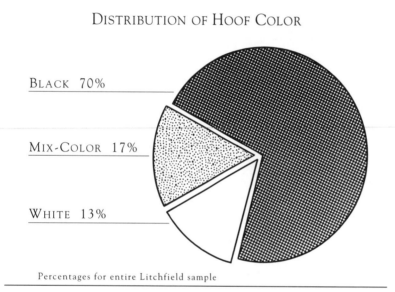

DISTRIBUTION OF HOOF COLOR

BLACK 70%

MIX-COLOR 17%

WHITE 13%

Percentages for entire Litchfield sample

Note that hoof color below the coronary band was always the same color as the hair immediately above the coronary band. This may indicate an attempt at camouflage, similar to the stripes found on zebras or the dorsal and leg stripes seen in some wild horse populations.[2]

Other observations that may be of interest to those who work with domestic horses: the color of the sole mirrored the color and color patterns of the outer wall, and pockets of discoloration sometimes seen in the soles of domestic horse hooves also appear in the soles of natural outback hooves.

Statistical treatments of the Litchfield data showed no measurable differences between hooves based on pigmentation, so it would seem that hoof color does not have anything to do with structural integrity or durability, as many horse enthusiasts believe today. These results are not included here because of their technical nature, but the distributions of data based upon hoof color, no matter how they were factored or correlated between the various measurement categories (e.g., toe angle to hoof color), were always the same in all three hoof color categories.[3]

SHAPE AND ANGLE OF GROWTH

The angle at which the hoof grows down below the hairline is a subject that has long interested me. In contrast to what many people may think, the hoof does not grow down and outward in several directions from the coro-

FIGURE 4-5

ANGLE OF GROWTH OF HORN TUBULES CONSTITUTING THE OUTER WALL

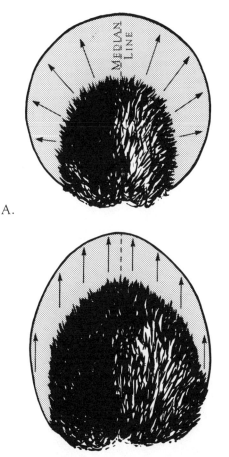

A.

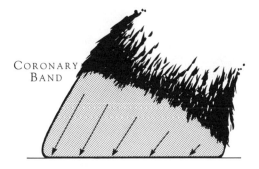

B. Anteroposterior angle of tubules decreases, angle of outer wall decreases

C. Horn tubules (i.e., grain) are parallel to each other and the hoof's median line

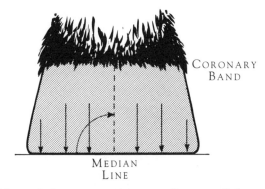

D. Horn tubules composing outer wall are parallel to each other and aligned at ninety degrees to ground during hoof's support phase.

nary band, as illustrated in Figure 4-5A. It grows down and forward from the coronary band to the ground. It does this at roughly the angle of the toe wall, when the hoof is viewed from the side (lateral profile), as seen in Figure 4-5B. Figure 4-5C shows the alignment of the wall's grain from above; the arrows indicate the direction of growth. Figure 4-5D shows it from the front.

Note in Figure 4-5B that the angle of growth of the hoof wall is steeper at the toe than at the heel—the grain is not parallel from toe to heel. Many people think it is or that it should be. It is formed this way for good reason. Anatomically, it has to do with the coffin bone underneath. Locomotively, it has to do with how the hoof strikes the ground, something that will be discussed later in this chapter.

The tiny fibers (called *horn tubules* by farriers and veterinarians[4]) that make up the grain of the outer wall and are "glued" tightly and densely

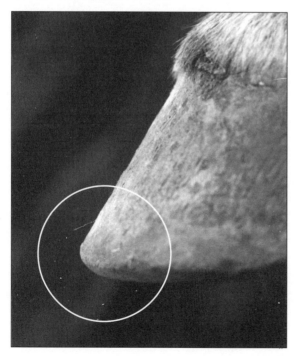

FIGURE 4-6

Tiny, fiberous, tubular bundles of cornified horn constitute outer wall of hoof. Note, in enlargement at right, that fiber bundles are densely packed in parallel fashion.

together by nature to form what we see as the hoof wall, grow down in roughly parallel fashion. This can be seen in the photo enlargement of a wild horse hoof taken at the BLM's facility in Burns, Oregon (Figure 4-6).

Underneath the hoof wall lies a bone, the *coffin bone*, as farriers call it. The outer surface of this bone looks like the hoof wall. The hoof wall is alive, and grows down and forward over this bone. How the hoof wall "slides" down over the coffin bone and down to the ground is one of nature's wonders. As it grows down, it conforms to the shape of the bone because that bone is what feeds and supports it on its journey to the ground. In other words, the shape of that bone inside is what determines the shape of the hoof wall.

WALL BEVEL

The bevel of the hoof wall refers to the bend, or turn, along the bearing surface of the outer wall. The term *wall bevel*, in spite of its common usage among farriers and some horse enthusiasts, is probably misleading. When

FIGURE 4-7

BEVEL OF OUTER WALL

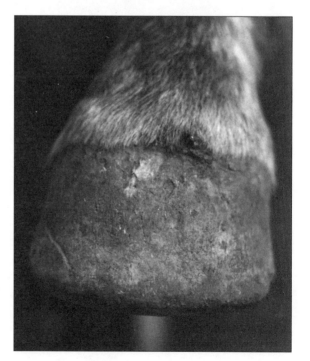

A. Bevel of toe wall (lateral view)

B. Bevel of medial (inside) and lateral (outside) walls

I think of a *bevel*, what comes to mind is the beveled edge of a chisel, and that imagery does not work for what I saw at Litchfield and in the outback. Rounded is a more fitting description, not necessarily the bevel shape that is apparent in a beveled-edge chisel.

Figure 4-7 shows a photograph of the sort of wall bevel observed in naturally shaped hooves. Something never seen is abrupt, sharp edges, precisely the type of chisellike bevel that would be worn away and honed smooth in wild horse country.

SOLE, BARS, AND FROG

As a rule, the sole of the naturally shaped hoof is, like the outer wall, uniformly smooth and tough as hard plastic. Loose or crumbly horn, seen commonly in the smelly hooves of domestic horses far between trimmings, is simply not seen in the soles of naturally shaped hooves. The sole is arched enough to assure itself, and the frog it surrounds, passive contact with the ground during the hoof's support phase in the natural locomotive process. I never saw a "cuppy"-footed (extremely arched or recessed) horse at Litchfield, nor did I see horses with dropped soles or flat feet. These conditions are anomalous to the natural world of the horse, even though they are apparent among domestic horses.

The bars of naturally shaped hooves extend from the heel buttresses forward to the frog apex and conform, more or less, to the shape of the frog (Figure 4-8). The bars can be thought of as short, narrow walls that divide the sole from the frog. Actually, they are extensions of the outer wall. Bars assist the arched sole in protecting the frog from direct, or active, contact with the ground. Near the frog apex, the bars generally do not protrude much above the surrounding sole but tend to lay flat and level with it. In contrast, near the heel buttresses, the bars tend to protrude in varying amounts below the adjacent sole. In effect, they help form the angle of the wall (seats of corn) where the outer wall turns abruptly inward. The small pockets formed here vary widely in size and depth from one hoof to the next.

Everyone who owns and rides a horse and takes the time to "pick" his or her mount's hooves has run into the so-called frog.[5] Cleaning the frog is usually a nasty, smelly affair, especially if it has been a while since the farrier put a knife to it and particularly where the climate is moist. Under such circumstances, it is hard to say what a naturally shaped frog is supposed to look like. Indeed, many horse owners do not know if the frog should even be trimmed at all, or what it should look like once it is trimmed.

The frogs that were examined at Litchfield were, without exception, neat and trim in

The bevel of the naturally shaped outer wall is well rounded at all points along its circumference. The degree of bevel of toe wall (A) is the same as the quarters and heels (B,C)

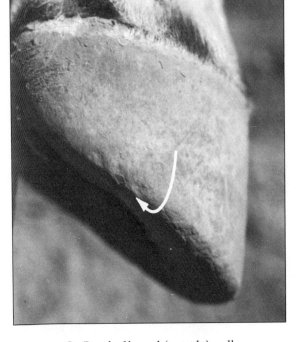

C. Bevel of lateral (outside) wall

CONFORMATION OF BARS IN RELATION TO FROG

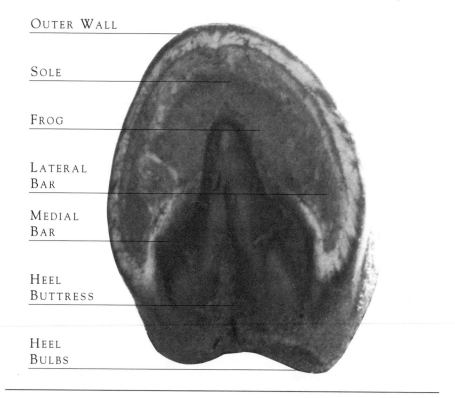

OUTER WALL

SOLE

FROG

LATERAL BAR

MEDIAL BAR

HEEL BUTTRESS

HEEL BULBS

appearance, as if an intuitive farrier had just finished an *aggressive* trimming job. The main difference between the two, after all the aggression is over, is that in natural outback hooves, the frogs appear to be pressed or worn very flat and feel dry and tough as rawhide to the touch (Figure 4-9). The freshly trimmed civilized frog—even though properly ravaged in uncivilized fashion—appears, in contrast, thick and rubbery, like the wet back of an

NATURALLY SHAPED FROG

FIGURE 4-9

Naturally shaped frog is not spongy and soft, but dry, flat, and tough. Note depth of frog cleft (A) and undifferentiated intermeshing of frog with heel bulbs (B).

A.

B.

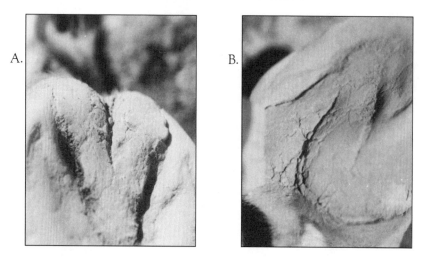

amphibious frog. In fact, a farrier would be hard pressed to trim a frog as flat as they are in the wild.

Although I examined hooves in both winter and summer, it was never clear whether frogs underwent a molting process or were kept constantly trim as a result of locomotive wear. I suspect the latter, but it is conceivable that both occur at the same time.

The naturally shaped frog is a bifurcated structure, consisting of two branches, or ridges, which emanate from a single ridge whose origin is the frog apex (Figure 4-9). The two ridges, or wings, are divided by a well-defined cleft (sometimes referred to as the sulcus), a little ditch of sorts, which measured from one-eighth to one-half of an inch in depth among the Litchfield horses.

Incidentally, that ditch turns out to be a little pedestal up inside the hoof—out of eyesight, of course, unless you dissect the hoof. Inside the hoof, it partly divides the mass of fattylike substance many farriers and some horse enthusiasts call the digital cushion (Figure 4-10). This cushion is like a hydraulic brake of sorts because it helps put the brakes on those bones in the hoof as they descend down toward the frog during the leg's weight-bearing phase in the natural locomotive process. But perhaps more important,

FIGURE 4-10

RELATIONSHIP OF FROG TO DIGITAL CUSHION

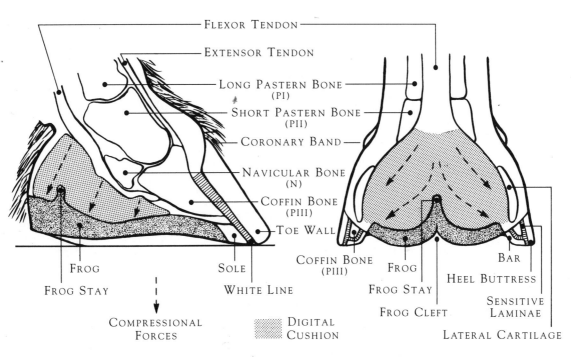

FLEXOR TENDON
EXTENSOR TENDON
LONG PASTERN BONE (PI)
SHORT PASTERN BONE (PII)
CORONARY BAND
NAVICULAR BONE (N)
COFFIN BONE (PIII)
TOE WALL
FROG · SOLE · COFFIN BONE (PIII) · FROG · BAR
FROG STAY · WHITE LINE · FROG STAY · HEEL BUTTRESS
COMPRESSIONAL FORCES · DIGITAL CUSHION · FROG CLEFT · SENSITIVE LAMINAE
LATERAL CARTILAGE

this frog pedestal, called the frog stay, helps divide the squished cushion spread outward into the heel buttresses above the little pockets (i.e., seats of corn) described earlier in the discussion of the bars. The relatively flexible frog is a sophisticated, dual-purpose, bifurcated widget with a cleft on one side and a pedestal on the other that enables the hoof sole to give and take like a trampoline.

The frog cleft, when the hoof is viewed from the rear, is centered between the heel buttresses (Figure 4-11). The frog itself is separated from

RELATIONSHIP OF FROG CLEFT TO HEEL BUTTRESSES

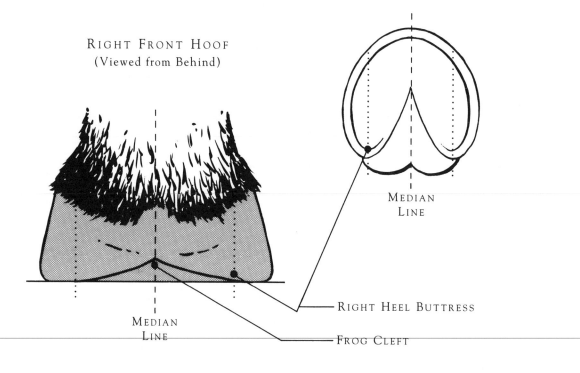

RIGHT FRONT HOOF
(Viewed from Behind)

MEDIAN
LINE

MEDIAN
LINE

RIGHT HEEL BUTTRESS

FROG CLEFT

FIGURE 4-11

the sole by two more small ditches called the collateral sulci, or frog commissures, which adjoin the bars. These ditches, or grooves, are deepest toward the frog apex, which itself is consistently the deepest point within the arched surface in the bottom of the hoof. Frog apexes generally range from one-quarter to three-quarters of an inch below the bearing surface of the outer wall.

FROG PASSIVITY

There has been considerable difference of opinion among farriers, horse-owners, and others as to whether or not nature configured the frog to press directly (actively) or indirectly (passively) against the ground during the hoof's support phase.

In the naturally shaped hoof, the frog and sole endure *indirect* contact with the ground. At the same time, the bearing surface of the entire outer wall, including the heel buttresses, undergoes *direct* contact. This is exactly what we would expect in view of the arched disposition of the bottom of the hoof. But what do I mean when I say "direct" and "indirect" contact with the ground?

The term *direct* means that the outer wall undergoes contiguous (active) contact with the ground. In contrast, the term *indirect* means that the frog undergoes passive contact with the ground when the horse exerts its weight upon the hoof. Thus, the brunt of the horse's weight is absorbed primarily by the outer wall and, secondarily, by the frog and sole. By way of analogy, think of the arch of the human foot, which remains passive to the ball (metatarsus) and heel (calcaneous) while we walk along. Anyone who has fallen arches is keenly aware of the difference.

Passive frog contact with the ground is another way of saying passive frog pressure. The frog is not squeezed directly against the ground from above or below, not anymore than your own arch is squeezed directly against the ground when you walk barefooted. The action and pressure is passive. I verified this among the Litchfield horses by pressing each hoof against a clipboard and looking at it from all sides, especially from the rear where the frog is most visible. In each instance, I was able to pass the one-eighth-inch-thick handle of a nailfile (i.e., about the thickness of two nickels stacked on top of each other) between the frog and the clipboard without the file getting jammed between the two from top to bottom. The gap, however, was never large enough between the rear of the frog and the clipboard below it for me to wedge my index finger between them. Of course, how much side to side play there was with the file depended upon the width of the frog, or more precisely, the distance between the adjacent heel buttresses.

Practically speaking, should the wild horse ever walk over a relatively large, hard and flat rock, or other such similar surface, its frogs would make little or no contact with that surface. But the same horse, when moving over somewhat softer ground, would endure considerable frog contact with the ground, but only in the passive sense. What one actually sees in the hoofprints made by wild horses on relatively "soft" ground are impressions of both heels and frog, with the heels sunk slightly deeper (and the toe deeper still).

Xenophon recognized over two thousand years ago the significance of passive frog contact with the ground when riding unshod hooves over hard, rocky ground:

> The feet should first be tested by examining the horn; thick
> horn is a much better mark of good feet than thin. Again, one
> should not fail to note whether the hoofs at toe and heel come up
> high or lie low. High ones keep what is called the frog well off the
> ground. . . . Simon says that their sound is a proof of good feet,
> and he is right; for a hollow hoof resounds like a cymbal as it
> strikes the ground.[6]

He goes on to recommend stabling horses on rocky surfaces as a means of toughening the hooves: "Stones strewn about in this way strengthen the frogs too."[7]

CONCAVITY

As stated before, the bottom, or sole, of the naturally shaped hoof is arched, or concaved, like the bottom of our feet. How this arch breaks down from one layer to the next is fairly well defined in naturally shaped hooves, and as horse enthusiasts, we ought to know what nature has in mind there. The gradations are illustrated in Figure 4-12A, an "exploded" view of the hoof, and in Figure 4-12B, a cross section (sagittal section).

The arching begins subtly at the junction of the outer wall with the white line, where the hoof makes active contact with the ground. It reaches

"EXPLODED" VIEW OF CONCAVITY IN NATURALLY SHAPED HOOF

FIGURE 4-12 A.

CROSS-SECTION (SAGITTAL) VIEW OF HOOF
SHOWING GRADATIONS OF CONCAVITY

FIGURE 4-12 B.

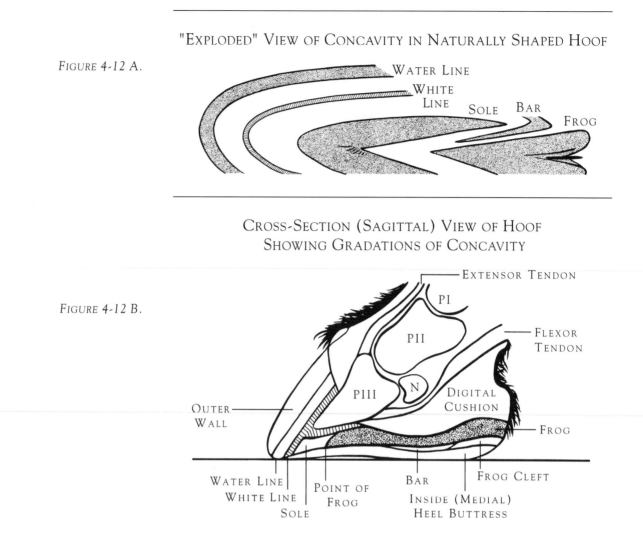

its highest degree of arch at the frog apex. Between these two extremes, there are a total of four distinct transitions, or gradations, in the hoof's arch:

1. Water line of the outer wall to white line
2. White line to sole
3. Sole to bar
4. Bar to frog/frog apex/frog cleft

Farriers should keep these gradations in mind when trimming hooves for natural arch.

TOE ANGLE

My first discovery, when I tried to make toe-angle measurements, was that my fancy hoof gauge was not capable of properly measuring the toe angle of a naturally shaped hoof. No hoof gauge manufactured today is. I eventually discovered that the bottom of the naturally shaped hoof wall is not flat or level, like a horseshoe, but complex, like a human foot. So to learn how to lay the hoof gauge against it meant figuring out first how the hoof rests against a flat surface. Also, the naturally shaped hoof is often asymmetrically shaped from the inside (medial) to the outside (lateral), so it was difficult to figure out where the center of the toe was and where to take a measurement. Eventually, this measurement was resolved, and I went on to gather my toe-angle data.

Table 4-2 itemizes the principal toe-angle findings for front and hind hooves measured at Litchfield.[8] These findings are expressed in two curves in Figure 4-13 to help visualize the ranges, with which all horse enthusiasts should become familiar.

As these figures show, the average toe angle for front hooves was approximately 54 degrees, the average hind about 58 degrees. Interestingly, hind-toe angles nearly always exceeded front toe angles; only in a small per-

TOE-ANGLE MEASUREMENTS FOR LITCHFIELD SAMPLE

TABLE 4-2

Hoof Angle [1]	Average Angle [2]	Range of Angles [2,3]
Front	54°	50° - 60°
Hind	58°	53° - 63°

1 Left or Right   2 All Ages Factored   3 Based on Normal Distribution (-2/+2 SD)

centage of hooves did they tend to be the same. This is significant in that front toe angles did not exceed corresponding hind toe angles.

Also of interest was that toe angle did not appear to be a function of relative heel length. For example, two hooves with the same heel length and identical toe lengths could have entirely different toe angles (Figure 4-14A). Similarly, two hooves with different toe lengths but identical heel lengths could have identical toe angles (Figure 4-14B).

Conclusions based on these observations are that the toe angle of the

DISTRIBUTION OF FRONT AND HIND TOE ANGLES FOR LITCHFIELD SAMPLE

FIGURE 4-13

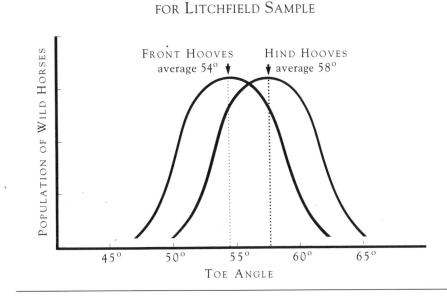

naturally shaped hoof is determined by the axis (the angle formed with the ground) of those bones inside the hoof, not the length of the heels relative to the length of the toe, or any other such mathematical factor. In the section on hoof sizes, heel lengths were found to be the same for virtually all hooves sampled. Even toe lengths hardly varied. What this probably means is that the higher the axis of the bones inside the hoof in relation to the ground, the higher the corresponding toe angle will be and vice versa. So forget about putting longer heels on domestic horses to increase their toe angles—that is not nature's way.

However, whatever determines precisely the angle of the digit bones and the toe wall, which we are actually able to measure, remains a mystery. Some authorities claim that toe angle is theoretically the same angle formed

FIGURE 4-14

A. IMPACT OF HEEL LENGTH ON TOE ANGLE

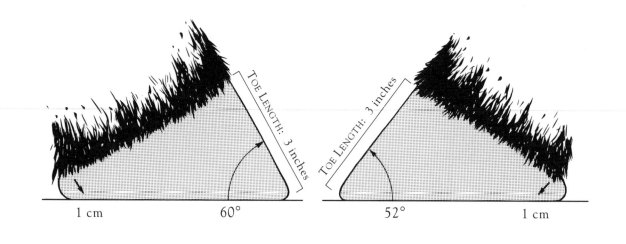

B. IMPACT OF TOE LENGTH ON TOE ANGLE

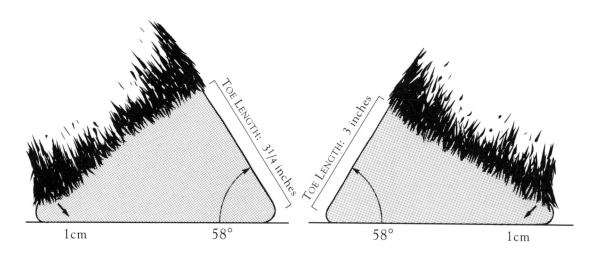

HOOF SYMMETRY AND ASYMMETRY

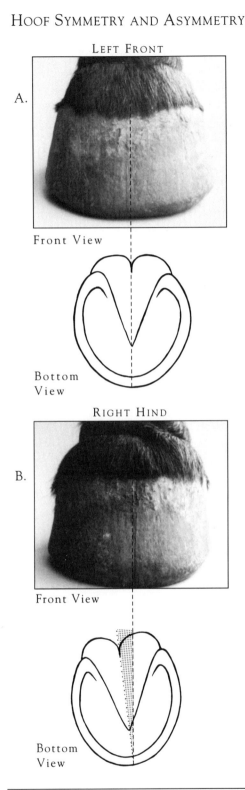

LEFT FRONT

A.

Front View

Bottom View

RIGHT HIND

B.

Front View

Bottom View

FIGURE 4-15

by either the scapula (shoulder) or femur (hip) with the ground, at least while the horse is standing at attention, on a flat surface.[9]

My own feeling is that the toe angle of the hoof probably does exist in such an equilibrium with the axis of the bones in the entire lower leg as well as the shoulder and hip. Those angles, however, may not be the same. Remember, the joints of the shoulder and the hindquarters, discussed in chapter 3, are not fixed; they are in a permanent state of semiflexion. Since this is the case with the shoulder and hindquarters, it may be that toe angles and semiflexed joint angles are meant to constantly *vary* in relation to each other, depending upon circumstances such as terrain, locomotive behavior of the moment, or the horse's conformation and temperament. To simply equate hoof angle to shoulder angle through a special measuring gauge and then shoe domestic horses accordingly is dangerously arbitrary. I know of no such ideal position in which to put every horse that would not compromise the inner or outer sense of balance in the vast majority. I think we are much wiser to consider the angle ranges given to us by the sound, athletic natural horse of the outback and to use them as general guidelines. We will discuss how to do that in the next chapter.

HOOF SYMMETRY AND ASYMMETRY

Hoof symmetry refers to the correspondence in size, form, and arrangement of parts or areas on opposite sides of the hoof's center line. The center line is an imaginary line that bisects the hoof right down the middle from toe to frog cleft. Draw a rectangle in your mind; now draw a line right down the middle of it, dividing it lengthwise in half. You'll find that one-half is symmetrical to the other half because there is correspondence in size, form, and arrangement of parts.

Hoof asymmetry is the opposite; there is no correspondence between the hoof parts on either side of the center line. Hold up the palm of your hand and look at it. Draw an imaginary center line straight down the center of it through the middle finger and palm. The thumb side of the line, obviously, is asymmetrical to the little finger side, since no two fingers are the same (nor is anything else on either side of the dividing line). The two sides are asymmetrical because they lack any kind of correspondence.

When examining front hooves at Litchfield, I found that the hoof's center line bisected the hoof in half when viewed from the front (See Figure 4-15A, above). The left side of the hoof was clearly symmetrical to the right side, just like it was when viewed from below (Figure 4-15A, below). This observation held true for all front hooves at Litchfield.

The hind hooves, however, presented a different picture. Examination showed the hoof halves to be symmetrical when viewed from below (Figure 4-15B, below), but asymmetrical when viewed from the front (Figure 4-15B, above). Apparently, this difference has nothing to do with hoof wear. Rather, it has to do with fundamental differences in conformation and in how the horse uses its front versus the hind hooves. In ways that I do not understand entirely, the growth orientation of the hind hoof wall—in relation to its sole, frog, and outer wall—is entirely different than that of front hooves. Figure 4-15 illustrates this difference.

HOW THE NATURAL HORSE SHAPES ITS HOOVES

The natural horse shapes its hooves with little or no conscious awareness that it is doing so. This may seem like an obvious statement, however, there are schools of thought that say otherwise. Not long ago, in an article in the *American Farriers Journal*, a shoer was quoted: "In wild horse herds, horses care for their feet through a fascinating instinctive process by which the lead mare takes the herd first to water to stand in, then to an area of rough boulders, and finally to an area of shale."[10] In response to this viewpoint, it must be said that in the horse's natural world, the animals act only in relation to the rhythms or cycles of nature. Accordingly, nature has equipped them with special instincts (e.g., survival and reproductive) to behave according to those cycles. Everything else (e.g., hoof wear) unfolds as a consequence of those behaviors, not the other way around.

Given this understanding of nature, I wanted to know how the wild horse hoof gets shaped in response to those rhythmic forces of nature. How does the hoof hit the ground, wear, and become balanced so that it and the horse are balanced together? Why are front hooves shaped different than hind hooves? Why isn't the bottom of the hoof flat like a horseshoe? Might it have something to do with the way the horse thrusts its body up, forward, and to the side? What about that toe-angle differential between front and hind hooves (Table 4-2)? Might that have something to do with collection?

BALANCED HOOVES, BALANCED HORSE

During the limb's support phase in the natural locomotive process, the weight of the horse is transferred downward through the limb to the coffin bone, which is housed within and supported by the hoof capsule. This is illustrated in Figure 4-16. The arrows in drawings A and B indicate the downward direction of the descending body weight along those bones. The term *support phase* simply refers to that period in the action of the leg when the hoof is making contact with the ground, and body weight is borne upon it and every other joint in the leg above. The hoof capsule is that part of the hoof that comprises all of the hard, horny, and insensitive tissues; this is the visible part of the hoof: the outer wall, bars, sole, frog, and probably the heel bulbs as well.

Figure 4-17 provides an interesting internal view of the hoof capsule and of all its inner surfaces that cannot be seen from the outside. The hoof capsule encapsulates everything that is soft and sensitive within it—like the shell surrounding the germ, yolk, and white of a chicken egg—as well as a

FIGURE 4-16
COMPRESSION IN THE HOOF

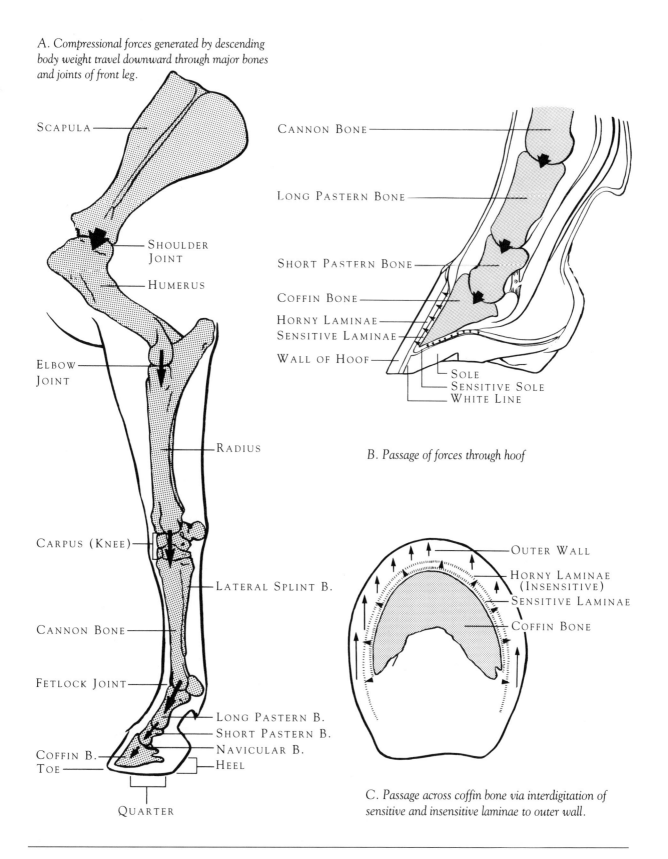

A. *Compressional forces generated by descending body weight travel downward through major bones and joints of front leg.*

SCAPULA

SHOULDER JOINT

HUMERUS

ELBOW JOINT

RADIUS

CARPUS (KNEE)

LATERAL SPLINT B.

CANNON BONE

FETLOCK JOINT

LONG PASTERN B.
SHORT PASTERN B.
NAVICULAR B.
COFFIN B.
TOE
HEEL

QUARTER

CANNON BONE

LONG PASTERN BONE

SHORT PASTERN BONE

COFFIN BONE
HORNY LAMINAE
SENSITIVE LAMINAE
WALL OF HOOF
SOLE
SENSITIVE SOLE
WHITE LINE

B. *Passage of forces through hoof*

OUTER WALL
HORNY LAMINAE (INSENSITIVE)
SENSITIVE LAMINAE
COFFIN BONE

C. *Passage across coffin bone via interdigitation of sensitive and insensitive laminae to outer wall.*

number of bones (coffin, pastern, and navicular) and blood. Many readers may not realize how many blood vessels are included in the hoof. Figure 4-20 is a photograph of a hoof showing only the blood vessels.

From the coffin bone, the path of the descending body weight is then transferred onto the outer wall via what is called "interdigitation of the sensitive and insensitive lamina" (Figure 4-16C). *Lamina* are amazing leaflike structures that actually bind the coffin bone to the outer wall. *Interdigitation* refers to how those tiny leaves intermesh so that bone and wall will stick together. The following excerpt from *Horseshoeing Theory & Hoof Care* explains this a little more clearly:

FIGURE 4-17

Horny capsule of hoof revealing frog stay and inner surfaces of outer wall and sole.

> The inner surface of the [hoof] wall is covered with many fine, flexible ridges of horn which course vertically along its surface. This inner layer is called the horny laminae, because of the many leaf-like layers of horn attached to each ridge. Between the layer of horny laminae and the coffin bone is a layer of soft velvety laminae. This layer of sensitive laminae is approximately one-quarter inch thick; it is flesh, not horn. It is firmly attached to the porous surface of the coffin bone. It contains a large supply of blood. Its many vertical ridges, also covered with minute leaf-like projections, mesh with the similar grooves and ridges of the horny laminae. If the "leaves" in one hoof were spread out, they would cover about 9 square feet. The wall is attached to the coffin bone by the meshing of the sensitive and insensitive laminae and their tiny leaves. The wall receives necessary moisture from, and shock is dissipated by, the large content of blood in the sensitive laminae.[11]

However, bear in mind that the hoof wall is not glued onto the bone like two boards nailed to each other; it also grows downward along the bone's surface. It is not stationary but is always growing.

Once the descending body weight is transferred onto the hoof wall via the "leaves," it is directed straight to the ground via the insensitive horn tubules, which constitute the bulk of the hoof wall. Recall that those insensitive horn tubules are visible on the outside of the hoof as the epidermis, or grain, of the outer wall (Figure 4-6).

At this point, the force of the body weight has reached the ground after traveling down the leg and into the hoof, across the leaves, and then down the outer wall of the hoof capsule via the horn tubules. This sets the stage for the actual shaping of the hoof.

The force of all this descending body weight, in passing through the limb onto the hoof wall, is resisted by the ground below. The ground, in this example, is the outback in wild horse society, not the swampy mud pack in the back forty nor the deep, sandy riding arena. The result of this resistance is that extraordinary compressional forces build within the hoof capsule. Also, everything is pretty tight at the bottom of the outer wall, underneath, where the descending body weight is concentrated against the outback as a result of compression. This is where the hoof gets ground and shaped.

The wild, free-roaming horse instinctively places its hooves under this descending body weight in the most advantageous, or balanced, way possible. It seeks balance in every step, collecting itself, too, if the locomotive requirements are extraordinary. Such balanced stepping requires precision, endurance, and an athletic body to be effective in the rugged outback.

FIGURE 4-18

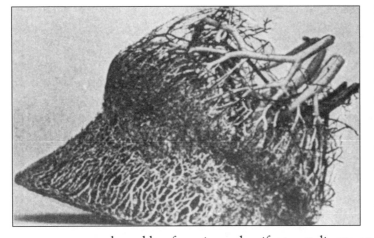

Blood vessels of hoof were injected with latex, and the rest of the parts dissolved in acid.

The actual grinding or shaping of the outer wall does not occur uniformly around its entire bearing surface. The bearing surface of the naturally shaped hoof wall, as observed in the wild horses at Litchfield, is not flat, like a level horseshoe. It is irregular and asymmetrical. This reflects the complex way in which the horn tubules composing the hoof wall are worn.

What makes the naturally shaped hoof precise and uniform yet diverse and full of variation and character must be understood in terms of how the horn tubules are compressed and worn. Apparently, the compressionary forces produced by the descending weight of the horse traveling downward through the limb are not transmitted equally around the hoof wall and down through the horn tubules. They are not transmitted equally because every horse is built differently and thinks differently. As we have seen during the natural locomotive process, these differences transmit themselves as individual locomotive styles. It follows that differences in locomotive style would surface in the hooves, since the hooves have to absorb the diverse locomotive pressure and energy. At the same time the compressionary forces are making an impression on the bottoms of the hoof wall, they also appear to be transmitting messages back up to the coronary matrix—that mysterious place where hoof horn is produced—advising it, somehow, to regulate the flow of growth sliding down the coffin bone. In addition, those forces also appear to regulate the degree of callousing or thickening that the cells of the horn tubules in the bearing surface must undergo in order to withstand abrasion and compression.

What all of this means is that the shaping process is really a filtering and sculpturing process. The compressionary forces are the forces of nature that make an impression on the hoof based upon the temperament, conformation, and socialization—in short, the "filters"—of the individual horse. The rhythms of nature command, the horse acts (filters), and the hooves respond. Natural hoof shape is a mirror that reflects the result of this process. The horn tubules, sculpted by this process, are the reality that we can touch, the reality behind the image in the mirror.

ACTIVE AND PASSIVE WEAR AREAS

I began to think of hoof shape as a type of filtering process through the horn tubules when I discovered that the bearing surface of the typical naturally shaped hoof exhibited both active (more protruding) and passive (less protruding) wear areas (Figure 4-19B). The areas of recession were not simply

RELATIONSHIP OF COMPRESSIONAL FORCES TO NATURAL ACTIVE AND PASSIVE HOOF WEAR

FIGURE 4-19

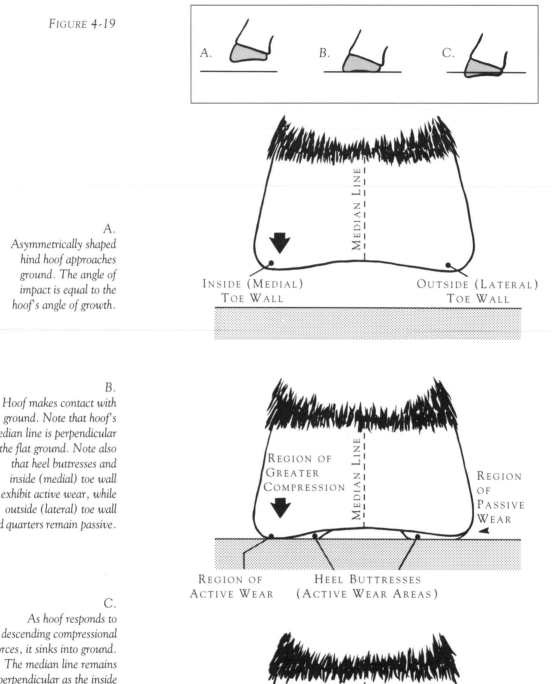

A.
Asymmetrically shaped hind hoof approaches ground. The angle of impact is equal to the hoof's angle of growth.

B.
Hoof makes contact with ground. Note that hoof's median line is perpendicular to the flat ground. Note also that heel buttresses and inside (medial) toe wall exhibit active wear, while outside (lateral) toe wall and quarters remain passive.

C.
As hoof responds to descending compressional forces, it sinks into ground. The median line remains perpendicular as the inside toe wall bears the brunt of the horses body weight. Note that the hoof has sunk or pressed straight into the ground (at the angle of impact), not rocked over on to its outside toe wall lopsidely by elevating its inside heel buttress.

broken away, they were worn differently. Like the frog and sole, they represent areas of passive wear. In contrast, protruding surfaces are areas of active wear since they endured the brunt of impact and support.

I do not believe that the active/passive wear areas have anything to do with relative strength or weakness. Some areas simply protrude more (e.g., the inside toe wall in Figure 4-19B) than others in order to give support in a manner like little pedestals. The specific locations of these active and passive wear areas varied widely from horse to horse across the Litchfield sample. This variation in shape, as explained in the previous section, resulted from the diverse influences of conformation and temperament among the horses sampled. Collectively, however, the locations of active and passive wear were so configured around the bearing surface of the outer wall as to balance each hoof in a manner that was uniform across the sample. This is explained further in a later section.

CALLOUSES

Another discovery relating to the shaping process fell right out of the first one. The active and passive bearing surfaces around the outer wall were not worn *into* the hoof. They *protruded* out of it like callouses. As farriers, we have been so used to grinding and nipping away the old, un-worn hoof horn that we have never noticed the areas of protrusion except as excessive growth.

In the natural horse world, the starting point is a work plate. This corresponds to the nail bed under our finger- or toenails. How much and how fast horn grows out of the work plate in the outback depends, partly, on how much the hoof is going to be used everyday and what areas will need more horn to keep the horse balanced according to its unique conformation and temperament. The work plate, thus, represents a kind of theoretical minimum amount of horn needed and out of which the active wear areas emerge. As the animal matures, the work plate matures and develops. Areas of protrusion begin to develop. I have seen this nascent progression in the hooves of the very young, who, following birth, lack much of the hoof character seen in older horses. But as they mature, they begin to develop the same exemplar full-bodied hooves as their elders.

Every protrusion and recession, then, corresponds to some attribute (conformation) or propensity (temperament) emanating elsewhere, above the hair line, in the horse's being. The natural gait complex is the vehicle that brings them out, developing the "swells." Collection, on the other hand, is what squeezes those swells into waves with crests (areas of active wear) and troughs (areas of passive wear). Without collection, the bearing surface of naturally shaped hooves would probably be as flat as the cold stretches of steel between the registered trademarks stamped on our abiotic, metallic horseshoes.

It is helpful to think of the tubules constituting the areas of protrusion (active wear) as callouses pressed out of front and hind work plates. To visualize this, think of callouses on your feet. Notice that they do not occur uniformly over the entire surface of the foot but just where you bear the most weight and compress or squeeze the foot the most.

The bearing surface (work plate) of the hoof wall works in basically the same way. Certain portions of the hoof wall tend to thicken more than others, depending on how the horse balances itself during the natural locomotive process. Those parts which are needed more to "balance" the horse, simply thicken (i.e., callous) and protrude more than the other parts.

SHAPED FROM WITHIN, WORN FROM WITHOUT

A third discovery stemmed, in part, from observations by Emery et al., that the hoof does not move, that is, slip or slide along the ground like a poled gondola, during its weight-bearing phase. It merely expands and contracts in place. This observation is consistent with the active and passive wearing that we see in all naturally shaped hooves. Obviously, notions of hoof wear in which the hoof is worn down by the ground as it slides or rolls over it, cannot account for the complex active/passive wear sites found on all matured, naturally shaped hooves. Consequently, the "stationary" hoof is shaped from within by those internal compressionary forces previously mentioned (filtered by socialization, temperament, and conformation), while the firm, stationary outback merely provides the necessary resistance and abrasion. Said another way, the natural hoof is shaped from within and worn from without.

ANGLE OF GROWTH EQUALS ANGLE OF IMPACT

According to various researchers, most of the horse's descending body weight is believed to be concentrated initially over the toe at the moment of impact and later over the entire outer wall. This observation is consistent with several of my own findings and helps to explain still another part of the natural shaping process.

First, the impressions made upon the ground by naturally shaped hooves in the outback are always deepest over the region of the toe, especially during extraordinary behavior. This can be seen in Figure 4-20 and also in the clay cast of a simulated hoof imprint I made using a freeze-dried hoof specimen (Figure 4-21). All over wild horse country, it is toe-down, toe-down, toe-down—none of that heel-first braking action we sometimes see in the hoofprints of domestic horses throttled up with resistance.

FIGURE 4-20

Wild horse hoof print showing greater degree of depression over toe wall.

FIGURE 4-21

Hoof print simulated with specimen. Arrows point to toe wall.

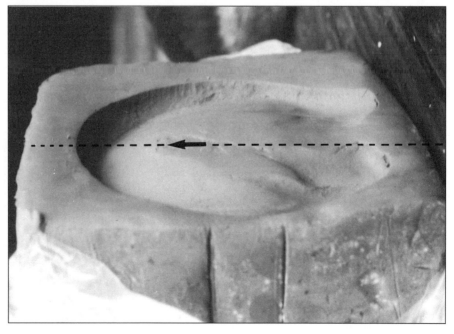

Second, the angle of the horn tubules (i.e., the grain) in hooves that I sampled at Litchfield lay uniformly at a steeper angle than the tubules found elsewhere around the outer wall (Figure 4-5). This higher angulation is related to the observation made by some researchers that the hoof strikes the ground directly at the same angle with the axis of the bones inside the hoof capsule. This places the brunt of weight bearing during impact directly over the toe of the hoof, which can be seen clearly in the cross section

ANGLE OF GROWTH EQUALS ANGLE OF IMPACT

FIGURE 4-22

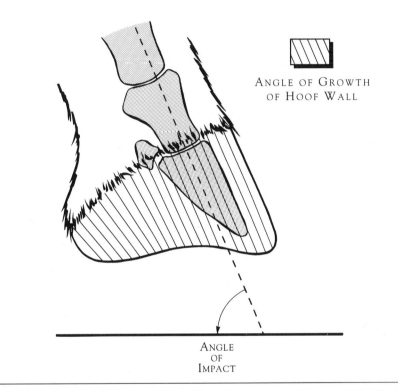

ANGLE OF GROWTH
OF HOOF WALL

ANGLE
OF
IMPACT

(sagittal view) of the naturally shaped hoof specimen in Figure 4-10. Note that the axis of the bone column parallels the angle of growth of the toe wall and, in turn, the hoof's angle of impact (Figure 4-22). This relationship was consistent in all the wild horse hoof dissections I conducted.

FRONT VERSUS HIND HOOF SHAPES

A question remained after I sifted through all the Litchfield data: Why did nature put a slightly smaller and narrower-toed hoof with a higher toe angle beneath the hindlegs, and a larger, broader one with a lower toe angle beneath the front? Given that the hindlegs are required to carry more body weight and provide most of the locomotive propulsion, it would seem logical that having a broader hoof in the rear would at least give the horse a larger base of support from which to work. But this is not the case.

LATERAL THRUST

One reason for the narrower hind-toe configuration may have something to do with the hind leg's pivotal role during the natural locomotive process. By pivotal, I mean the hind legs are anatomically designed to initiate move-

FIGURE 4-23 A.

Horse and rider at lateral trot in left lead.

ment that is not just straight ahead, for example, lateral variations of the natural gaits, turns, or lead changes. But the hind legs also encourage movement that is not straight to become straight and ensure that "straight-ahead movement" does not drift off course. In other words, the narrow-toed hind hooves are specially adapted to support the hind legs' efforts to provide *lateral thrust*.

Figure 4-23A illustrates how this specialized narrow-hoof configuration works in action: in this figure, a horse is being ridden laterally, left to right, at the trot on its left lead. I have seen rival monarchs use this interesting "forward-while-moving-sideways" pace on more than one occasion. They employ it quickly and with great precision and coordination in order to position themselves together, head to tail, for the purpose of nonviolent "discussions" prior to merging their respective bands in the face of a common enemy. I have also seen it used playfully among foals as they side pass beneath their mothers to escape the encroachments of other siblings in the family band.

Figure 4-23B simulates the flight of the leading left hind hoof of the horse moving laterally in Figure 4-23A. Note that the hoof does not actually land on its outside (lateral) wall, nor does it push off exclusively upon its inside (medial) wall. Rather, it endures the main brunt of impact, as well as the main pressures associated with departure, while the entire outer wall is essentially level on the ground. Note further that throughout its entire weight-bearing and support phase, the hoof remains stationary and motionless. The hind leg

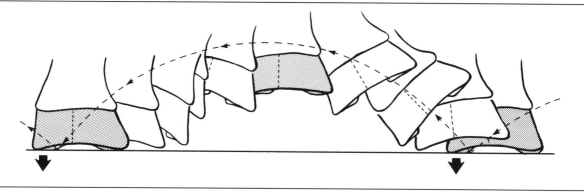

FIGURE 4-23 B.

Action of left hind leading foot. Heavy arrow indicates region of greatest compression during support. Note that median line is perpendicular during hoof's support phase. Compare with left hind hoof in figure 4-19.

simply rotates laterally right over the top of it. Not until breakover along the inside toe wall occurs, does the hoof appear to repeat its lateral trajectory.

The pressure generated concentrates right over the toe, even at the lateral. The narrower hind-toe configuration merely facilitates the lateral action of the hoof as it lands and breaks over, but the weight is still concentrated mainly over the toe at impact. Evidence shows that most of that pressure may be concentrated more to the inside wall than anywhere else along the outer wall (see Hoof Symmetry and Asymmetry, page 83). This was indicated by the arrows in Figure 4-19 beneath the inside toe wall of the naturally shaped hind hoof. Regardless of where the compressional forces concentrate themselves most around the outer wall, the hoof still remains flat and stationary upon the ground during support.

Looking at Figure 4-23B, it is not difficult to see why a narrow toe con-figuration in the hind hoof clearly supports the types of lateral thrusting and lateral breakover that are common when the horse turns or moves laterally. The hoof, like the horse's leads, merely follows along the same lateral trajec-tory as the leading hind leg. But what about those "rounder" front hooves and front legs? They also appear in the photograph to be striking and thrust-ing laterally along with the corresponding hind hooves.

The front hoof does appear to strike and depart from the ground very much like the hind hoof. But, unlike the hind hoof, the front hoof does not endure the same levels of compression, lateral or otherwise, because the front leg is not equipped to deliver it to the front hoof. As mentioned in the previous chapter, the front leg has only one main center for propulsion: the semiflexed shoulder joint. The hindquarters, in contrast, have three: the massive hip joint, the stifle, and the hock. The hindquarters, hindlegs, and hind hooves are designed to create, transfer, and endure grinding, compres-sional forces. The front end is not. So what do those round hooves and long, straight, front legs do?

FIGURE 4-24

The front end, with its long, straight legs and round hooves, seems

AXIS OF DIGIT BONES IN RELATION TO HOOF ASYMMETRY

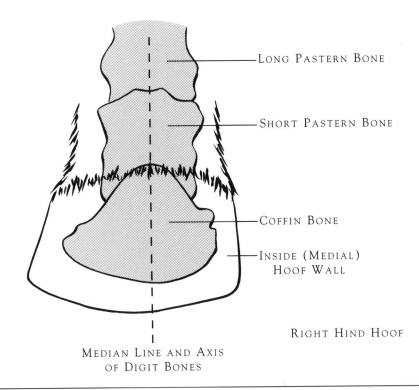

LONG PASTERN BONE

SHORT PASTERN BONE

COFFIN BONE

INSIDE (MEDIAL) HOOF WALL

RIGHT HIND HOOF

MEDIAN LINE AND AXIS
OF DIGIT BONES

intended for support. The front assembly can be seen as a pedestal and stabilizer rolled into one. Specifically, front hooves are designed to support and stabilize that big flying-through-the-air horse body, while the hindquar-ters lift and propel most of the weight. This is contrary to popular opinion, which suggests that the front legs play an important role propelling the horse forward. But it seems to make more sense that a slightly larger, rounder hoof would be adapted up front to enhance the support process.

HOOF ASYMMETRY

Hoof symmetry and asymmetry complement the support and propulsory actions of front and hind legs as follows:

front hoof symmetry + front leg = support + stability

hind hoof asymmetry + hind leg = propulsion + lateral thrust

FIGURE 4-25

The naturally shaped hind hoof, when viewed from the front, is divided asymmetrically by its center line into two, disproportionately shaped left (medial) and right (lateral) halves. In contrast, the front hoof is divided symmetrically into two, proportionately shaped halves. The asymmetrical

SHAPES OF FRONT AND HIND HOOVES IN RELATION TO COFFIN BONES

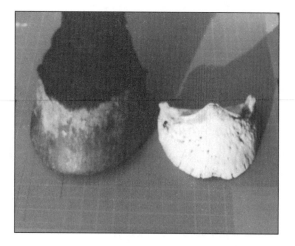
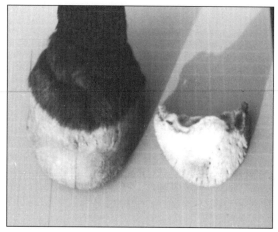

FRONT HOOF AND COFFIN BONE   HIND HOOF AND COFFIN BONE

division of the hind hoof does several things. First, it usually produces a higher angled inside wall than outside wall when viewed from the front (see Figure 4-1, front view). Second, this asymmetry puts the inside half of the hoof capsule and its corresponding toe wall directly beneath the hind leg rather than the outside half during lateral thrusting (Figure 4-23B). Third, it also has the effect of putting the inner side of the hoof more closely under the axis of the bones themselves (Figure 4-24).

Note also, in Figure 4-25, that the asymmetrically shaped hind hoof, with its steep-angled inside wall, mirrors the asymmetrically shaped coffin bone and its higher angled inside wing within its hoof capsule.

The front hoof's symmetry is consistent with the front leg's preemptive role of providing support and stability, in lieu of propulsion, in the natural locomotive process. In this interpretation, a larger, rounder, and more symmetrically shaped front hoof would appear to make the most sense. This symmetry extends equally to the coffin bone, where the inside and outside wings of the bone measure approximately the same angle (Figure 4-25).

TOE ANGLE AND THE COLLECTION CONNECTION

It makes sense that hind hooves would have higher toe angles than corresponding front hooves, when we recognize the following: (1) a more elevated hoof axis complements the increased up-and-down action of the hind legs seen during collection-based behavior, and (2) it favors the increased loading of body weight upon the hindquarters. The steeper the angle the horn tubules form with the ground, the better they are prepared to withstand the pressure of additional body weight.[12]

In connection with this, I believe there is a relationship between collection and higher hind toe angles. In sifting through the Litchfield data, a number of interesting trends emerge that support this hypothesis. One is mentioned here to illustrate this connection.

One of the variables I sought to investigate at Litchfield was body weight: Does a horse's weight influence the conformation of its hooves? And, if so, what was the collection connection? I tested for toe length, toe angle, and hoof size (in this example, how big the bottom of the hoof is in

FIGURE 4-26

IMPACT OF BODY WEIGHT ON DIFFERENT HOOF
MEASUREMENT CATEGORIES

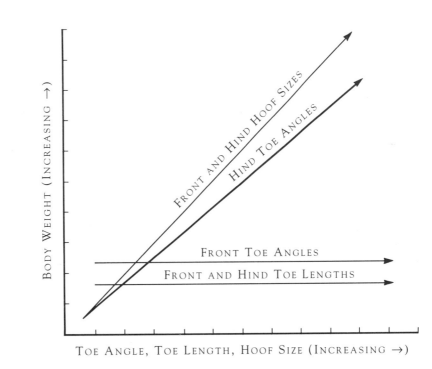

terms of volar surface area), to see if weight affected any of these in either front or hind hooves. Figure 4-26 shows these findings graphically. The impact of age was factored out so as not to complicate the picture unnecessarily. Results showed that both front and hind hooves tend to get bigger across their bearing surfaces (i.e., hoof size) as the body gets heavier. Interestingly, though, toe length was not affected. Apparently, a larger base of hoof support is needed to offset heavier horses, but at the same time, the feet are relatively short.

Results also showed that hind toe angles increased significantly with greater body weights, but that front toe angles remained the same. What this means is that the "extra work" associated with the body weight is handled by the hind hooves, but probably only during collection-based, extraordinary behavior. If it were otherwise, both front and hind hooves would have increased toe angles.

SUMMARY

Naturally shaped hooves are the product of natural equine locomotion occuring in a dry, abrasive environment as exemplified by the hooves of wild, free-roaming horses in the American West. Two basic, archetypal hoof shapes can be identified, front and hind, which have the following general characteristics: (1) left and right pairs that are symmetrical in terms of size and shape, (2) fronts that are normally larger and rounder than hinds, and (3) hind toe angles that are higher than front toe angles.

PROVIDING NATURAL CARE FOR THE DOMESTIC HORSE

Jim Hansen

General
Care of
the Horse

THIS CHAPTER, along with chapters 6 and 7, is intended to help bridge the gap that exists between the world of the natural horse and the world of the domestic horse. At times, the gap seems unbridgeable given the confines of our civilization. But there is much concern for the state of the domestic horse, and I hope that, with the efforts of interested horse enthusiasts, this gap can be bridged. Ideally, everyone intererested in the natural horse should visit the outback and become familiar with nature's rhythms. Unfortunately, this is not always possible. In lieu of a trip to the outback, this chapter attempts to provide some general recommendations for the care of the domestic horse.

PROVIDING A WATERING HOLE

Most horse owners recognize the importance of providing their horses with dry, firm ground on which to live and move about. Excessive moisture is a mortal enemy of natural hoof shape. Although wild horses spend very little time standing in water or mud, normally just long enough to drink and take an occasional mud bath, a watering hole of some sort plays an important role in evoking natural watering behavior in these animals. Such behavior, like all natural locomotive behaviors, contributes vitally to the shaping of the hooves, and accordingly, we should afford the domestic horse the same opportunity.

If a stream, pond, lake, or other large, natural body of water is not available to a horse, provide a nice muddy area around the watering tank or trough but definitely apart from the feeding area. Make it large enough for the horse to stand or roll around in. I recommend burying the watering tanks in the ground, so the horse will have to spread apart its front legs to drink and exercise its strong, powerful neck.

If possible, provide a sand pile adjacent to the watering area so the horse, after bathing in the mud, can roll in the sand to dry off. Horses like this, especially mares and foals. This natural watering behavior produces healthy, lustrous coats.

Let the horse determine its own daily watering schedule by making the watering hole accessible to it day and night. It is normal for the natural horse to stand in water only long enough to quench its thirst, usually minutes at most, in the outback. So, notwithstanding a horse with inflamed hooves, I would not be overly concerned about the animal turning the experience into some kind of water sport that goes on and on to the detriment of its hooves, much like those of us who enjoy soaking in the bathtub or jacuzzi until our skin shrivels.

The wild horse may not enter the watering hole on a daily basis, especially during winter months. In the mind of the natural horse, watering behavior translates to being vulnerable, either to natural predators or to more dominant bands attending the same watering hole. Thus, the experience is normally abbreviated in the wild by these constant threats.

Do not wash or hose off the horse's hooves routinely to make them look fresh and clean. As Xenophon noted, "daily washing is bad for the hooves."[1] Let the horse clean its own hooves nature's way.

PASTURE, EXERCISE, AND DIET

In addition to providing the welcome soft mud, sand, and moisture around the watering hole, the horse owner should make sure that the remainder of the pasture is dry and that the ground is firm, even rocky in places. With naturally shaped hooves, there is no need to worry about stone bruises from strewing rocks over the pasture, much as Xenophon recommended to his readers over two thousand years ago.[2] A varied terrain, including rocks of all sizes, is natural to the horse, so try to make the pasture both interesting and challenging in many respects. A diverse landscape strengthens not only the horse's limbs and hooves, but also its mind and character. Wild horses love to climb, jump, and run as they graze, playing and sparing with each other just like young children, and a physically challenging environment helps bring out the animal's natural instincts and corresponding locomotive behaviors. Obviously, a rectangular pasture, flat, and devoid of rocks, hills, trees, and brush is unnatural to the horse. Yet, sadly, this is typical of the dull, empty environments in which most domestic horses live today.

The same sort of dry, firm, rocky terrain of the natural pasture applies to the corrals where horses work, train, and compete. Arenas filled with deep sand, fancy spongelike bark, or any other soft materials seriously compromise the firm ground preferred and needed by the naturally moving horse—so do unyielding city streets, which, unfortunately, many carriage horses are expected to work today.

Lots of daily exercise is important and so is a variety of nutritious feeds. In the wild, a horse cannot eat without exercising its entire body at the same time. And because of its freedom to move about, it is ensured a variety of foods to eat. Wild horses simply do not stand in one place at a feed box or hay manger to eat just one or two things. While this may seem obvious, too

Jim Hansen

many domestic horses have no choice but to stand around idly, in close confinement for most of their lives, eating the same thing. We need to develop creative alternatives to this unfortunate stable custom.

Alternatively, a good-sized pasture containing a variety of plants and grasses known to be edible and nutritious to the horse is what we must strive to provide for the animal. This is an area in which more research is needed to discover what the natural horses in the outback eat. Perhaps we can plant this food in our own pastures, or feed manufacturers can incorporate them into their commercial feeds. If, on the other hand, the horse is stabled full time in close quarters—a practice I strongly advise against—then, at the very least, provide it with plenty of exercise each day and multiple daily feed rations, consisting of three or more hays plus grain, bran, vitamin supplements, water, and a salt lick.

PARASITE CONTROL

My feelings on parasite control have changed considerably after my experience among wild horses. The general feeling throughout the domestic horse world is that worming procedures are necessary because of the horse's close confinement and proximity to its feces.

This concern is understandable; however, I am not sure it is necessary, given my observations in the outback. Wild horses frequently walk over their own, and each other's, feces as they move about their home ranges, routinely seeking out stud piles on which to defecate. These animals are not walking knee deep in their waste, as many domestic horses are unfortunately obliged to do on a daily basis, nor are they walking in it all the time. But follow them closely in their tracks through the home range, and you will see it is virtually impossible for the animals to avoid walking on their dung at least

part of the time. Particularly distressing to me was the first time I witnessed these perfectly healthy animals actually eating their own feces (called coprophagous behavior), and not becoming ill.[3]

Concluding from my own observations, I suggest that nature seeks an infestation balance of sorts, that is, a level of parasites in the horse's digestive tract that is somehow essential or necessary for normal digestion and metabolism. How it is kept in check, however, is perplexing. Perhaps diet, the effects of the sun, organisms in the soil, and balanced living explain the animal's health. Wild horses, particularly in Montana, have been known to eat the inner bark of certain trees that contains low levels of arsenic—an ingredient known for its antiparasitic qualities. Certainly, more research in this area is in order.

I have never accepted as desirable the current practice of subjecting horses routinely to pesticides for parasite control. Now, I am more skeptical of their use as an instrument of natural care, even though I, like most other horse owners, use them. So, what possibly lies ahead in the way of a natural parasite control regimen? A more varied diet, perhaps including vegetable matters used commonly by wild horses; the use of natural bio-organisms in stalls, like those presently being experimented with in waste management for city dumps; plenty of wholesome sunshine and fresh air; responsible stall hygiene, including adequate drainage; and sufficient levels of balanced exercise. Collectively, all of these practices may yet lead us away from the conventional pesticide wormer.

THE CONFORMATION AND LOCOMOTIVE STYLE MYTHOS

What is troubling in the domestic horse world are the concepts of "good" and "bad" conformations, "appropriate" locomotive styles, and "desirable" personality types. Such notions are disturbing because they are the misperceptions of human beings out of touch with what it means to be natural. Among wild horses, good or bad conformations, ineffective locomotive styles, and dysfunctional personality types do not exist. Notwithstanding the relatively few unfortunate equine anomalies that occur sporadically in the outback, nature selects for a broad range of physical and temperamental types, all of which appear to be perfectly suitable for a rugged life in the wild. Variation is clearly nature's way. Natural grace and beauty are in the eyes of the beholder.

For example, I have seen relatively small, aggressive, and rather nasty studs intimidate into submission what many horse enthusiasts would consider to be the quintessential monarch—a physically large and powerful stallion with striking presence. In awesome contests for harem mares, these little fellows tend to emerge victorious just as often as not. So stereotypes of the exemplary equid only crumble before the reality of the horse's natural world. In the outback, we see horses with phlegmatic and high-strung personalities coupled with long backs, short backs, and virtually every other conformation imaginable in between. All roam about happily and all survive equally well, the perfect embodiments of sound, healthy, and athletic horses we horse enthusiasts would like to have in our charge.

Against this reality of the horse's natural world, however, we find the unfortunate expectation among many equestrians, and their various official organizations, that only certain locomotive styles and physical (breed) types are appropriate for certain types of athletic endeavors. Various breeding and training practices attempt to mold the domestic horse into these paragons of equestrian specialization. Much of this, however, threatens to subvert nature's tendency to select for diversity of conformation. Each horse does things differently according to its own unique wholeness.

Instead of respecting and promoting diversity of conformations within each domestic breed, we demand that each horse, to be appropriate, stand straight, be coupled from fore to rear in a particular way, and be levelheaded too. When nature has failed in these endowments, we resort to mechanical means (e.g., corrective shoeing) to make the animal stand straight or move more according to our arbitrary precepts, or even drug it to make it more

Jim Hansen

compliant, more cooperative, or more excited, as the requirement may be. If still not satisfied, we may even try to breed the desired trait in or out.

Now and then, equine anomalies occur in the domestic horse world that cause us to doubt our own stereotypes of the ideal horse, or at least question that which we think horses are supposed to be able, or unable, to do. In one case, in the 1984 Olympics, the smallest horse in the field of entrants for one of the jumping competitions, ridden by the largest rider (a male rider from Australia), won the gold medal. Alois Podhajsky, in his

memoirs, noted how he and his much-ridiculed, and very long-backed gelding, Nero, nicknamed the "sausage," routed the field of favored contenders in the individual dressage competitions by winning the bronze medal. These horses, and others too numerous to mention here, clearly point out nature's real penchant for diversity of conformation in athletic excellence.

Obviously, more openmindedness is in order among equestrians, trainers, and breeders when assessing a horse's athletic potential based upon conformation, temperament, and locomotive style. To be respectful, compassionate, and understanding toward the horse's natural physicality and personality, whatever that might be, will help to enhance the diversity and colorfulness of every equestrian specialization and experience and will also spawn a new order of horsemanship.

RIDING AND TRAINING

Attention to riding and training practices is also very important. The more we can engage and develop the horse's natural locomotive abilities, especially collection, when we ask it to work for us, the better off the horse and rider. Indeed, this ought to be a goal of every equestrian.

Newcomers to the horse world should try to find a teacher who is knowledgeable about the natural gaits and behavior of the horse. Reading is another excellent way to get started, since in any creative undertaking, which is exactly what riding and training should be, words can help to convey images that will enable the newcomer to conceptualize the learning process that lies ahead long before the foot ever hits the stirrup. As it is, untold numbers of people come to the horse for the first time without a realistic idea of what to expect and, in the process, often get seriously injured.

Never learn to ride on an untrained horse. Insist that the teacher instruct on a horse that has been trained fully, and preferably by the teacher. Tragically, too much time, money, and broken bones have been sacrificed to unqualified, and qualified, teachers with unschooled horses. The widely heard argument that peripatetic students will only "ruin" the teacher's alleged schooled horse through ignorance is wholly unfounded and, in my experience, belies the person's incompetence as a teacher or the lack of a truly schooled horse.

Lastly, forsake the use of violence in deference to reason. Remember, horses are unique with minds of their own and need to be related to as such if we are ever to have enjoyable and productive relationships with them. When those angry impulses surface because the horse is not cooperating, nature is trying to warn us that we are getting out of balance, out of tune, out of harmony. Don't lose your temper with the horse—this will ultimately defeat your best intentions. The use of force and violence only means one thing: the rider has not learned to communicate honestly with the horse.

SUMMARY

Most of what is included in this chapter is meant to bring into question some current practices of horse care. Not all horse care practices are bad; some have evolved for very sound reasons. But for those practices where the intent is bad or the results are harmful or ineffective, it is time to go back to nature and think things over.

Jim Hansen

Hoof Care
the
Natural
Way

BY NOW WE HAVE A FAIRLY GOOD IDEA of the type of hoof intended for the wild, free-roaming horse and also how it is intended to be used. The purpose of this chapter is to provide the domestic horse with the same kind of hoof. A strategy and step-by-step method for trimming and shoeing is detailed based upon the research conducted at Litchfield Corrals and my personal experience as a farrier. It is my hope that this information will prove helpful to farriers, horse owners, trainers, veterinarians, and anyone else seeking to improve the lives of domestic horses by providing more natural hoof care.

STRATEGY FOR TRIMMING A NATURALLY SHAPED HOOF

The principal idea behind generating naturally shaped hooves in the domestic horse is simple: to help the animal move in the way that nature intended. The trimming and shoeing process described here is geared specifically toward this end. Implicit in this hoof-shaping strategy is the assumption that naturally shaped hooves cannot *make* the horse move naturally. We cannot expect the domestic horse to benefit fully from having balanced, naturally shaped hooves if the animal is going to be subjected repeatedly to imbalanced use.

In chapter 4, findings based on the Litchfield data were presented. These findings form the basis of the method of trimming and shoeing domestic horses presented in this chapter. These findings were tested on hundreds of horses in my charge over a three- to four-year period. All breed types were involved, including over 200 barefooted Peruvian Pasos on one ranch. Notwithstanding a few horses who had been suffering from many years of unsoundness, all horses trimmed down nicely according to the method presented here and remained, or went, sound. I should add, however, that this is not a guide to learning the art of horseshoeing, and I advise strongly that the recommendations included here be put to use only by experienced shoers or their supervised students. At the same time, every serious horseman and horsewoman should try to familiarize themselves with at least the main concepts that follow and as much of the detail as they find helpful.

In shaping a natural hoof, it is helpful to keep the following points in mind:

~The hoof should be shortened, especially through the toe, as much as possible without causing lameness or penetrating sensitive tissues. A natural hoof is a short hoof, lacking the excess baggage and weight of unstable and unsightly old-growth horn found in unnaturally shaped, long-toed hooves. Not only does a short, compact hoof translate to less resistance during breakover and less work overall for the horse to move it during the natural locomotive process, it is also a more durable one, less likely to split and unravel.

~The shoer should discriminate between front and hind shapes. Recall from chapter 4 that hind hooves, when viewed from beneath, are narrower from side to side across their quarters and toes than their more rounded fore counterparts.

~The hoof should be trimmed so that the horn tubules visible in the outer wall as grain will be aligned perpendicularly (at right angles) to the ground when the hoof, planted firmly upon a flat surface, is viewed from the front (see Figures 4-5 and 4-6).

~Hind hooves should be trimmed to have higher toe angles than corresponding front hooves (Table 4-2). This angle differential is extremely important to the overall natural locomotive process and to collection in particular.

SIX-STEP METHOD FOR TRIMMING

Basically, there are six steps to trimming naturally shaped hooves:

1. Assess the hoof for naturalness of toe length, toe angle, and hoof balance. In other words, for overall size, shape, and proportion.

2. Remove old-growth horn from the sole to expose the "white line," especially around the toe.

3. Shorten the toe and both quarters.

4. Rasp outer wall to encourage straight-line growth.

5. Trim frog; trim heel buttresses if necessary to balance hoof.

6. Contour the bearing surface of the outer wall consistent with horse going shod/unshod.

MEASURING THE HOOF

FIGURE 6-1

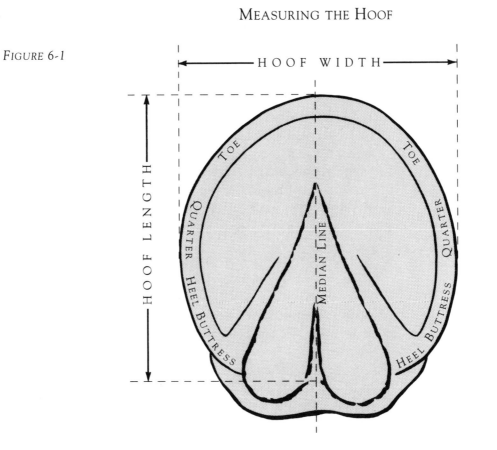

VOLAR PROFILE

Measure hoof width from quarter to quarter, perpendicular to hoof's median line, at point of widest bend. Measure hoof length from point along toe wall that intersects hoof's median line to point on median line parallel to heel buttress.

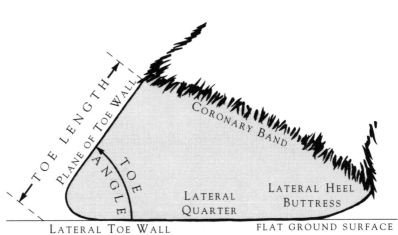

LATERAL PROFILE

Measure toe angle using a farrier's protractor, which must set flush upon both heel buttresses and at least one toe wall (medial or lateral side). Measure toe length from the coronary band down to the point where the plane of toe wall intersects the flat surface supporting the hoof.

Practically speaking, horseowners, veterinarians, and farriers should find this method basic, straightforward, and simple. Personally, I have found that it works well, especially when there is close cooperation between the farrier, horse owner, trainer/rider, and veterinarian. The six steps are explained in detail below.

STEP 1
ASSESS THE HOOF FOR NATURALNESS OF TOE LENGTH, TOE ANGLE, AND BALANCE

Before trimming work begins, assess the hoof for naturalness of toe length, toe angle, and overall balance, as well as for shape and size across its bottom (volar profile). This is an important preliminary step in the shaping process, since what is learned here will determine precisely how the hoof will be trimmed.

TOE LENGTH AND TOE ANGLE

To begin, measure the hooves for toe length and toe angle. Figure 6-1 illustrates how these and other measurements for the Litchfield horses were made. It is important that you try to replicate these measuring techniques as close as possible in order to be consistent and to ensure compatibility with the data.

Now refer to Figure 6-2 to compare your measurements with my findings. The bell-shaped curve is a simple, convenient way to compare averages and ranges for naturally versus unnaturally shaped hooves. The numbers below the curve are designated in inches and degrees. You might compare this figure with Tables 4-1 and 4-2 to see how I derived the curve.

For example, your horse may have a front toe angle (left or right) of 54 degrees and a hind toe angle of 58 degrees. First, find those numbers in the ranges below the curve. Now look above. According to the curve, both angles are considered to be "very natural." Now, measure the toe lengths. They may measure three and one-quarter inches long; according to the curve, both are "very natural."

If the toe lengths and toe angles measured are not natural at this point, do not worry about it. We will address this problem later.

HOOF BALANCE

The balanced, naturally shaped hoof was discussed fully in chapter 4 (see Balanced Hooves, Balanced Horse, p. 84). In view of that discussion, a hoof can be said to be balanced when:

1. The horn tubules (grain) constituting the outer wall are approximately parallel to each other and perpendicular to the flat ground (or level supporting surface) when the hoof is viewed from the front.

2. The center line divides the front profile of the front hoof into two *symmetrically* shaped halves.

3. The center line divides the front profile of the hind hoof into two *asymmetrically* shaped halves.

4. Front and hind toe length and toe angle measurements fall within the ranges specified for naturalness—preferably "very natural" to "natural"—in Figure 6-2.

To check for hoof balance, have the horse stand on a flat surface; a

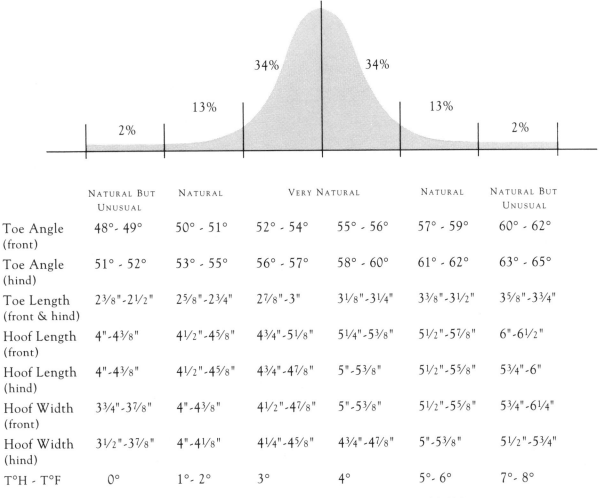

BELL CURVE FOR NATURAL HOOF SIZE AND ANGLE

	NATURAL BUT UNUSUAL	NATURAL	VERY NATURAL		NATURAL	NATURAL BUT UNUSUAL
Toe Angle (front)	48°- 49°	50° - 51°	52° - 54°	55° - 56°	57° - 59°	60° - 62°
Toe Angle (hind)	51° - 52°	53° - 55°	56° - 57°	58° - 60°	61° - 62°	63° - 65°
Toe Length (front & hind)	2³⁄₈"-2¹⁄₂"	2⁵⁄₈"-2³⁄₄"	2⁷⁄₈"-3"	3¹⁄₈"-3¹⁄₄"	3³⁄₈"-3¹⁄₂"	3⁵⁄₈"-3³⁄₄"
Hoof Length (front)	4"-4³⁄₈"	4¹⁄₂"-4⁵⁄₈"	4³⁄₄"-5¹⁄₈"	5¹⁄₄"-5³⁄₈"	5¹⁄₂"-5⁷⁄₈"	6"-6¹⁄₂"
Hoof Length (hind)	4"-4³⁄₈"	4¹⁄₂"-4⁵⁄₈"	4³⁄₄"-4⁷⁄₈"	5"-5³⁄₈"	5¹⁄₂"-5⁵⁄₈"	5³⁄₄"-6"
Hoof Width (front)	3³⁄₄"-3⁷⁄₈"	4"-4³⁄₈"	4¹⁄₂"-4⁷⁄₈"	5"-5³⁄₈"	5¹⁄₂"-5⁵⁄₈"	5³⁄₄"-6¹⁄₄"
Hoof Width (hind)	3¹⁄₂"-3⁷⁄₈"	4"-4¹⁄₈"	4¹⁄₄"-4⁵⁄₈"	4³⁄₄"-4⁷⁄₈"	5"-5³⁄₈"	5¹⁄₂"-5³⁄₄"
T°H - T°F	0°	1°- 2°	3°	4°	5°- 6°	7°- 8°

All measurements left or right hooves, ages 5+ (adults). Based on Litchfield data.

FIGURE 6-2

concrete slab, large board, or flat piece of firm ground will do. One of the remarkable things I discovered at Litchfield about naturally shaped hooves is that they will all sit balanced on a flat surface in essentially the same way regardless of differences in each horse's leg and body conformation. An imbalanced hoof can be distinguished readily from a balanced one without having to be concerned about variations in the horse's stance stemming from conformation-based differences, provided the hooves are examined one by one on a flat surface. Therefore, let the animal stand in a comfortable posture. It does not have to stand "straight," and the hooves can face in any direction. We are not really concerned here with how each hoof is positioned under the horse's body, nor how it sits in relation to the leg. All we want to know is how the hoof rests on a flat surface. With this done, we can now subject the hooves at hand to the visual inspection.

With the horse's hoof on a flat surface, examine the hoof's angle of growth. First examine the hoof and grain closely from the front (anterior profile). The horn tubules should be laying perpendicular (at right angles) to the hoof's supporting surface. This can be either eyed, or the toe wall can be marked with a heavy felt pen. I have devised a convenient strip test to do this, which is conducted as follows:

1. Cut a narrow one-eighth-inch-wide strip from a roll of masking (or, preferably, duct tape) and place it over the median line of the toe wall. Use

STRIP TEST FOR HOOF BALANCE

FIGURE 6-3

Place test strip over median line in front (anterior) profile of hoof (A); snip strip off at toe. Strip should be perpendicular to flat supporting surface. If strip is skewed to left or right, hoof is imbalanced.

Figure 6-1 to locate the median line, which extends from the bottom (volar) profile to the front (anterior) profile. Figure 6-3 shows how I have done this with a hoof specimen removed from a domestic horse. Note that the hoof must be dry, or the tape will not stick.

2. Then, cut the tape off near the bottom of the hoof so that it will not drag on the ground and work loose. The strip, when affixed, should be roughly parallel to the horn tubules of the toe wall.

3. Next, return the hoof to the flat supporting surface and view it from the front. If the hoof is balanced, the strip should be roughly perpendicular to the ground. If, however, the strip is skewed either to the left or to the right, then the hoof is probably imbalanced and will require special attention later.

4. Now, look at the hoof from the outside (lateral profile) to check the angle of growth in that view. The strip should lie in a straight line from the hairline (or coronary band) down to the bevel of the hoof wall without curving outward (concaved) as we see often in foundered or badly flared hooves (Figure 6-4A), or inward (convex), as seen in snub, bull, or "beak-nosed" hooves (Figure 6-4B).

5. Further, the tape should lay at a slightly higher angle, or slope, than the horn tubules visible anywhere else from the quarters to the heels, espe-

FIGURE 6-4

A.

Concaved hoof walls are not natural and usually indicate excessive toe length.

B.

Convex hoof walls are equally unnatural and may result from excessive toe lengths caused by poorly fitted horseshoes or trimming where the toe is "snubbed" but not shortened.

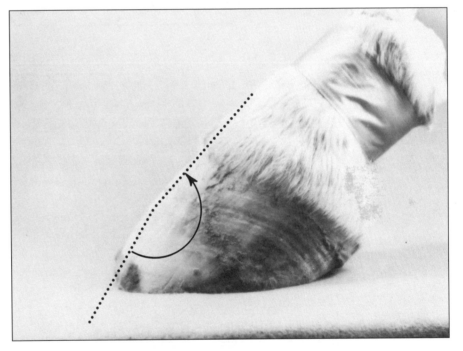

cially at the heel, where the grain will tend to lay at a conspicuously lower angle than anywhere else (Figure 4-5B).

If these conditions of hoof growth (front and side) are met, and the hoof's toe-length and toe-angle values fall within the "natural" to "very-natural" regions of the curve in Figure 6-2, then the hoof can be considered balanced.

HOOF SIZE AND SHAPE
The last task in Step 1 is to assess the bearing surface (volar profile) of the hoof for naturalness of size and shape. To do this, first measure the bottom of the hoof lengthwise and crosswise as shown in Figure 6-1. Then, compare this data with the curve in Figure 6-2.

Considerable variation is allowed in hoof size measured lengthwise and crosswise across the bottoms of naturally shaped hooves. Calculations show that for any given toe length, a broad range of bearing (volar) surface areas are possible. For example, for adult Litchfield horses with toe lengths measuring three inches, bearing surfaces varied by as much as fourteen square inches.

Again, for the hooves at hand to be considered natural, they should measure somewhere within the "natural" to "very natural" ranges. Only

FIGURE 6-5

Naturally shaped front hooves are wider and longer than their hind counterparts; however, both typically are equally wide across the heels.

RELATIONSHIP OF HEEL BUTTRESSES TO FRONT AND HIND BEARING SURFACES

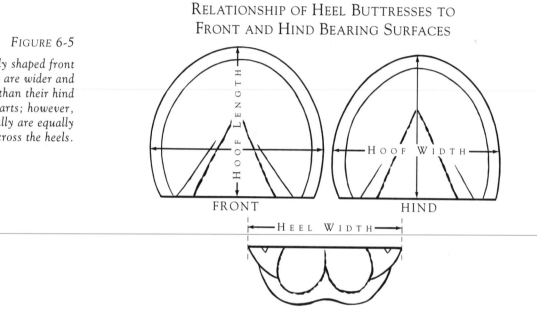

ponies, draft horses, and horses suffering from severe hoof pathologies (e.g., severe laminitis), should fall outside these guidelines.

The main differences between front and hind hoof shapes when viewed from below (volar) were described in chapter 4 (Figure 4-1, p. 69). The naturally shaped hind hoof is narrower across the toe and quarters than its fore counterpart. At the same time, it is also somewhat shorter lengthwise from toe to frog cleft. This can be seen in the ranges given in Figure 6-2. Surprisingly, calculations for heel width (data not summerized in Figure 6-2), on the average, tended to be the same for both front and hind hooves. This, when considered in relation to other side-to-side dimensions across the bottom of the hind hoof, indicates a proportional reduction in hoof size forward of its heels, which explains why the surface areas of front hooves are greater, on the average, than their corresponding hinds. It is as though nature has kept the rear portions of front and hind hooves the same size and shape, but found it necessary to attach different size and shape "toes." This can be seen in Figure 6-5. In chapter 4, I attempted to account for this in terms of the natural locomotive experience (see Front and Hind Hoof Shapes, page 70).

Figure 6-6 represents composite front and hind (volar) shapes computed from all the averages itemized in Figure 6-2. Note that each image suffices for either a left or right hoof. This is because, on the average, I found no significant differences in their respective shapes between paired left and

FIGURE 6-6

A. COMPOSITE VIEW OF BOTTOM (VOLAR) OF
NATURALLY SHAPED FRONT HOOF

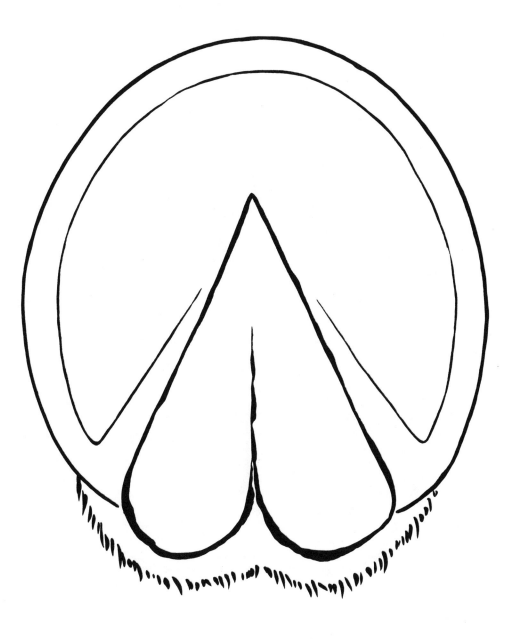

Figure 6-6

B. Composite View of Bottom (Volar) of
Naturally Shaped Hind Hoof

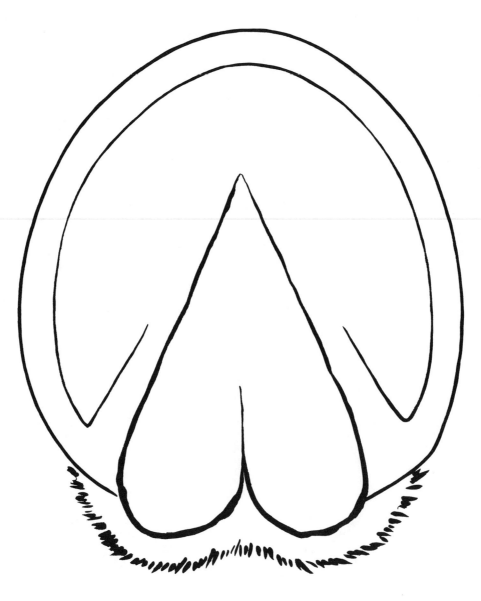

right hooves. The shoer can use these as templates to compare with the hooves to be trimmed and, later, when shaping horseshoes.

On the average, little noticeable variation in hoof proportion from these composite front and hind shapes (seen in Figure 6-6) was found among the Litchfield horses. As a rule, changes in hoof size (volar) length-wise across their bottoms were more or less accompanied by proportional changes in all the other side-to-side hoof measurements.

STEP 2
REMOVE OLD-GROWTH HORN FROM THE SOLE

Once the hooves have been measured and assessed for naturalness of size, shape, proportion, and balance, they are ready to be trimmed. In this step, the task will be to remove as much old-growth horn from the sole as possible (Figure 6-7A). This may require the combined use of the hoof knife, sole knife, and nippers to clean out the sole and expose the white line around the toe and quarters (Figure 6-7B). The projected cutting site along the white line is marked with a felt pen in Figure 6-7C. Once the white line can be seen clearly, the shoer is ready to proceed to the next step.

Remember, in wild horse hooves, the horn of the sole is quite hard or calloused and somewhat arched (concaved), as can be seen in Figure 4-2

PREPARING THE SOLE FOR THE HOOF NIPPERS

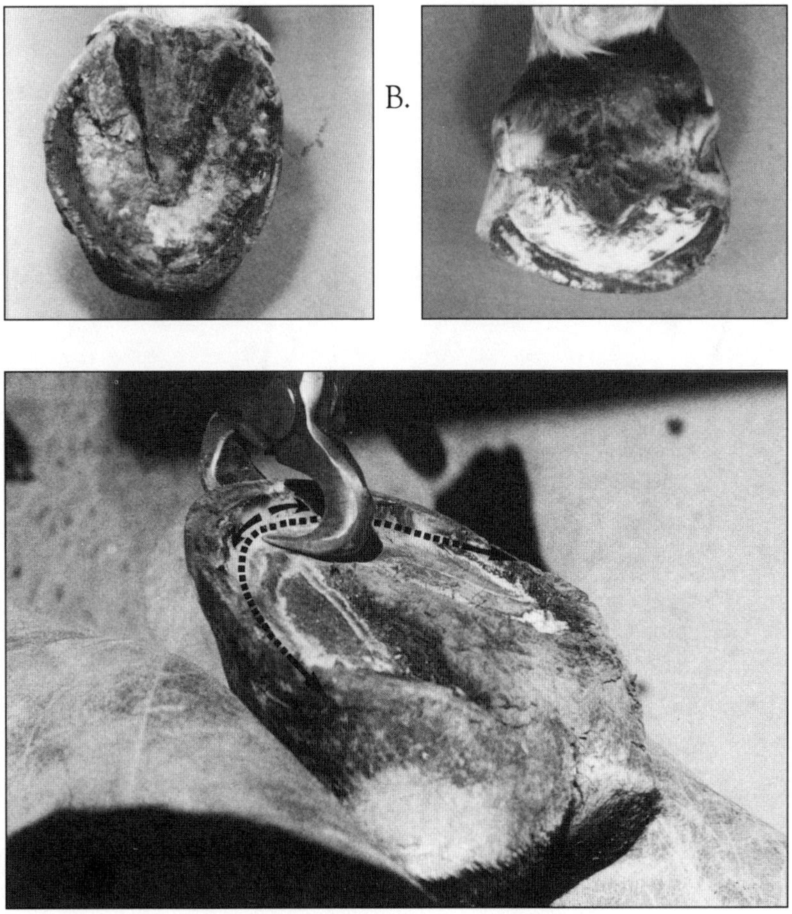

FIGURE 6-7

Unnaturally shaped hind hoof illustrates long, unsightly outer wall and flakey sole (A). Same hoof with sole excoriated of dead, excess horn, exposing cutting site around toe wall and quarters (B). Nippers applied to exposed toe wall at white line (C). Note that heel buttresses are not included in cutting perimeter at this stage.

and Figure 4-12. This unique structuring and palpable firmness serves the naturally shaped hoof in several ways. First, it serves to shield the sole's own sensitive structures within the hoof-capsule from enduring direct contact with the ground. Second, it assists the bars in ensuring that the frog and its sensitve structures will also sustain only indirect (passive) contact with the ground. Third, it aids the coffin bone in deflecting compressional forces onto the outer wall, so essential to the natural shaping of the hoof.

In contrast, the soles, typical of many, if not most, domestic horse hooves, are not calloused at all, but are flaky, moist, often palpably soft and rival the frog in terms of general foulness. All of this must be cleaned out.

From experience, I have found that barefooted domestic horses will eventually develop a tough, thickened sole, like the wild horse, if the outer wall is kept trimmed short and the ground of the pasture is maintained in a relatively firm, dry consistency most of the time.

STEP 3
SHORTEN THE TOE AND QUARTERS

It has been shown in chapter 4 that the junction of the white line and water line around the entire outer wall marks the first stage of concavity in naturally shaped hooves (Figure 4-12). Here, the outer wall emerges naturally to

FIGURE 6-8A

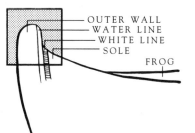

FRAMEWORK OF THE CUTTING SITE

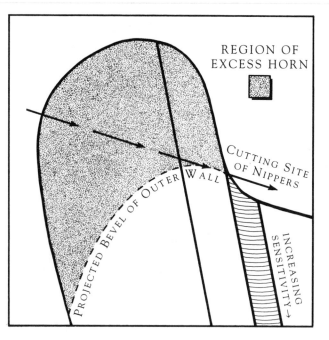

protrude below (i.e., distal or inferior to) the white line. Accordingly, the white line represents the boundary above (toward the sole) which the hoof nippers should never cut, less we risk quicking the hoof and laming the horse (Figure 6-8A). With this barrier in mind, lower the toe wall with the hoof nippers and then rasp it lightly to give it a smooth, even finish.

My dissections of wild horse hooves reveal that the calloused sole provides a distinct, insensitive barrier of cornified horn for a thickness of at least one-quarter inch. This can be seen in the sagittal section in Figure 4-10 and in the close-up in Figure 6-8B. Similarly, this cornification is commensurate within the white line at thicknesses of at least five-eighths of an inch and in the frog at one-half inch thicknesses beneath the point of frog.

Now, ascertain whether or not the toe wall can be shortened further. Experience must guide the shoer in making this decision, however, the ranges for front and hind toe-length values given in Figure 6-2 are also helpful, especially in regard to the quicking of horses. This unfortunate problem usually stems from the shoer's uncertainty about how much to shorten the

FIGURE 6-8B

Sensitive and insensitive structures affected by reduction of toe and sole through corrective trimming. This cross-section provides an important view into the work plate discussed in chapter 4, page 89.

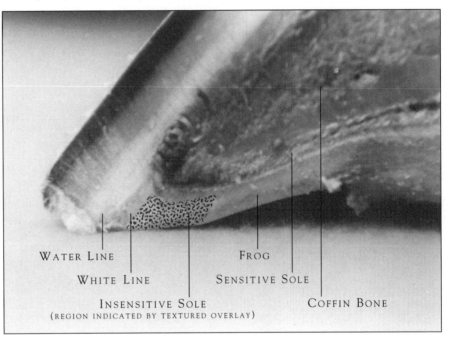

WATER LINE   FROG

WHITE LINE   SENSITIVE SOLE

INSENSITIVE SOLE   COFFIN BONE
(REGION INDICATED BY TEXTURED OVERLAY)

hooves. Approaching the quick is not a pleasant notion in the minds of many shoers, and the temptation to leave the toe too long, because it is easier and safer to do so, is understandable. But shortening the hoof through the toe as much as possible—without quicking the hoof and causing lameness, of course—is a fundamental goal in this trimming strategy and must be done.

The shoer ought to be able to shorten most toes (front and hind) to somewhere within the "very natural" range, that is, down to three and one-quarter inches (Figure 6-2). Some hooves will fall into the "natural" range, or three and one-half inches. Hooves that only shorten to the "natural-but-unusual" range, that is, to three and three-quarter inches, are still okay but borderline. Any hoof that resists being shortened to this length, without quicking it, may be suffering a pathology (e.g., laminitis due to founder), in which case a veterinarian should be consulted and radiographs considered before attempting to trim the hoof further.

Figure 6-9 may also help ascertain if the hoof has reached a natural toe length. Basically, the graph shows that toe lengths, on the average, tend to increase directly with hoof size (volar) in naturally shaped hooves. Note, however, that all these toe lengths are relatively short (i.e., not more than three and a half inches). Although I found many exceptions to this trend among the Litchfield sample, the correlation is still useful when faced with hooves that contradict the trend blatantly. For example, while I would expect that many hooves with relatively large bearing (volar) surfaces would

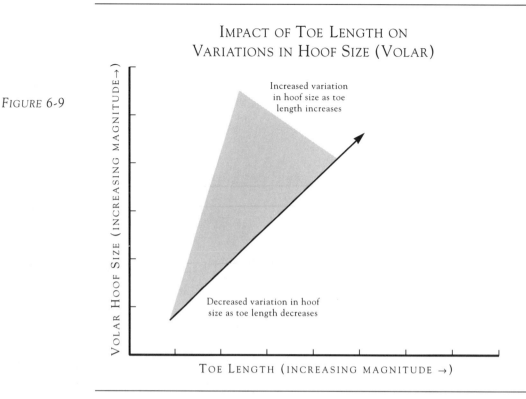

Figure 6-9

IMPACT OF TOE LENGTH ON
VARIATIONS IN HOOF SIZE (VOLAR)

Increased variation
in hoof size as toe
length increases

Decreased variation in hoof
size as toe length decreases

VOLAR HOOF SIZE (INCREASING MAGNITUDE →)

TOE LENGTH (INCREASING MAGNITUDE →)

have relatively short toe lengths, as is often the case with wild horses, I
would be leery when confronted with a relatively long-toed hoof (e.g., three
and a half inches) having a relatively small bearing surface. In other words,
it is not unusual to find longer toe lengths in wild horse populations associated with relatively large bearing surfaces, but abnormal to find such hooves
with relatively small bearing surfaces.

STEP 4
RASP THE OUTER WALL

Earlier, I characterized the growth of the naturally shaped hoof wall as
occurring straight down from the hairline to the turn of the wall (bevel),
neither dished (concave) nor bulged (convex). Accordingly, rasp the
outer wall anywhere around its entire circumference in order to achieve
the same straight-line effect. This does not mean thinning down the
outer wall unnecessarily. On the contrary, most wild horse hooves that
I have examined have relatively thick outer walls, in some cases, as thick
as three-quarters of an inch outside the white line. Thick outer walls are
natural and desirable.

The main idea here is to encourage more natural straight-line
growth where indicated by altering the angle that the horn tubules form
with the ground. As Emery et al., point out in *Horseshoeing Theory and
Hoof Care*, "Rasping the sides and quarters of flaring feet also simulates
natural wear and shape. Such manicuring encourages more vertical growth
of the wall and thus greater strength. It also allows for more secure nailing
in many cases."[1]

Lowering the toe wall sufficiently will facilitate much of the needed
change, especially in the long run, because the entire hoof wall is automati-
cally put at a higher growth axis. But rasping the outer surface of the hoof

CORRECTIVE TRIMMING FOR
CONCAVE AND CONVEX HOOF WALLS

FIGURE 6-10

A.

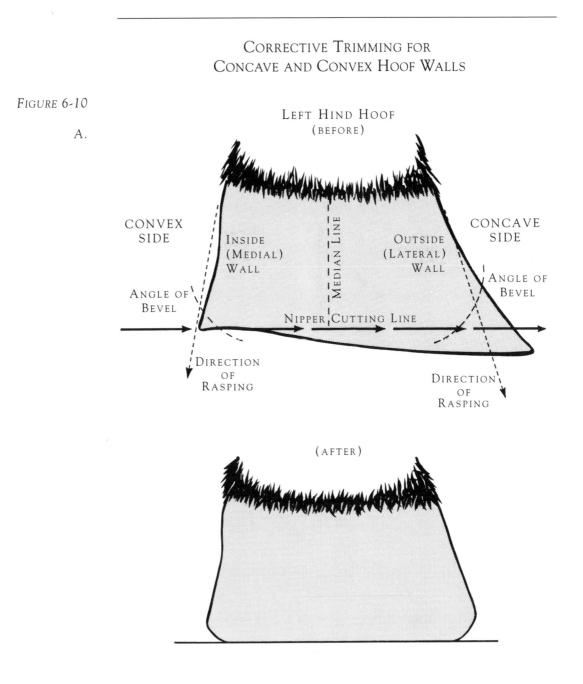

LEFT HIND HOOF
(BEFORE)

CONVEX
SIDE

INSIDE
(MEDIAL)
WALL

MEDIAN LINE

OUTSIDE
(LATERAL)
WALL

CONCAVE
SIDE

ANGLE OF
BEVEL

ANGLE OF
BEVEL

NIPPER CUTTING LINE

DIRECTION
OF
RASPING

DIRECTION
OF
RASPING

(AFTER)

B.

BEFORE: *Left hind hoof
specimen with badly
flared inside (medial)
toe wall.*

AFTER: *Same hoof with
wall nipped and rasped.*

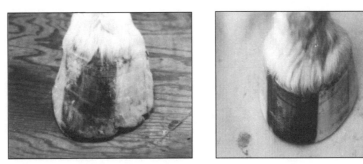

BEFORE

AFTER

wall helps too, since the underlying horn tubules will be encouraged to grow downward and forward instead of collapsing downward and outward like the walls of an Indian tipi (Figure 4-5A). In practice, this may involve the removal of relatively large portions of the outer wall in some hooves, but only light, localized raspings in others. For example, hooves that are badly flared may need considerable rasping to promote more vertical growth (Figure 6-10A, B). Conversely, hooves that are unnaturally dished (concaved) will receive less attention with the rasp, since the angle of growth of the horn tubules is already much too vertical (Figure 6-10A). Treat "beak-nosed" hooves like dished hooves—avoid rasping their outer walls altogether.

If straight-line growth cannot be established in the framework of one trimming session without weakening the outer wall or quicking the sensitive lamina within, then rasp away as much as seems safe and wait until new growth emerges. Baring some underlying pathology, future trimming sessions should gradually yield improved results, especially if the toe wall is consistently kept to a short, natural length.

STEP 5
TRIM FROG AND LOWER HEEL BUTTRESSES IF NECESSARY TO BALANCE HOOF

With the toe wall shortened and the outer wall rasped to encourage straight-line growth, the time has come to pare the frog and then balance the hoof if necessary by trimming the heel buttresses.

TRIMMING THE FROG

FIGURE 6-11

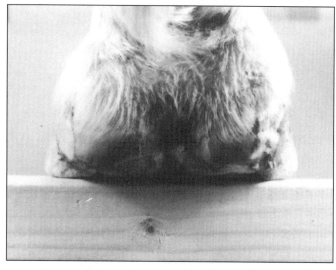

Before trimming the heels, trim the frog thoroughly at this time with the hoof knife. The naturally shaped frog is a bifurcated structure, so we want to accentuate its natural divisions, that is, the cleft and commissures, as much as possible (Figure 4-9). When finished, the point of frog should be roughly level with the sole (Figure 4-12A, B), and the frog's wings just passive to the bars. The rear of the frog should be passive to the heel buttresses when the hoof is viewed from behind (Figure 6-11). The latter can be verified easily by laying a flat stick or ruler over the frog and both heel buttresses. If passive, the frog should barely touch the ruler but not prevent the ruler from making simultaneous contact with both heel buttresses. Trimmed this way, the entire body of the naturally shaped frog will nearly always be ensured of indirect (passive) contact with the ground when the horse's weight is exerted upon the hoof.

TRIMMING THE HEEL BUTTRESSES FOR HOOF BALANCE

Next, place the hoof back on a flat surface and give it the strip test as in Step 1 (see page 110). Make sure that when sighting the hoof, both heel buttresses have active contact with the supporting surface. If the hoof is balanced when viewed from the front, both tape strip (or marker line) and

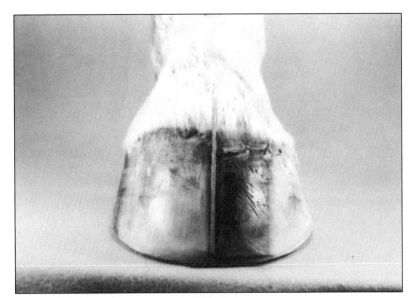

FIGURE 6-12

Balanced hoof with strip test passed in front (anterior) view.

horn tubules should be perpendicular to the flat surface supporting the hoof (see Figure 6-12).

If, however, the strip (or marker line) is askew, then check to see if either the inside (medial) or outside (lateral) half of the toe wall needs further reduction. If one side does, then either trim it down carefully with the nippers, or rasp it down in small increments; either way, do this, if possible, until the strip becomes perpendicular (Figure 6-13).

Remember, both heel buttresses must be in active contact with a flat surface when the strip's (marker line) orientation is being evaluated. It is not necessary, however, for both quarters or, for that matter, the entire toe wall, to have direct contact with the supporting surface, since a three-point base of support—for example, the inside or outside toe wall and both heel buttresses—is often the case with naturally shaped hooves, particularly hind ones that are asymmetrically shaped.

If the toe wall cannot be lowered farther without quicking the sole adjacent to the toe, then rasp down the longer of the two heel buttresses in small increments until the strip becomes perpendicular. In the event, however, that there is too little buttress to begin with, avoid rasping altogether. A heel wedge may be necessary later to balance the hoof.

Once the hoof is balanced from side to side when viewed from the front, measure its toe angle again to confirm that it is natural. If the toe angle falls somewhere within the "natural" range in the curve in Figure 6-2, that is, between 50 to 59 degrees for fronts, and 53 to 62 degrees for hinds, then consider the angle to be acceptably natural and the hoof balanced.

If, by chance, the toe angle measures above the upper limits of the ranges in Figure 6-2, that is, "natural but unusual" or greater, it may be too

FIGURE 6-13

Hoof balanced using principles of natural trimming method.
BEFORE: *Right hind hoof is imbalanced in front view; strip,skewed to outside, results from unnatural wall flare.*
AFTER: *Same hoof corrected after removing over 1½ inches of toe horn.*

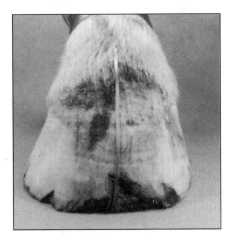

BEFORE

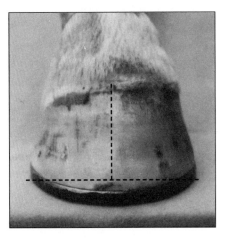

AFTER

high. In this case, rasp down both heel buttresses *evenly* to get the toe angle down into a more natural range. It is possible, however, that a toe angle will measure above 60 degrees (front or hind) and still be natural. But to be so, the heels should not be excessively long, just long enough to afford the well-trimmed frog passive contact with the ground. Remember that the toe angle appears to be a function of the relative position of the coffin bone and not relative heel length (Figure 4-14). Lest we get into deep trouble at this point by contradicting what is a fundamental principle of natural hoof shape, namely, a short hoof, it is probably wise not to burden the heels with too much responsibility for angling the hoof.

If the angle of the toe falls below 50 degrees (front or hind), it is probably too low to be considered natural. In this case, either the toe wall has not been lowered sufficiently, too much heel buttress has been removed (in which case, they will be passive rather than active in relation to the frog), or the hoof is simply unnaturally configured due to a pathology or some kind of injury. Accordingly, either lower the toe wall further, or if this is not possible—and providing that the toe angle is less than 50 degrees—apply a horseshoe later with wedged or stacked heels to help elevate the hoof's low toe angle. More often than not, however, patience and new growth will eventually allow the hoof's angle to be raised without resorting to wedges, angled pads, shoes with stacked or caulked heels, or other mechanical aids.

Another dimension of the Litchfield hoof survey was to compare front and corresponding hind toe angles. Indirectly, differences between the two afford another means to corroborate hoof balance. Figure 6-2 expresses these angle differentials, toe angle hind minus toe angle front (T°H - T°F), as a simple curve. In my own work, I look for an average angle difference of about three to four degrees for any given horse but expect there to be no difference at all in some hooves ("natural but unusual"), and as much as seven to eight degrees difference ("natural but unusual") in others. For the most part, however, angle differences should range somewhere between two to five degrees to be considered natural. If this is the case with the hooves at hand, we can assume that they are now balanced from front to rear (anteroposteriorly) and side to side (mediolaterally).

STEP 6
CONTOUR THE BEARING SURFACE OF THE OUTER WALL

This step precludes a horseshoe from being applied. If a shoe is to be applied, then skip this step and go on to the next section. To finish the hoof without a shoe, the entire bearing surface of the outer wall must first be rounded off. Start with the rough side of a farrier's rasp, working the tool downward toward the ground, that is, obliquely against the grain of the outer wall. Sharp or pointed edges have to be worked completely out of the wall's projected bearing surface. Next, using the fine side of the rasp, smooth down the loosened horn produced by the rough rasping.

Following the raspings, hone the outer wall with sandpaper. I have found that sanding the wall helps to prevent splitting and is the only effective way to duplicate the rounded character of the naturally shaped hoof wall seen in the outback. Begin with a narrow strip of medium-grade paper attached to a U-shaped handle (such a sanding device is available from Advantage-Line Horseshoeing Tools). Work the tool back and forth over the bearing surface of the outer wall, just like shining a shoe with a buffing cloth. Finish polishing the hoof with a disc of fine-grade paper mounted on a circular, rubber pad (rubber-backed sanding discs are available in different diameters from The 3M Company). Use this flexible pad also to hone the concaved surface of the hoof wall and the sole.

The job is finished when the bearing surface of the outer wall is thoroughly rounded, smooth, and uniform—just like the domestic horse hoof in Figure 6-14. This represents the work plate discussed in chapter 4 (see page 89). If this is the first trimming the horse has received, and the hooves are not yet naturally shaped and balanced as described above, do not worry about it. They will be better the next time. The hooves will respond to the efforts made to improve them by growing down at the new angles established by the shoer. As new wall grows down, the shoer can continue to alter its angles, size, and shape to make the hooves even more natural.

FIGURE 6-14

TRIM JOB FINISHED

BEFORE   AFTER

Working to make the hooves progressively more natural is my definition of "corrective trimming/shoeing."

Also, do not be overly concerned with contouring the work plate further to induce active and passive wear areas (see page 88). Just make sure the hoof is balanced and the bearing surface of the outer wall is well rounded, and then quit. It is now up to the horse and its rider, working as a team, to squeeze out those crests and troughs described in chapter 4.

SHOEING THE HORSE

If the horse is to be shod, then the shoer should skip Step 6 and monitor the hoof instead for naturalness of size and balance as per Step 5. Once this has been done, the hoof is ready to shoe.

SELECTING A HORSESHOE

Before applying a horseshoe to a naturally shaped front or hind hoof, a decision must be made as to what type of shoe to use. The vast selection of horseshoes available today is staggering. But how many of these would be truly appropriate for a naturally shaped hoof?

In selecting a horseshoe, seek a balance between weight, thickness, and durability. For example, choose a thinner and lighter shoe over a thicker and heavier one if the lighter one will hold its shape and support the hoof adequately. A thinner shoe makes for a shorter toe, and a shorter toe translates to less resistance and less work for the horse during the hoof's breakover phase; moreover, there is less weight for the horse to carry around on its feet.

Avoid using a shoe that either imbalances the hoof by causing an otherwise balanced hoof to fail the strip test; alters the hoof's natural toe angle by making it too low or too high; or mechanically obstructs the animal's natural gait complex by inducing aberrations in locomotive style, disrupting the normal stride patterns of the three natural gaits, or hindering collection.

For your information, Advantage-Line Horseshoeing Tools, a company specializing in unique farriery equipment and supplies, is currently developing a new line of hoof care products to assist the shoer in simulating natural hoof wear based, in good measure, upon the wild horse–natural horse paradigm. Immediately relevant here is an exciting, new, lightweight horseshoe that is neither nailed nor glued onto the hoof. It is textured around its entire bearing surface like a wild horse hoof, and can be used in conjunction with a program of going barefooted.

Also in the experimentation stage is an interesting new rasp, which, by its unique shape and action, will aid the shoer in producing the well-rounded bevel that is characteristic of the natural outback hoof. Further information on these and other fascinating products will be available nationally and worldwide through different farrier and equestrian supply houses, as well as through advertisements in various horse-related magazines and professional journals. It is this type of innovative new thinking that will do much to propel the wonderful possibilities of the horse's natural world into the mainstream of the domestic horse world.

SHAPING THE HORSESHOE

Once the appropriate horseshoe has been selected, it must be fitted to the trimmed hoof. The front and hind illustrations in Figure 6-6 can serve as guides or templates in giving the shoes their basic shapes. These shapes can be modified later at the anvil to accommodate subtle shape nuances.

In terms of relative front-to-hind shoe sizes, the shoer will find that, on the average, approximately 60 to 70 percent of all front horseshoes will have to be made larger than corresponding hinds in order to fit the hooves properly. Actually, my statistical findings indicate that approximately 90 percent of all naturally shaped front hooves exceed their corresponding hinds in hoof size (volar). But of these, approximately 20 percent are marginal in terms of actual surface area. Therefore, a shoe size that fits the front hoof can also be shaped and expected to fit the hind hoof adequately in approximately 30 to 40 percent of the horses a farrier will encounter.

Consistent with the templates in Figure 6-6, which, again, are based on all the statistical averages for the measurement categories in Figure 6-2, the shoer will want to shape the basic hind shoe somewhat differently than its fore counterpart. Specifically, the expanse between the inside (medial) and outside (lateral) branches forward of the heels should be less in hind shoes than in corresponding fronts. The expanse between the heels, however, should be approximately the same for both fronts and hinds, on the average but not always. Accomplishing this will involve considerable hammering or flattening of the typical front keg shoe (if hinds are not available) directly over the toe between the two front nail holes to match the roundness of the toe in the naturally configured front hoof. In contrast, the shoer will need to flatten both the inside (medial) and outside (lateral) branches of the hind shoe, roughly between the first and last nail holes on each side, while essentially leaving the toe of the shoe alone. The narrowness of the branches may necessitate using a slightly smaller shoe size than was used for the fronts.

The shoer should give the entire outside circumference of the shoe's bearing surface a chamfer, if this has not already been done by the manufacturer, so that the outside bearing edge has an oblique, preferably well-rounded bevel (Advantage-Line Horseshoeing Tools is developing such a shoe based on the principles of natural hoof shape). The idea is to give the bottom of the shoe, where the outer wall meets the ground, the same type of bevel or roundness seen in wild horse hooves (Figure 4-7).

Finally, in view of the potential importance of hind-hoof asymmetry to the natural locomotive process (i.e., lateral thrust), the shoer should resist the temptation to either shorten or taper the inside (medial) branch of the hind shoe more than the outside (lateral) branch. Ostensibly, both practices stem from shoers trying to reconcile asymmetry in the front (anterior) profile of hind hooves with symmetry as it unfolds in their bearing surfaces (volar profile). Although the naturally shaped hind hoof is often asymmetrically shaped when viewed from the front (anterior) and from above (superior), its bottom (volar) profile will always be symmetrically shaped, or very nearly so. Practically speaking, this means that the circumference of the outer wall, on either side of the hoof's center line (volar profile), should measure approximately the same length, just as in symmetrically shaped front hooves. Accordingly, the shoer will want to shape both branches of the hind shoe identically, so that when set on the hoof, it will be divided in half by the hoof's median line (Figure 6-16).

OTHER SHAPING CONSIDERATIONS

As explained in chapter 4, the natural hoof shows active and passive wear patterns occurring along the bearing surfaces of outer walls. Active wear areas occur as protrusions, or crests, on the bearing surface of the naturally shaped outer wall, apparently squeezed out of an otherwise flat hoof by forces of compression acting downward within the wall. Passive wear areas occur as recessions, or hollows, between the active wear areas. Much like callouses on the human foot, the active wear zones bear more of the horse's weight than the interjacent recessions or regions of passive wear. While these active/passive wear patterns tend to occur with relative subtleness in most front and hind naturally shaped hooves, they are, nevertheless, important. Unfortunately, unless the wear points have been identified first in the barefooted horse, it is impossible to predict where to forge them in the shoe. The best the shoer can do in the absence of such knowledge is to keep the shoe level and give the entire outer edge of the ground-bearing surface a sufficient chamfer.

FITTING THE SHOE TO THE HOOF

Once the shoe has been shaped and before it is nailed on, spread the branches just enough to afford ample support to the quarters and heels (Figure 6-15A). This would also include an eighth- to a quarter-inch edge of shoe protruding beyond each heel buttress (Figure 6-15B). Again, these are the areas of the hoof that will undergo the greatest degree of contractive/

Figure 6-15

Provide a sufficient edge of shoe to support the natural contractive and expansive action of the hoof.

A.

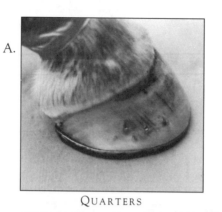

QUARTERS   HEEL

B.

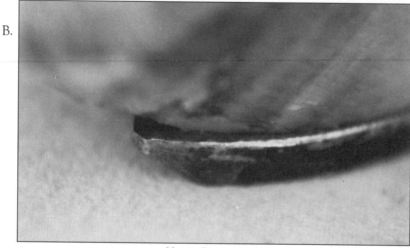

HEEL BUTTRESS

expansive action stemming from the trampoline effect of the sole and frog; consequently, they need that extra steel on which to slide outward and inward. Otherwise, the hoof might collapse over the branches of the shoe, a condition destructive not only to the natural configuration of the heel buttresses, but also to the entire natural action of the hoof.

NAILING ON THE HORSESHOE

If a conventional nail-on horseshoe, as opposed to a boot or glue-on variety, is to be applied, set the nails no farther back on the hoof than the widest bend of the quarters. Figure 6-16A shows this positioning for symmetrically shaped hooves; Figure 6-16B illustrates positioning for asymmetrically shaped hooves. Such positioning will enable the shoer to set the nails up high enough in the hoof wall—approximately one-half to one inch— to establish a strong clinch. Also, nails placed farther back than this may obstruct, to the limited extent that it occurs, the natural expansive/contractive actions of the hoof from side to side across the heel buttresses.

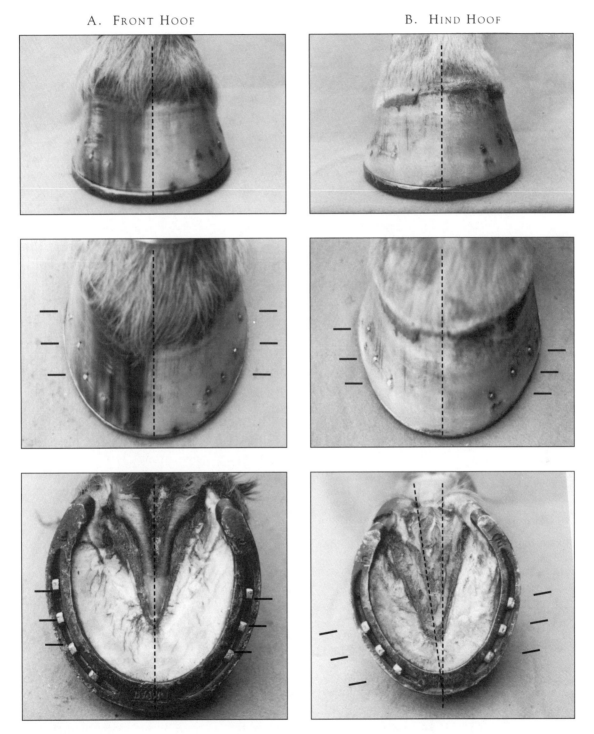

FIGURE 6-16
RELATIVE POSITION OF NAILS IN SYMMETRICAL AND ASYMMETRICAL HOOVES

A. FRONT HOOF B. HIND HOOF

Front is symmetrically shaped relative to its median line (top); accordingly, nails are spaced evenly across median line (middle). Symmetry is mirrored in bottom (volar) profile, where nails are also spaced evenly on both sides of median line (bottom).

Hind hoof is asymmetrically shaped relative to its median line (above). This is particularly apparent from above (superior profile), where nails reveal staggered arrangement across hoof's median line (middle). However, symmetry emerges in bottom (volar) profile, where nail placement aligns evenly across median line.

USING RESETS

Avoid using previously used shoes, or resets, unless they exhibit even, or symmetrical, wear around their entire circumference. Resets that are worn more to one side than the other, like those removed from asymmetrically shaped hind hooves, may tend to imbalance that type of hoof further by making them more lopsided in the direction of heaviest wear.

Remember that the naturally shaped hoof tends to generate extra horn in those areas of the outer wall sustaining the greatest levels of compression. This callousing, or horn buildup, protects the hoof and keeps it balanced at the same time. The impact of compression on the shoe, however, is the reverse of what we see on the hoof itself. The bottom of the shoe tends to wear away most where compression is greatest. Obviously, since no horn buildup is possible on the shoe, the shoe continues to wear away unevenly from side to side, in effect, lowering and imbalancing the hoof on the side that is normally reinforced with horn. If reset, the hoof, even if retrimmed for balance, is immediately imbalanced by the asymmetrically worn shoe because it will tend to tip over onto the worn area of the shoe. This action, in turn, causes the horse instinctively to counteract the imbalance by applying more pressure to other areas of the hoof, if it can. This migration of compression within the hoof capsule, culminating in the displacement of one series of crests and troughs from one locality to another, was apparent to me in the dysfunctional hooves of wild horses long held captive at Litchfield. But I have also seen it occur among domestic horses in which a hoof trimmed and shod a particular way by one farrier alters its wear patterns after being trimmed and shod another way by a second farrier.

RIDING AN UNSHOD HORSE

I have been asked the following question many times: Is it harmful to ride an unshod horse? Unfortunately, this is a difficult question to answer, although, personally, I am dubious about riding any horse that is not shod without first doing a lot of thinking and planning with the farrier. First, some research needs to be conducted to determine whether or not the structural integrity of naturally shaped hooves is really capable of sustaining the weight of an adult rider.

Whether or not the cornified epithelium, comprised of the hoof wall, sole, and frog, is naturally capable of thickening enough—as opposed to just growing longer—to withstand the increased compression caused by the added weight of a rider is not clear to me. I think such callousing is possible, although no study that I am aware of has investigated this possibility definitively.

Although history suggests that horses have been ridden barefooted with some measure of success, it also indicates that there have been problems. The ancient Greeks and Romans rode unshod horses, as did nineteenth-century North American Indians and American cowboys. But how many of these horses experienced lameness as a result of being ridden unshod?

The anthropologist John Ewers, who did extensive research with the Blackfeet and their horse culture, wrote that to "repair a worn foot that caused a horse to limp with pain, the Blackfoot [Indian] owner made a raw-hide protective shoe from a piece of thick hide from a freshly killed buffalo bull" (Figure 6-17). But he adds immediately that "when the hoof grew out, the shoe was discarded."[2] Similarly, the Sioux Chief Luther Standing Bear wrote, "I learned [as a child] to look after my horse when he was troubled with sore feet, and how to make horseshoes of buffalo hide."[3] The explorer Inaz Pfefferkorn stated that "for want of horseshoes, they [the Apache in Sonora] cover their horses' hoofs with thick horse or oxhide to protect them."[4] In 1832, an army patrol led by Captain Bonneville observed that a

RAWHIDE HORSESHOES SIMILAR TO
BLACKFOOT TYPE, ARAPAHO

FIGURE 6-17

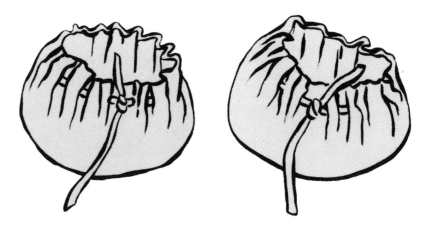

Crow Indian war party had covered the hooves of their horses with "shoes of buffalo hide" to protect them from the "sharp and jagged rocks."[5] Even white traders and explorers, including Lewis and Clark, adopted the Indian practice of using rawhide horseshoes. Their journals indicate that during the 1806 expedition through Yellowstone Valley, at least one horse wore a "moccasin of green buffalo skin" to relieve its worn feet.[6] Interestingly, the explorer William Parker observed the wife of a Comanche Indian chief "leading a horse and mule slowly backwards and forwards through a slow fire" to facilitate "hardening the hoofs by exposing them to the smoke and vapour of the wild rosemary-artemisia."[7] (I would not recommend this, nor do I approve of hot fitting.)

Apparently, the ancient Greeks, lacking horseshoes in their day, developed ingenious stable customs to toughen their horses' hooves. Xenophon described one such practice:

> The same care which is given to the horse's food and exercise, to make his body grow strong, should also be devoted to keeping his feet in condition. Even naturally sound hoofs get spoiled in stalls with moist, smooth floors. The floors should be sloping, to avoid moisture, and, to prevent smoothness, stones should be sunk close to one another, each about the size of the hoofs. The mere standing on such floors strengthens the feet. Further, of

course, the groom should lead the horse out somewhere to rub him down, and should loose him from the manger after breakfast, so that he may go to dinner the more readily. This place outside of the stall would be best suited to the purpose of strengthening the horse's feet if you threw down loosely four or five cartloads of round stones, each big enough to fill your hand and about a pound and a half in weight, surrounding the whole with an iron border to keep them from getting scattered. Standing on these would be as good for him as travelling a stony road for some part of every day; and whether he is being rubbed down or is teased by horse-flies, he has to use his hoofs exactly as he does in walking. Stones strewn about in this way strengthen the frogs too.[8]

An argument commonly heard today purports that it is okay to ride a horse without shoes on soft ground (e.g., sand, sawdust) to mitigate concussional shock, save the hooves from excessive wear, and, thus, prevent lameness. In my opinion, this suggestion is more problematic than riding the barefooted horse on relatively firm ground, which is what Xenophon advocated and did. Soft ground, which may relieve some minor concussional stress to the hoof incurred at impact and perhaps some of the intensified effects of abrasion normally associated with movement over relatively hard ground, only aggravates matters for the horse in the long run. Why? Because the hoof no longer has the type of firm support it needs to support the natural action of the legs and body. Hard ground does not actually hurt the horse's hooves or pain the animal. This is because the horse does not slap its hooves against the ground, like a person striking a tabletop with a fly swatter; rather, it presses its body weight down upon the hooves, squeezing them against the ground. It is this pressing action, corresponding to compression transmitted downward through the leg, that is primarily responsible for shaping the hoof. It is doubtful that a hoof can even sustain its natural shape in the absence of firm ground. Thus, riding over soft ground carries with it a host of potentially grave problems, ranging from imbalancing the natural loco-motive process to imbalancing and misshaping the hooves.

The problem with shoeing a horse to protect its hooves is that while it effectively checks the loss of any horn due to the added weight of the rider, it, unfortunately, also checks the loss of horn that would be lost due to normal wear and growth.

Until appropriate research is conducted that will indicate the limits of the naturally shaped hoof's durability, the best approach is to refrain from riding any horse that is unshod unless you have the close cooperation of a knowlegeable and open-minded shoer. To start, riding for short periods of time (a few minutes per day at first) and for very short distances upon ground that is neither too wet, too soft (deep sand, mud, or bark), nor too hard (concrete or street pavement) would not be harmful. For hooves with tender soles, pea gravel will probably be a major obstacle. Here is where the new Advantage-Line barefoot-horseshoe will be useful. At any rate, allow time for the hoof capsule to transform itself. Be patient. Give your horse a chance to get used to it, like you would yourself if you were going barefooted for the first time.

HOOF DRESSINGS

One area of traditional hoof management concerns the use of hoof dressings. Generally speaking, these are either emollients that impart moisture to dry, brittle hooves or plastic resins that either block or form osmotic barriers that discriminate between unwanted, extraneous moisture trying to enter the hoof from the environment and water molecules exiting the hoof

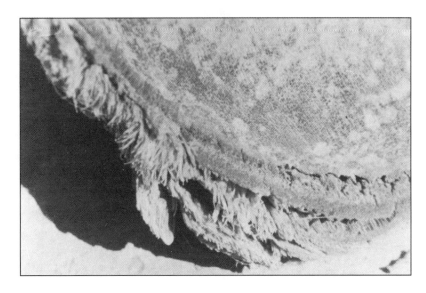

FIGURE 6-18

Weak, brittle hoof suffering the effects of excess moisture (above). Note unraveling of outer wall in close-up of same hoof (below). Similarly, hooves subjected repeatedly to hoof moisturizers (e.g., pastes and oils) can also be expected to undergo the same type of horn quality degeneration.

through normal perspiration. From what we know of the physiology of the naturally shaped hoof, hoof dressings would seem to be unnecessary in a natural hoof care program. They invariably do more harm than good because they tend to soften the hoof by either moisturizing it (oils, pastes) or by blocking normal perspiration through the outer wall (plastic resins).

As we know from observing the wild horse in the open range, a relatively dry, tough, and thickened hoof capsule is essential if the hoof is to withstand the extraordinary frictional wear incurred by the natural locomotive process over dry, firm ground. At the same time, balanced locomotion over relatively hard, dry ground is essential to producing a naturally shaped hoof, including healthy blood circulation within it and the transpiration of blood gases across its outer wall.

My experience with hoof dressings has been that, if they in fact do anything at all, they tend to soften and weaken the hoof wall, not strengthen it or improve its natural capacity to flex and spring back into place. While hoof dressings can look sleek when first applied, their side effects can slowly cause the horn tubules to unravel and the hoof to split and come apart (Figure 6-18).

Conversely, hoof dressings that allow transmission of blood gases through osmosis are somewhat promising. These discriminate between water as a gas, exiting the hoof via perspiration, from water as a liquid, trying to enter the hoof from the environment. But can they endure the enormous frictional wear the outer wall incurs as the hoof strikes the ground and body weight is pressed down upon it? If not, and I suspect this to be the case, then the outer wall's bearing surface still remains a viable portal through which harmful moisture can enter.

My feeling is that by giving the horse ample dry pasturage, sufficient balanced exercise, and a well-rounded, nutritious diet, all hoof dressings should be rendered unnecessary.

RETRIMMING THE HOOVES

For reasons that are not entirely clear, much of the domestic horse world revolves around the belief that horses need trimming every six to eight weeks. Some horse owners have their horses' hooves attended to when the horse begins to trip, when the hooves start to look peculiar, or when the horse owner realizes it's been a while since the last time he was trimmed. But most adhere to the prescribed interval of two months before soliciting the farrier's services. How frequently should horses be trimmed to keep them short, calloused, balanced, and naturally shaped? According to Emery et al.:

> The frequency with which a horse should be shod depends entirely on the individual's rate of growth, the amount of expansion and weakness of the horn at the quarters and heels, and the use to which he is put. When one is trying to effect a change in shape, particularly when trying to develop stronger heels and quarters, shoeing should be done fairly often.[9]

Although the authors put a time frame around this, I suggest we stop thinking in terms of time intervals and instead think in terms of what is natural and unnatural. Thus, if a hoof's growth has not changed significantly from its work plate dimensions in five years, that is okay. That is common in the outback. But, if the work plate is not natural five minutes after the shoer has left, that is not okay.

My feeling is that the horse should be trimmed from a holistic perspective, that is, in relation to a number of interconnecting factors, some of which do not even mention the word hoof. All however, have to do with the horse's natural world:

1. The hooves are always ready to be trimmed when their toe lengths fall outside the natural ranges specified in Figure 6-2. These ranges do not allow for a whole lot of leeway because nature intends for horses to have short toes all of the time. Personally, I prefer to keep horses in my charge with toe lengths that do not exceed 10 percent of their minimum work-plate lengths. The minimum work-plate toe length may be defined as the shortest length that a hoof can be trimmed through the toe without penetrating sensitive tissues or causing lameness. In most cases, hooves not allowed to exceed a 10 percent ceiling above the work-plate toe length

will measure within the "natural" to "natural-but-unusual" ranges in Figure 6-2. A short hoof configuration is possible and will go a long way toward minimizing the ill effects of excess growth upon the hoof's overall structural integrity. It will also support the natural locomotive process as nature intended, thus, aiding and benefitting the horse's natural propensity for athletic excellence. So, whenever a hoof grows beyond approximately 10 percent of its minimum natural toe length, it is time to trim it back.

Consider the trimming steps discussed earlier. Most hooves I have encountered could be trimmed down to a minimum work plate of three and one-quarter inches, which is a reasonable length and probably average for most domestic horses. I doubt that toe lengths much shorter than this are possible to achieve through trimming in most adult domestic horses. Only through sufficient levels of intense natural wear can the domestic horse's outer walls, soles, and frogs develop sufficiently compressed and calloused horn to be shorter and not sensitive.

In an effort to establish reasonable guidelines for retrimming the hoof based on excessive growth, I have created a chart that gives recommended toe-length limits (Figure 6-19). These limits are based upon the sample averages and ranges for toe lengths calculated from the Litchfield data, and which I have tested on hundreds of domestic horses. They will ensure that most hooves will stay within the "natural" toe length ranges seen in Figure 6-2 all, or most, of the time. Figure 6-19 tabulates maximum toe-length differentials in one-eighth of an inch increments, based upon the Litchfield data for hooves of varying minimum work-plate toe lengths. Using this

---

CALCULATING MAXIMUM TOE LENGTHS FROM WORK-PLATE VALUES

FIGURE 6-19

Calculate maximum toe length from the work-plate toe length established by the farrier. When hoof exceeds this measurement by ten percent (10 %), it is ready to be retrimmed. Ten percent differentials calculated from work-plate values derived from the Litchfield data are tabulated in accompanying chart for reference.

Work-Plate Toe Length [1]	Maximum Toe Length BASED ON 10% DIFFERENTIAL [2]
3 inches	3 1/2 inches
3 1/8	3 3/8
3 1/4	3 1/2
3 3/8	3 5/8
3 1/2	3 3/4
3 5/8	3 7/8
3 3/4	4

[1] Adult (5 years plus) horses only
[2] Maximum toe length = work plate toe length X 1.10 (10% increase)

---

chart, it can be seen that the hoof of a horse measuring three and one-quarter inches (toe length) will be excessively long when it reaches three and one-half inches, or 10 percent longer than its minimum work-plate length. The shoer or horse owner may want to refer to these calculations when structuring a trimming schedule.

2. As with toe length, the hooves will probably be ready for trimming when their measurements for toe angle and hoof size (i.e., volar length and

width) fall outside the natural ranges specified for naturally shaped hooves in Figure 6-2.

3. Hooves may need to be trimmed if their front and hind toe angle differentials are not natural (Figure 6-2). For example, if front toe angles for most horses in the shoer's charge measure repeatedly at the same or higher values than corresponding hind toe angles, something is wrong. On the average, hind toe angles should exceed front toe angles by approximately four degrees (Table 4-2 and Figure 6-2).

4. Trim the hooves if they fail significantly to pass the strip test for hoof balance (Figure 6-3).

5. If most front hooves fail the strip test for symmetry, and most hind hooves fail the strip test for asymmetry, something is wrong. Review the natural shapes (volar) for front and hind hooves (Figure 4-1 and Figure 6-6), rasping procedures for straight-line growth (Figure 6-10), and the possible consequences of shoe shaping in contradiction to hoof asymmetry as it unfolds across the bearing surface of the hind hoof (Figure 6-16).

6. Evaluate the trimming job if natural active wear areas dissipate, become passive, or migrate to other locations on the hoof wall or horseshoe, especially if such changes unbalance the hoof from side to side (mediolaterally). Evaluate the equestrian experience of the horse (chapters 3 and 7).

7. Evaluate the hooves if the horse cannot properly execute its natural gait complex, especially collection, either at liberty with other horses or when under saddle with a knowledgeable and competent rider. Check for unnaturally shaped hooves (e.g., long toe configurations), mechanically obstructive shoeing (e.g., excessive wedge padding), or drugs.

8. Evaluate the trimming/shoeing job if the horse goes foot-lame for any reason.

MOVEMENT AND NATURAL HOOF SHAPE

Since imbalanced or unnatural locomotion is a major enemy of natural hoof shape, efforts to trim the hooves into a natural shape can be seriously undermined if the horse is going to be ridden without regard for the natural gait complex. One of the first things that happens to wild horses when they are removed from their natural habitat and placed in BLM holding corrals is a steady deterioration of their hooves. This results more from an erosion of their natural gait complex (see chapter 3) than from restricted movement.

Lacking the framework of the family band, which is destroyed by current BLM confinement methods, normal socialization between captured wild horses is unable to continue as it did previously in the rangelands. Consequently, the natural gait complex, that is, the natural locomotive system through which social behavior is normally channeled, more or less collapses. What ensues is a vicious cycle from which the horse seems incapable of escaping. First, a plethora of unnatural stride patterns (e.g., four-beat canter, hare-hopping) and locomotive styles (movement with little or no collection, or hurried movement marked by interference) arise in direct response to an array of equally unnatural locomotive behaviors (depression, anxiety, confusion). These, in turn, precipitate unnatural hoof shapes and conditions (long toes, flared hooves, quarter cracks) virtually never seen in the outback.

What all of this means is that the quality of the locomotive experience is of much greater significance or importance in shaping the hooves than the distance traveled by the horse or the amount of use the hooves are given. This appears to be true no matter how far or fast the animal travels over a period of time. If the animal is not moving naturally because there is no motivation or incentive for it to do so, then its hooves will inevitably reflect the inertia of its unnatural state by undergoing unnatural, and probably harmful, changes.

For this reason, we can assume that imbalanced equestrian practices will probably have the same imbalancing or destructive effects upon the hooves of the domestic horse. Thus, a horse that is ridden unnaturally, or is confined perpetually in close quarters, will develop misshapened hooves no less actively than a misguided farrier's rasp. Nevertheless, a naturally shaped hoof is always in the best interest of every horse, regardless of how the animal will be ridden or worked because it is an extremely efficient and effective design based on an athletic locomotive system that is right for the animal. See chapter 7 for more specifics on the natural way to ride.

LAMENESS AND THE NATURAL HOOF SHAPE

In concluding this chapter, I want to emphasize that prevention is the best medicine in treating ailments of the horse, including hoof-related problems. We should try to provide for the animal's basic needs while respecting its natural limitations. This means becoming more knowledgeable about the horse's natural locomotive behaviors. In turn, this will enable us to act less from a framework of unsubstantiated opinion, arrogance, indifference, or uncertainty and more from a responsible and educated perspective. It is appropriate education and personal accountability, followed by thoughtful change, that will lead us directly down a path of prevention.

The vast majority of lameness in the domestic horse world cannot be understood properly or completely without considering the effects of abuse. Although many might argue to the contrary, most lameness among domestic horses is really more an issue of ignorance, violence, and complicity than it is of veterinary medicine; veterinary schools, clinics, and slaughterhouses are simply the processing stations that have to deal with it. What is not an issue here are injuries that stem from unfortunate accidents, where the horse enthusiast made an honest miscalculation or innocently followed the bad advice of someone whom they trusted. What is of concern is abuse that results from neglect and bad intent.

Most domestic horses suffer from disabilities as a result of vicious abuse and neglect. I have not seen a single shellacking ever given to a horse in which the offender had any kind of honest rapport with his or her mount; there is always the delusion that the horse had it coming or wasn't trying hard enough. Nor have I ever heard of a horse with "high heels" being accompanied by its master in the same dynamic footwear (Figure 6-20). Both "horse masters" have the earmarks of animal abusers or animal abusers in the making.

Unfortunately, equine lameness has also become a booming business in the horse world. Whether we like it or not, there is a lot of money to be made at it. Accordingly, a plethora of farrier-related treatments and tech-

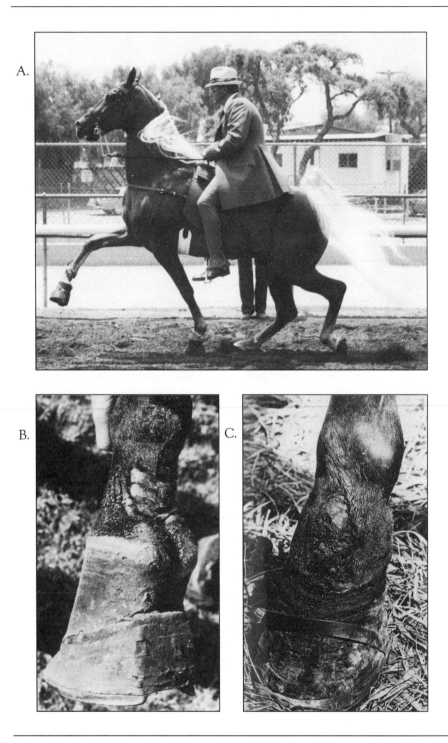

FIGURE 6-20

Not at all natural, Tennessee Walking horse(A) is set up in "high heels"—in reality, a combination of wedge pads (B) that artificially raise the hoof's toe angle. The purpose of padding, which is aided by special weighted horseshoes and a stringent metal band to prevent the shoe and pads from coming loose, is to accentuate the horse's artificial gait, called the running walk. As can be seen, the effect of such mechanically obstructive shoeing and unnatural, imbalanced horsemanship is notorious: ulcerated pasterns, heel bulbs, and coronary bands (C), and chronic lameness in many instances. Note pastern chains (A), calculated to induce pain and force the horse to artificially raise its forehand to allow high-heeled front hooves to step higher. Note also footfall sequence and compare with Figure 3-2 to see how the horse's natural walk has been altered.

nologies have arisen in response, including high-tech pads, bar shoes, quarter-crack clamps, and other gadgets, all of which must somehow try to reconcile the dark shadows of lameness, looming everywhere in the horse world, with the immediate and often arrogant demands of some equestrians. Without passing judgment on the relative value or efficacy of any of these numerous farrier-related treatments for hoof-based lameness—some of which appear to be truly helpful in mitigating the horse's suffering—I would prefer to merely recapitulate the premise of this book: In the long run, there is no substitute for a better understanding of the horse's natural world. This, I hope, will become the cornerstone of education and prevention in the treatment of lameness, as in every other dimension of the domestic horse's life.

The sooner the farrier can restore natural hoof shape, and the equestrian and veterinarian can remedy the source of the hoof inflammation—whether it be dietary or locomotory—and encourage the animal to move within its natural gait complex, the better off the horse will be.

SUMMARY

The naturally shaped hoof is an indispensible dimension to the natural horse paradigm. Without it, natural locomotion is rendered impossible. With it, the image of the natural horse can be brought one step closer to life. This chapter has sought to show the reader that there is a way to transform the unnaturally shaped hoof of the domestic horse into the reality of the natural hoof. The farriery process, described at length above, is one important way to assist in that transformation. Another important way is through the diligent and skilled work of the natural rider, a job made impossible in the absence of naturally shaped hooves.

Jim Hansen

7

A
Natural
Way to
Ride

IN THIS CHAPTER, the approach to horsemanship of the *natural rider* is closely linked with the principles of the natural equine state as discussed in chapter 3. This is done within the framework of a conceptual model that explores the extraordinary communication network existing between such riders and their athletic mounts. Here, the equestrian goals of the natural rider are aligned with the natural locomotive behaviors of the horse. Such well-known equestrian concepts as "going with the herd instinct," "relative dominance," "the aids," and "reward and punishment" provide familiar as well as useful vehicles with which to enter the world of the natural rider. But first the natural rider is contrasted with the unnatural rider, for the difference is striking.

THE NATURAL RIDER VERSUS THE UNNATURAL RIDER

What separates natural riders from other equestrians are the unique mental bonds they are able to establish with their mounts. These bonds are based on mutual respect and trust, not force, violence, or coercion. Their relationships are marked by unusual self-discipline and cooperation, cognizance of and compassion for each other's physical and mental limitations, and ultimately, athletic grace and fluidity. Natural riders are able to forge such extraordinary relationships by, first, avoiding the pitfalls of projection, that is, by not confusing the horse's identity with their own, and, second, by becoming knowledgeable of the natural equine state, which is referred to throughout this book as natural locomotive behaviors.

PROJECTION:
THE FOREMOST ENEMY OF NATURAL HORSEMANSHIP

Projection is the act of ascribing one's own human qualities—values, beliefs, and expectations—to another living thing, in this case, the horse. Many unnatural riders today are unconscious of their projections as they relate to their horses and do not realize what the consequences of those projections are on the animal's behavior. They assume that the horse sees and responds to the world as they do. The horse, however, perceives reality in its own unique way, which is different than the way human beings sense the world around them. "But to mention man and animal in one breath is nearly always dangerous, for one either does injustice to the animal by humanizing it and thus misunderstanding its essence, or one romanticizes man; there are essential qualities and ways of behavior, physical and psychological characteristics known in animals, and only in them, which are simply not part of man, however much one might attempt to transfer them to him and thereby to ennoble him."[1]

Understanding the horse and how its instincts and perceptions influence its actions, via the natural locomotive behaviors, seems incomprehensible to the unnatural rider, whose expectations of the animal are based largely upon his or her own perceptions of reality. The horse is expected to behave according to the rider's own consciousness or intuitions of equine reality. To do otherwise usually means punishment, either physical or verbal. Projection, then, inevitably leads to subjugation.

Not surprisingly, the potential for a relationship marked by the horse's trust and respect for its rider is, from the outset, supplanted by confusion, fear, and resistance: Confusion because the horse does not understand what its rider wants it to do, fear because its instincts tell it that what it has been asked to do is unnatural, and resistance because its instincts warn it to find some means of escaping the rider's unreasonable demands. Collectively, such behavior is perceived by the unnatural rider as obstinance, worthy of punishment and proof of the animal's ignorance and inferiority. Thus, it is not uncommon to see, ushered in with the use of force, wholly unfair indictments of the animal's psychology. According to Handler, "People think that a horse is stupid when it shies from a flying sheet of paper only to leap into the path of a moving car, but one must remember that fear, developing at times into outright panic, is a fundamental characteristic of the horse."[2] So, not only is the horse victimized by the unnatural rider's projections, since it is not permitted to act upon its natural instincts, but it is also blamed contemptuously for trying to do what is only right for its species. In the end, projection has the ugly effect of turning the horse's natural world upside down, wherein natural behavior is met with disdain and violence, while unnatural behavior is rewarded by threat of punishment.

In contrast, the natural rider becomes educated about the natural equine state and so is better prepared to avoid the pitfalls of projection. The rider realizes that there is no need for the animal to think or act like a human in order to form an effective equestrian partnership. This awareness supplants the vicious cycle of confusion/fear/resistance that plagues the unnatural rider from the start. The natural rider knows, for example, that fear, especially unmitigated fear or panic, is necessary, important, and integral to the animal's inward sense of safety and survival and should not be dealt with through violence. He or she knows that arresting this fear and putting the animal at ease is possible without the use of force and violence.

To accomplish this, however, he or she must learn to identify with the horse's way of looking at the unknown. In this way, the horse's fears can soon be anticipated by the rider and dealt with systematically, much as wild horses do in their natural habitats, until the unknown is no longer perceived as threatening or harmful. Indeed, mitigating fear is the first order of training, since the "physical relaxation and spontaneity we strive for in training presuppose a degree of mental calm."[3]

NATURAL LOCOMOTIVE BEHAVIORS: GATEWAY TO THE HORSE'S MIND

In lieu of ascribing human qualities to the essence or nature of the horse, the natural rider tries to understand how the horse perceives its world: how it senses things around it, how it responds to those stimuli with distinct body postures and vocalizations, and how it physically moves its body to go from one place to another. Such knowledge is indispensable when training under saddle begins later. Alois Podhajsky wrote in his treatise on natural horsemanship:

> If success is to be obtained the highest standard of understanding must be reached between the two living creatures concerned. This is as true for the commanding partner, the rider, as it is for the executing one, the horse. The rider must be a psychologist in order to understand, from the smallest signs, the behavior of his horse and act accordingly. To be successful he must have the same qualities as a good teacher and know how to make himself understood by the pupil entrusted to his care.[4]

Much attentive thought goes into this observational process, which enables the natural rider to, as Handler described, "view the horse as a whole [before] attempting to bring his physical and mental qualities into harmony through the course of training."[5] Any other approach to formulating a system of horsemanship would be contrived, thoughtlessly insensitive, awkward and mechanical, and not very natural for the horse. Warns Museler in Riding Logic, we must realize that the horse "is a sensitive creature and a living being with its own psychology and [is] not to be used as if it were a piece of machinery."[6]

The natural rider begins his or her education with the natural behaviors exhibited by wild, free-roaming horses. It is these behaviors, or more precisely, their underlying behavioral impulses—the instinct to survive— that inspire the natural locomotive process. Knowledge of natural equine behavior opens the door to the way the horse sees, hears, and responds to its world. This knowledge allows the natural rider to share in the emotional life of the animal and to understand such matters as why it fears things the way it does, so that later, through training, the rider can help it to overcome its fears in an ambience of compassion, mutual respect, and trust. Identifying with the horse in this way represents the cutting edge of natural training.

This approach eventually enables the reflective, natural rider to match his or her equestrian goal with locomotive behavior. Although relatively time-consuming, the process does work and is far superior to a relationship marked by force, violence, and cruel dominance.

THE MEETING OF MINDS: A CONCEPTUAL MODEL

The fluid manner in which natural riders and their horses are able to merge together, both mentally and physically, to perform as athletes reflects not only the way in which they communicate but also the extraordinary honesty, trust, and respect that pervade their relationships. Such a relationship results from a combination of many things, including self-discipline, compassion, cognizance of another living thing's physical abilities and intuitions, and a well planned *training methodology*. The following is a model that represents this unification process. Figure 7-1 provides an overview for this discussion.

As the illustration indicates, first study the horse's *natural locomotive behaviors*—how it breeds, eats, and plays—as well as the panoply of body postures and vocalizations that are normally associated with them. To do this, it is best to observe groups of horses at liberty, preferably bands of wild, free-roaming horses, recognizing that the horse is instinctively a herd and band animal and does not tend to act as naturally when isolated from others.

Next, study the natural gait complex of the horse: What are its natural gaits? How does the animal engage them with collection during extraordinary locomotive behavior? Why does the horse activate certain gaits in response to specific locomotive behaviors? For example, when does the horse use the extended trot as opposed to the canter? With what frequency and duration are the various gaits normally executed, especially in relation to collected behaviors? For example, how long can a horse be expected to engage itself at the extended trot? These and similar questions are of great concern to the natural rider, whose second objective is to know as much as possible about how the horse physically moves its body in relation to its natural behaviors.

Finally, from this knowledge of the horse's natural behavior and locomotion, formulate a training method or gymnastics program that will best satisfy the working requirements of necessary equestrian goals. In order to implement this program, a relationship based on relative dominance must be sought with the horse. This is accomplished through the pecking order system that underlies the natural social structure of all wild equids. The natural rider is able to participate in this process by means of the aids and a well-calculated system of rewards and punishments. These concepts are defined later in the chapter.

EQUESTRIAN GOALS

As shown in the model, the natural rider predicates all training upon the horse's natural locomotive behaviors. This is why it is so important that the

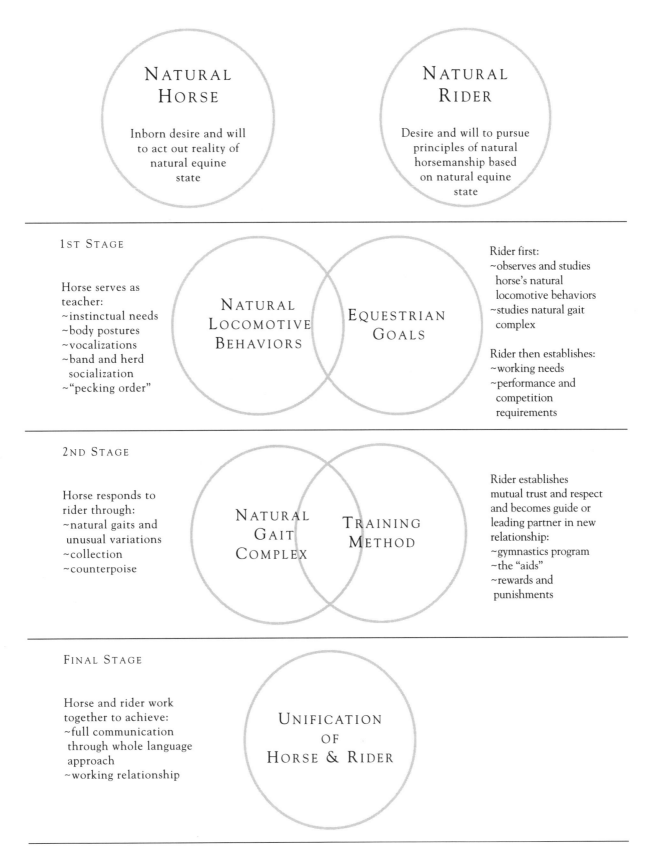

FIGURE 7-1
CONCEPTUAL MODEL: UNIFICATION OF HORSE AND NATURAL RIDER

NATURAL HORSE

Inborn desire and will to act out reality of natural equine state

NATURAL RIDER

Desire and will to pursue principles of natural horsemanship based on natural equine state

1ST STAGE

Horse serves as teacher:
~instinctual needs
~body postures
~vocalizations
~band and herd socialization
~"pecking order"

NATURAL LOCOMOTIVE BEHAVIORS

EQUESTRIAN GOALS

Rider first:
~observes and studies horse's natural locomotive behaviors
~studies natural gait complex

Rider then establishes:
~working needs
~performance and competition requirements

2ND STAGE

Horse responds to rider through:
~natural gaits and unusual variations
~collection
~counterpoise

NATURAL GAIT COMPLEX

TRAINING METHOD

Rider establishes mutual trust and respect and becomes guide or leading partner in new relationship:
~gymnastics program
~the "aids"
~rewards and punishments

FINAL STAGE

Horse and rider work together to achieve:
~full communication through whole language approach
~working relationship

UNIFICATION OF HORSE & RIDER

horse's natural instincts and behaviors be understood, for without this pathway into the animal's mind and its natural world, it is virtually impossible for the rider to decide intelligently if the equestrian goals included in the training program are even compatible with the horse's locomotive capabilities. Every equestrian goal, such as jumping or turning on the hindquarters, should be exhibited naturally by the horse when at liberty. If it is not, then the rider must justify why he or she is expecting the horse to engage in unnatural behavior, especially when such behavior may be injurious to the animal. For example, circus acts frequently violate the natural behavior and will of the horse, especially when trainers ask it to jump through rings of fire or off of high towers into shallow pools of water (Figure 7-2) — in short, by commanding it to engage in life-threatening acts. These are the kinds of outrageous goals the natural rider knows to avoid.

FIGURE 7-2

Although horses naturally love to frolick in water, I have never known wild ones to dive from high precipices into bodies of water—as this mule and other horses are compelled to daily by circus-style road shows. This animal climbed a 30-foot ramp in order to dive into a pool six feet deep. Electric prods are believed to provide the incentive, and the horses sometimes have dogs or monkeys chained to their backs.

When the natural rider is finally confident that the full range of equestrian goals is compatible with the horse's natural abilities and that he or she understands fully, in principle, the various elements of the natural gait complex, then the task of training the horse is in order. In fact, at this stage, integrating locomotive behaviors with equestrian goals becomes the central feature of the natural rider's training program. This assumes, of course, that the rider has already learned to ride naturally.

LEARNING TO RIDE

Learning to ride a horse should always precede learning to train one. How can an inexperienced person, who has never felt the natural locomotion of a horse under saddle, possibly guide or impart that feeling to an animal who has never learned to carry the weight of a rider? Clearly, both partners are equally unknowledgeable and equally unqualified to teach each other. For this reason, the natural rider should begin by learning to ride on a calm, schooled horse, preferably well along in years and experienced with unknowledgeable student riders. At the same time, the horse's trainer should be at horse and rider's side. This person, who knows the horse best, should be a knowledgeable and skilled natural rider who can patiently guide the motivated student in his or her efforts to learn to feel, become balanced with, and, eventually, move in harmony with the equally patient and knowledgeable, schooled horse. Such an arrangement is extremely important because the trainer is able to demonstrate by personal example, if need be, the nuances of riding technique to the student, especially when problems arise, as they always do. As Podhajsky explains:

> The chief asset in the training at the Spanish Riding School is the fact that the instructor trains the young rider on a horse that he, himself, has trained, so that he knows all his strong and weak points. When the instructor has not trained the horse himself, he should ride the horse himself, before starting to train his pupil, in order to get to know his capabilities. This will give the pupil confidence that he will not be asked to do anything that the horse cannot perform, and . . . give him ideas how best to remedy difficulties that are sure to occur in the process of training.[7]

Two or more years of steady work on different horses—and always under the immediate tutelage of each animal's respective trainer—is usually necessary before the student rider becomes experienced enough to assume the role of trainer. The continued assistance of experienced trainers will likely be required for some time after this transition has occurred. Such a protracted approach to learning constitutes the essence of "horsemanship by tradition."

TRAINING THE HORSE
GOING WITH THE HERD INSTINCT

Because the horse is governed by its herd instincts, training a horse, like learning to ride—or just riding—is done best in a group situation. This means riding with, or training, more than one horse and rider at a time. In this way, the trainer/rider can take advantage of the horse's natural propensity to lead or follow. Natural riders know that by carefully observing natural rivalries between horses at liberty, their relative positions of dominance can be emulated later when riding, teaching, or performing in group situations, such as placing more dominant individuals ahead of more acquiescent individuals in tandem routines. This practice is also employed in the riding, training, and stabling of the stallions at the Spanish Riding School in Vienna.[8] Thus, less experienced riders/horses are "cast along" with the natural flow of the group, which is always led by more dominant and experienced horses, who, in turn, are ridden and directed by more dominant and experienced natural riders. This group-experience approach to horsemanship has many potential benefits, to which the literature of classical horsemanship clearly testifies. It is successful in promoting harmony between horse and rider, not only because it eases many of the natural rivalry-based tensions that would otherwise tend to surface between horses, and thus plague their riders, but also because it represents an alternative to isolating horses from each other.

RELATIVE DOMINANCE:
NATURE'S WAY OF RELATING TO THE HORSE

The natural rider, in asserting his or her training prerogatives on the life of the horse, does so by first establishing a position of higher *relative dominance*, which is nothing more than finding a place above the horse in its natural pecking order system of social hierarchy. The natural rider participates in the pecking process in the same way that any horse newcomer would have to in the wild. This type of behavior goes on all the time among wild, free-roaming horses as their bands undergo changes in size, sex ratio, and relative dominance. What happens during the pecking is not usually physical combat, wherein one animal defeats another by maiming it, but rather a battle of gestures or posturings that tend to exhaust or impress an adversary.[9] Apparently, once the process has been worked out (only a few seconds or minutes may be required), all that is needed are subtle persuasions now and then to reinforce one horse's position over another. The final result of these interesting interplays is a kind of negotiated peace, in which fear and long-lasting tensions are obviated by mutual trust and respect. Not surprisingly, I have found that wild horses are always eager to get the details of their pecking orders worked out so that they can resume a more peaceful coexistence.

The natural rider recognizes this dynamic in the horse's social hierarchy from his or her observations and studies of the natural equine state and, as a result, has learned to trust the pecking process to the extent that he or she is willing to participate gallantly in it. I say "gallantly" because the tactics involved sometimes require a showy display of heroic bravery, attentiveness to an adversary's readiness to acquiesce, and good old-fashioned chivalry. Showmanship is extremely important in all of this. Exactly how the natural rider will conduct him- or herself, however, will depend largely upon the personality, temperament, age, and sex of the horse. For example, a vocal, rearing stallion may require a loud, sharp voice from the trainer accompanied by an active display of the whip, whereas an easily frightened or flighty mare may need a steady, calm voice and passive display of the whip. What is important is that the horse respect the trainer. Indeed, much caution and discretion must be exercised in this process, because the rider is really selecting an equestrian partner at this stage, and if the animal is begrudged by the misplaced use of force and violence, trust, respect and harmony may be lost to fear and subjugation.

The natural rider also knows that relative dominance is invariably related to alliance behavior among horses. Not all horses get along with each other and will forge alliances with others to keep antagonists and enemies, real or imagined, at bay. Surprisingly, this is typical of subdominant mares in wild horse bands, wherein two or more mares may exclude one or more other mares from their "group," even though, collectively, all the mares form a single band led by a dominant mare and a still more dominant monarch. What alliance behavior, among other things, means to the natural rider is this: not all horses and natural riders will be compatible. So the natural rider knows that to arbitrarily single out a given horse to train and ride may be asking for long-term trouble. In all likelihood, only through the pecking process will the natural rider and horse discover if their respective personalities will meld and facilitate an enjoyable, effective, and lasting equestrian partnership. As Podhajsky notes:

The success of training can always be decisively influenced by the selection of the right riders for the right horses. An overly energetic rider on a highly strung horse may lead to disastrous results; similarly, a phlegmatic rider with a lazy horse will soon be lost in sleepy, indifferent movements. It can also happen that a rider takes an aversion to some particular horse and vice versa. Better progress can often be obtained by exchanging horses and riders.[10]

So, as with any two "dueling" horses, the natural rider and his or her mount must peck their way into a lasting, peaceful relationship. Specifically, they do this by means of the aids, a unique language based primarily upon the sense of touch and a rather complex system of rewards and punishments, through which the aids are administered.

THE AIDS: A LANGUAGE OF FEELING

The aids are the sensual means or channels of communication—sight, hearing, and touch—through which the natural rider and horse "speak" to each other (Figure 7-3). Learning the language of the aids is not unlike learning to communicate in a new language. Because the principal medium of this language is touch, and not the spoken word, both horse and rider must learn how to "feel" what the other is trying to "say." In this sense, aids communication between horse and rider is one of language experience: the mediums of communication, primarily the rider's touch, attempt to induce a body posture in the horse that will elicit a memory response, or feeling, known already to the animal either from its past, real-life experiences, or its collective unconscious, that is, the mental history of its species wherein the natural locomotive behaviors or instincts are matrixed.

The natural rider's challenge, then, is to learn which combinations of physical stimuli will resonate in the mind and body of the horse and, ultimately, elicit, with impulsion, the desired locomotive behaviors as prescribed by the equestrian goals. As Handler explains:

> We call these stimuli—in the order in which they are instilled in
> the horse in the course of his training—leg, hand, and seat aids.
> Each produces a basic reaction from the horse: the legs tend to
> impel him forward, the rein to hold him back, and the seat either
> to drive him forward or, in given circumstances, to restrain him.
> Since each of the aids offers considerable diversity in intensity,
> point of contact, and direction of stimulus, a whole scale of possi-
> ble combinations may be used by the rider to affect given muscles
> and achieve the desired movement of his mount.[11]

Consider the various aids necessary for encouraging a horse to move at the trot, a two-beat movement in which each hind hoof moves simultaneously with a diagonally paired front hoof. The natural rider understands that he or she must, by means of the aids, adapt his or her body posture to the same posture that the horse would assume at the outset of trotting. This is because the footfall sequence of the trot follows naturally from the trot's postural impulse, not from kicking or spurring the horse in its sides in order to make it go, as we see so often among horse enthusiasts.

Figure 7-3 illustrates how the natural rider positions his or her body using the leg, seat, and back aids in order to evoke the trot posture in a horse. In this example, the rider has asked for the trot on the horse's left

FIGURE 7-3

AIDS INITIATING THE TROT

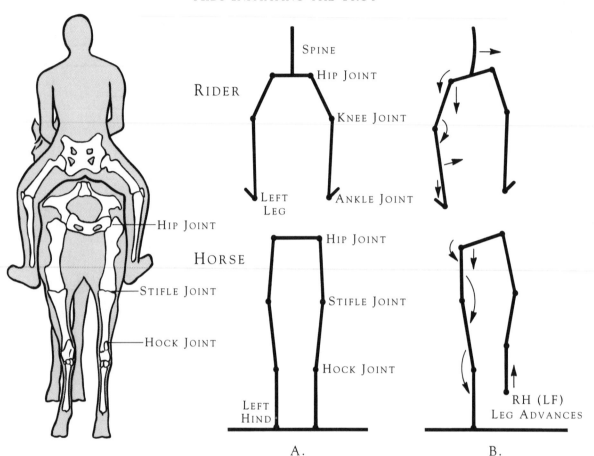

A.　　　　B.

A. *Horse and rider with pelvises and major joints aligned at standstill.*

B. *Rider lowers pelvis on left side, semiflexing rider's three major leg joints. Horse responds—through systematic development of counterpoise—by semiflexing its three major leg joints and tilting pelvis on left side.*

lead. Specifically, the left thigh (leg aid) drops straight down, which pulls or tilts the pelvis (seat aid) downward on the rider's left side. At the same time, the rider's left leg bends at the knee so that the calf and heel (leg aids) rest lightly against the horse's left flank, that is, just behind an imaginary vertical that passes through the horse and rider's combined center of gravity. Also occurring simultaneously is the contraction of the rider's abdominal muscles on the right side, which helps elevate the right half of the rider's pelvis. This action allows the spine (back aid) to sway sufficiently to the right so that the rider's upper body will remain upright and balanced over the horse.

Each leg, back, and seat aid initiated by the rider elicits an identical postural response from the horse. This occurs much like two persons dancing together, in which one partner "leads" the movement and the other "follows." Thus, in response, the horse bends (semiflexes) the three major joints of its left hind leg and simultaneously presses the left hoof against the ground, thereby establishing propulsion and the left lead sought by the rider.

This action also tilts the horse's pelvis on its left side, aided by the contractive action of the abdominal muscles, which assist in elevating the pelvis on its right side.

It may be noted by some that these natural aids for eliciting a trot response, which are based primarily upon the natural action of the horse's pelvis and semiflexor joints, contradict the commonly held belief that the gait is properly initiated and sustained by a back-and-forth and up-and-down, thrusting of the pelvis, which is alleged to follow from the vigorous, up/down action of the horse's back. But the up-down action of the horse's back is much more complex than most equestrians seem aware. In fact, the natural action of the horse's back follows from the action of the pelvis, which is not simply an up-and-down movement, but a combined sideways (lateral) and up-down action. Instinctively, however, most unnatural riders know better and, to avoid physical discomfort, will resort to the post (i.e., rising seat) or slow canter. In contrast, the natural rider tilts his or her pelvis alternately left to right like that of the horse and rides the trot comfortably at all tempos.

The effect of these combined posturings is to produce the trot gait such that the action of the human body is in harmony with the natural action of the horse. By applying these aids subtlely, the rider is virtually assured of an ordinary (e.g., calm, free-forward riding) locomotive response from the horse. By increasing their intensity, however, the experienced rider is able to induce collection in the horse and thereby engage in extraordinary locomotion (e.g., an extended trot or trot on the spot).

It is no wonder, then, that this rather delicate business of aligning stimulus to response can entail years of hard work and study before the horse and its rider are able to think and act as one. Nevertheless, it happily represents a language that the horse can participate in too, especially when things go wrong.

For example, because the various postures that the rider asks the horse to assume have precise meaning in the mind of the animal and will evoke in it, with impulsion, the desire "to do," as Xenophon rightfully put it, "what the animal himself glories and delights in,"[12] misapplication or over application of the aids will tend to elicit confusion and subtle resistance in a normally well-treated horse. Before the rider is able to induce body postures that are either grossly unnatural to the horse or overly tax the limitations of its unique conformation or athletic development, the horse will, because of its respect and trust for the rider, responsibly take the opportunity to signal quiet protests: "I cannot bend this much through my hindquarters"; "I cannot extend my trot any farther or any longer"; "You are engaging me on the wrong side." These warnings are immediately picked up by an understanding, sensitive natural rider as subtle perturbations in the animal's muscular ring, which correspond directly to the horse's inability or refusal to bend, extend, or engage, thus, alerting the rider precisely where to adjust his or her aids. Further, the amplitude of the perturbations, which the rider feels through counterpoise (defined below), will indicate to what degree the aids must be adjusted. If the rider is too overbearing, the horse can get more vocal by means of tail swishing, squeeling, biting, or bucking. Thus, in the same way that the natural rider can elevate the aids to a degree of punishment, so the horse can turn a slight twitch in its back—an aids harbinger of more violent behavior to come—into a violent buck to punish the rider for his or her transgressions.

The great value of the language-experience approach is that the horse is able to communicate resistance to its rider as soon as unnatural or excessive demands are made. The natural rider is able to respond instantaneously to the horse by adjusting his or her usage of the aids. In effect, the aids dialogue between horse and rider represents an equilibrium, or *counterpoise*, between opposing stimuli, which, over a period of years, is carefully and systematically refined through hard work. In Handler's words, "The use of the aids becomes increasingly complicated and refined in the course of training as the requirements of given movements become greater, until finally such harmony is achieved between rider and horse that one has the impression that the rider only thinks and that the horse effortlessly carries out his thoughts."[13]

REWARDS AND PUNISHMENTS

Inseparable from the aids is the system of rewards and punishments through which the aids are administered by the natural rider. It is this system that enables the rider to let the horse know that all of its cooperation has not been taken for granted. Indeed, intrinsic to the successful administering of the aids, and the forging of a healthy equestrian partnership, is the natural rider's unremitting persistence in letting the animal know how he or she feels the relationship is going moment by moment. At the same time, the system enables the horse to respond to how it feels about the relationship, for when the rewards and punishments are discharged with fairness, understanding, and compassion by the natural rider, "a horse," Gueriniere noted over 200 years ago, "will perform his tasks with cheerful acceptance, verve, and brilliance rather than with resistance and resignation."[14] I have found the nuances of reward/punishment to be as diverse and complex as the myriad personalities of horses and riders who strive to communicate through them. Briefly, they might be defined as follows.

A *reward* is a simple gesture or act of kindness, which will convey to the horse a sense of the rider's approval for having cooperated in some measure. Rewards, always more important than punishment, might include praise, petting the horse's neck, feeding a favored tidbit, or simply the cessation of work. Which reward should be given, and how it will be given, will depend largely upon the personalities of both horse and rider as well as the quality of their rapport. Rewards follow, not precede, acts of cooperation.

A *punishment*, in contrast, is an act or gesture that lets the horse know, unequivocally, that the rider is not happy with its actions. Like rewards, punishments also follow the act in question. "The severity of a punishment," wrote Gueriniere, "must be matched to the horse's temperament. A gentle remonstrance applied at the proper psychological moment will often suffice."[15] In this way, punitive measures are kept to a minimum, and, according to Handler, "respect is established negatively by fear of punishment, and positively by trust, affection, and anticipation of rewards."[16]

Although the line between them is at times thin, rewards and punishments differ from the aids in that they are used to reinforce or discourage a horse's behavior, rather than to induce the behavior, which is the purpose of the aids. The natural rider understands this difference and, accordingly, uses rewards and punishments as a means of clarifying the aids language experience. A thorough education in the horse's natural locomotive behaviors is necessary for a natural rider to be able to distinguish between behavior that is natural but defiant (e.g., relative dominance), and, therefore, in need of punishment, and behavior that is resistant and unnatural, precipitated by the rider's unreasonable demands, contradictory to the natural equine state, and, therefore, not in need of punishment at all. As Gueriniere reminds us, "If a horse disobeys, it is generally because he has simply not understood what the rider wants or because of some physical deficiency."[17]

SUMMARY

Properly used, the aids language experience and its related system of reward/punishment are employed first within the context of a well-planned and time-tested training methodology. Like the aids language itself, the training method should be thoroughly understood—in principle and practice—by the natural rider before ever trying to train a horse. Training a horse, like teaching a person to ride, presupposes that the trainer/rider has already learned to ride naturally.

Appendix B lists a number of books that either explain or summarize a training methodology oriented toward the natural equine state. Caution is advised against using them alone as a means to learn either to ride or to train. While they are helpful in orienting the reader toward natural methods of training/riding, generally speaking, the authors assume that the reader will be under the tutelage of an experienced rider/teacher. The novice cannot be expected to deal effectively with all the situations that will arise when working with an untrained animal. As I have written in chapter 5, the inexperienced rider puts him- or herself at great personal risk when trying to learn to ride without the presence and guidance of an experienced professional.

Those horsemen and horsewomen who have spent years trying to learn to ride or train their horses and who are not satisfied can be assured that the world of the natural rider is good news. I have seen untold numbers of riders spend year after year getting nowhere with their horses: one trainer after another, one teacher after another, one excuse after another, and, not infrequently, one horse after another. Yet, in a mere fraction of the same time, natural riders are able to turn out schooled horse after schooled horse—and schooled riders too, if circumstances permit—without the frustrations and disappointments typical to so many equestrians. It appears that the main watershed between the quintessential natural rider and most other equestrians is the natural rider's ability to identify closely with the horse through its natural locomotive behaviors. Part of this identification process, no doubt, is intuitively based, but a much larger part appears to result from education about the natural behavior of the horse and guidance from experienced, accomplished riders.

E P I L O G U E

A NEW ERA OF HORSEMANSHIP

THE DOMESTIC HORSE WORLD needs to usher in a new order of horsemanship based upon the paradigm of the natural horse and rider. The benefits to be reaped from doing so are potentially great, and the methods of achieving this new order have been identified in this book.

Such change can, and will, occur if more horse enthusiasts are willing to recognize the shortcomings of their current methods of horsemanship and horse care. Each needs to ask: Is this system of horsemanship founded upon the natural capabilities of the horse, or is it merely alleged to be? Every system of horsemanship practised in the horse world today should come under scrutiny.

I suggest a forum, such as a magazine or newsletter, be established so knowledgeable or interested horse enthusiasts can speak out about this alternative direction. Such a forum could facilitate the transmission of new information concerning the natural state of the horse, as well as pave the way for the licensing or certifying of qualified riding teachers and horse trainers experienced in and knowledgeable about the principles of natural horsemanship.

New legislation is needed to protect the horse from abusive systems of horsemanship. Most horse abusers get away with their actions because no one is there to hold them accountable. What is worse, many of their cruel practices are accepted at large for no reason other than that they have been around a long time and are entrenched in pomp and tradition. Their shortsightedness stems from the fact that they do not know what is naturally best for the horse and so lack the necessary vision to help bring about constructive change.

I recommend strongly that persons who engage in training and teaching be licensed or certified. A few years ago, Les Emery—author of *Horseshoeing Theory and Hoof Care*—and I envisioned the creation of an institute for the study and promotion of the principles of the natural equine state and natural horsemanship. Such a center for the study of hippology would demonstrate that a range of horse enthusiasts coming from diversified backgrounds can flourish as natural riders in an atmosphere of disciplined and compassioned respect for the horse. Moreover, if discrepant equestrian theories and practices, such as dressage, western, jumping, and racing, were scrutinized within the academy's holistic focus of balanced, natural horsemanship, much could be offered through an open forum to improve horsemanship in these fields.

I still hold strongly to the vision behind such a learning center. But whether or not such a facility will come into existence depends upon others accepting the value of the natural rider/horse paradigm.

My continuing source of inspiration? Not in the barns and pastures of the domestic horse world, but way out in the outback—in the land of the spirit of the natural horse.

APPENDIX A

DOMESTIC AND WILD HORSE ADVOCATES

I have taken liberty in this second edition to make considerable changes in this appendix. I will refer readers here to two organizations for the sake of wild and domestic horse protection. Ms. Sussman has been the Director of the International Society for the Protection of Mustangs and Burros for over twenty years. Velma Johnson, its first president, led the movement resulting in the current wild horse protection laws. Ms. Duxbury, Director of Project Equus, has been a front line animal protection activist for as many years and can assist concerned horse enthusiasts both within the domestic and wild horse realms. Both of these women fully embrace the principles of natural horsemanship.

Wild horse protection in this country is in trouble. The conditions which ISPMB and others of post-World War II fought to change—horrible cruelty at the hands of unchecked mustangers—are different now than then. Today we have unwittingly "protected" the wild horse to the extent that its "natural order" has been set asunder. To fight alleged over-population, wild horses are removed in waves from the rangelands and then consigned to vast, concentration camp-like holding centers where they stand idly around and absorb vast quantities of tax payer dollars. Or, they are adopted by earnest and well-meaning, but frequently unqualified, horse lovers, who cannot manage their new charges effectively. There is now ample evidence that the plight of many of these horses is less than desirable. I propose a dramatic change in management. Space does not permit full delineation of the ideas here, but a brief overview is possible. First, let us create entirely new herd management sectors in suitable environments that are capable of carrying a given number of horse families. All wild horses would be removed to these management areas—vast tracts of Great Basin lands.

Second, within each sector, let there be concentrically configured protection "zones." Each zone, from core to periphery, would be graded by protection priorities and management strategies. Within the central zones, we would maximize natural orders of predation to control wild horse population while minimizing direct human influences. Other wild life forms, such as deer, antelope, and mountain lions, would be encouraged and protected as well. These areas would be restricted; other than scientists conducting studies, the rest of us would be limited to the outer zones. The latter could be operated like public parks, including wild horse resource centers serving the public. Supervised educational excursions into wild horse country could be mounted from these centers; conceivably, use-fee revenues might pay for the whole program by visitors, thereby relieving the federal tax base commensurately. The peripheral outer zones would closely resemble the current BLM Herd Management Sectors, except that removal campaigns would—as I envision them—amount to very little. We would retain the Adopt-Horse-Program, but it would be put back in the hands of ISPMB (where it originally started). The public would still be able to adopt wild horses, although the numbers would be greatly reduced by the inner zone predations. Highly competitive, selective criteria for ownership would be strengthened to prevent neglect and abuse.

INTERNATIONAL SOCIETY FOR THE PROTECTION OF MUS-TANGS AND BURROS. Involved with all facets of wild horse and burro protection and preservation. Contact: Karen Sussman, President. Public membership welcome. 6212 E. Sweetwater Ave., Scottsdale, AZ 85254. (602) 991-0273   E-mail: 103053,1112@COMPUSERVE.COM

Karen Sussman and wild horse mare, Shooting Star

"Jaime Jackson has captured in his new book the true essence of the wild horse. Only those people who share their lives with these animals or live amongst them know the infinite connection between the souls of humankind and the horse. The wild horse re-unites us with our kinship to nature."

Karen Sussman

PROJECT EQUUS. Dedicated to the protection of all horses, and the study and advancement of the principles of natural horsemanship. Education, legislation, and investigations. Contact: Robin Duxbury, President. P.O. Box 6989, Denver, CO 80206-0989. (303) 388-0219   E-mail: equus@projectequus.org   Web-site: www.projectequus.org

"It was Christmas 1993 when I was presented with a book that would forever change my course in animal protection. The book was *The Natural Horse*, by Jaime Jackson. Project Equus is dedicated to the foundations of natural horsemanship: The natural horse. One cannot understand natural horsemanship, as it is currently presented by many popular trainers, without first understanding natural horse behavior—not domestic horses, but wild horses. What works for them is the first lesson to be learned in natural horsemanship."

Robin Duxbury

THIS APPENDIX lists a number of books (by no means a comprehensive list) that describe the training of horses with at least some of the principles of the natural equine state in mind. I have gone through them, studying each closely, and recommend them to readers wanting to know more about the world of the natural rider. But none is without criticism, however, and I have made accompanying remarks. To this list I have added several other books that do not focus upon training, but are helpful in that they deal with the anatomy of human and equine movement, as well as the behavior of the horse.

Handler, Hans
THE SPANISH RIDING SCHOOL
New York: McGraw-Hill, 1972

The best book on the subject of classical riding anywhere. Also the most expensive and hard to find, since it is out of print. Handler builds a strong case for a classical riding tradition, then offers the reader a clear overview of how his riding staff at the Spanish Riding School conducted their training. But he offers no pretense that the work is a training method, as other writer's of lesser books love to do. Colorful and interesting and worth reading if a copy can be found.

Hunt, Ray
THINK HARMONY WITH HORSES:
AN IN-DEPTH STUDY OF HORSE/MAN RELATIONSHIP
n.p.: Panorama West, 1987 (Reprint)

Hunt is held in high regard by Western enthusiasts everywhere. I have read it closely and can appreciate his departure from the mechanics of training to enter the mind of the horse. In recommending it, however, I would urge the reader to question what might be the justification of behavior modification techniques in order to be at one with the horse. Nowhere does the author refer to the natural world or behaviors of the horse as a guiding light, and we must, therefore, raise the tough question: To what end "harmony with horses"?

Klimke, Reinert
BASIC TRAINING OF THE YOUNG HORSE
London: J. A. Allen & Co., 1989

Klimke, a German, was winner of the Individual Gold Medal in Dressage
at the 1984 Olympics. I mention his book because, unlike most other books
written by eminently qualified European horseman down through the years,
Klimke is still alive and has a golden opportunity to change history by revis-
ing his book so that it does not insult the scores of horse enthusiasts who
look to him for help. Obsession with equestrian "authorities" by large sectors
of the publishing world has left a vast desert of unaccountability between
horse enthusiasts in trenchs who want clear answers to their questions and
their dressage superstar heroes who continue to go round and round on their
silver-studded longe lines.

Museler, Wilhelm
RIDING LOGIC
New York: Arco Publishing, 1984

German equestrian of the Hitler period, Museler had a penchant for natural
based horsemanship and thoughtfulness to give credit to the horse for aiding
him in developing his insights. Mysteriously, this book seems to change with
each new edition, although Museler is no longer with us. Unfortunately, like
virtually every other book on horsemanship that comes from the classical
dressage world, there is no way for the average aspiring horse enthusiast to
use it practically. Museler illogically fails to give appropriate time frames for
training sequences and fails also to stress the importance of learning to ride
by tradition and example as the appropriate way to use his book.

Podhajsky, Alois
THE COMPLETE TRAINING OF HORSE AND RIDER
New York: Doubleday, 1967

An ambitious book by the former director of the Spanish Riding School.
Unfortunately, the book fails to deliver an earnest attempt to present uni-
fied instruction in schooling of horse and rider. Nevertheless, Podhajsky
clearly knew what he was doing and was not afraid to give credit to the
horse, which he did in all his books (e.g., MY HORSES, MY TEACHERS),
as the one who knows most.

Schuksdziarra, Heinrich and Volker
ANATOMY OF RIDING
Briarcliff, New York: Breakthrough Publications, 1985

Excellent book to read and study by apologetic German father-and-son team
trying to atone for Museler's and others' unsound advice concerning "back
bracing," the great cornerstone of the classical seat, unfortunately set in sand.
Although excellently and sensitively written, the authors fall one step short of
mentioning the natural world of the horse, its anatomy and natural movements.

Smythe, R. H.
THE HORSE: STRUCTURE AND MOVEMENT
London: J. A. Allen & Co., 1972

Not a book on riding, but I have found it useful to understand the locomotive process in relation to the horse's anatomy.

Suenig, Waldemar
HORSEMANSHIP
New York: Doubleday, 1956

Difficult to follow and poorly organized, but Suenig realized the importance of balanced, natural locomotion and our need to get in harmony with it.

Warrening, George H.
HORSE BEHAVIOR: THE BEHAVIORAL TRAITS AND ADAPTATIONS
OF DOMESTIC AND WILD HORSES, INCLUDING PONIES
Park Ridge, New Jersey: Noyes Publishing, 1983

An excellent attempt to lay out in categories the various behaviors of the horse so that we can make sense of them. Worth looking at as an introduction to the subject of equine behavior.

Watjen, Richard L.
DRESSAGE RIDING
London: J. A. Allen & Co., 1979

Here is advice from the classically trained German horseman who once "guest instructed" at the famed Spanish Riding School. I vowed to read his book from beginning to end, but gave up in the first chapter, after facing a deluge of undefined terms or definitions so contradictory from one phrase to the next as to wear down my patience. Nevertheless, close scrutiny reveals that Watjen, in spite of his obsession with a Napoleonic riding wardrobe, was aware of the horse's natural world and used it for justification of his riding principles.

Wynmalen, Henry
THE HORSE IN ACTION
New York: Arco Publishing, 1973

A must to keep around and study since Wynmalen attempts to delineate all the gaits of the horse, no easy feat to try to do on one's own. But on what, after his chastising in the opening pages of Eadweard Muybridge for using unruly horses and grossly incompetent riders/drivers in his 1899 classic ANIMALS IN MOTION, does he base his own study of equine movement?

Xenophon
THE ART OF HORSEMANSHIP
Trans. by M. H. Morgan. London: J. A. Allen & Co., 1962

Simple but effective presentation of honest, natural horsemanship and horse care. Written over two thousand years ago, Xenophon's treatise is still worth looking at since his basic ideas have not fallen by the wayside, but have proven to be seminal.

Notes

INTRODUCTION

1. You may obtain information regarding the federal government's Adopt-A-Horse Program by contacting any office of the BLM or by writing directly to: U.S. Department of the Interior, Bureau of Land Management, Washington, D.C. 20240.

2. BLM officials estimated each horse's age through an evaluation of the animal's dentition (i.e., the kind, number, and arrangement of the teeth) as well as how the teeth wear, erupt, and shed. The Official Guide for Determining the Age of the Horse (1981), published by the American Association of Equine Practitioners (AAEP), is their standard reference. This method of aging, however, has been criticized by scientists of the National Academy of Sciences (NAS), who pointed out to the BLM in a government sponsored document, "We do at this point recommend one additional study to investigate the validity of the tooth-aging technique in equids. A precise understanding of herd age structure is important to a thorough assessment of population dynamics and there are some uncertainties about the validity of the tooth-eruption and wear criteria for wild horse and burro age determination. Hence, the criteria need to be investigated and either verified or changed." (Report No. BLM—TE-82-001- 4700, *Wild and Free-Roaming Horses and Burros*, U.S. National Research Council, Washington D.C., Oct. 1982). The 1981 AAEP guide was handed to me by a BLM veterinarian five years after the NAS report; since many of the proposed NAS wild horse–related research projects, ostensibly including age-determination, were dropped abruptly during the Reagan Administration, it's highly unlikely that age criteria have been scrutinized and modified to date (1989).

3. Oberbereiter Karl Mikolka, formerly of the Spanish Riding School in Austria, wrote in a personal letter to me several years ago: " 'Classical horsemanship' are words without meaning in this country, where everyone wants to steal information from authorities to claim it as their own, or in order to make a fast buck."

1. Wild asses do roam the Great Basin area along with wild horses, although most of these peculiar animals are found in more southerly ranges. So the stories go, these asses are thought to be the feral offspring of abandoned stock—jacks—used by miners, dating back to the 1849 Gold Rush. In fact, they do interbreed with their relatives on occasion; I personally witnessed a band of wild horses that included one mare mule, who apparently was sterile, since no foal was at her side. I was able to measure and photograph her hooves along with the others of the band; this data may be of interest to mule shoers. Please contact the author through Northland.

2. The correct scientific name for *Eohippus* is *Hyracotherium*. According to Zarn, et al., "This [i.e., the name *Eohippus*] came about because early scientists (1838) did not recognize that the fossil remains of a small animal found near Suffolk, England, was related to horses and compared the remains to the Hyraxes, which the fossils closely resembled. Hyraxes are comparable in size and external appearance to rodents and lagomorphs. When similar fossils were found in North America at a later date, the principle of evolution had become well established and they were recognized as horse ancestors. Charles Marsh of Yale University gave them the euphonius name *Eohippus*. Since *Hyracotherium* is much the older of the two names, under the rules of zoological nomenclature it is the correct one to use" [Mark Zarn, Thomas Heller, and Kay Collins, "Wild, Free-Roaming Horses—Status of Present Knowledge," *Technical Note 294,* (Washington, D.C.: U.S. Department of Interior and U.S. Department of Forest Service, March 1977), 11]. To order copies of *TN 294*, direct inquiries to: DSC, Federal Center, Building 50, Denver, CO, 80225.

3. Efforts to restore Przewalski's horse to its natural habitat are now being undertaken jointly by several countries, including the U.S. See Food and Agricultural Organization Staff, *Przewalski's Horse and Restoration to Its Natural Habitat in Mongolia* (Lanham, Maryland: UNIPUB, 1987).

4. For a discussion of horses in the New World during the Age of Discovery, see BLM *Technical Note 294* in the bibliography; the authors cite Simpson (1951), Ryden (1970), Haines (1971), Smith (1969), McKnight (1959), and Denhardt (1948).

5. The mustangers took their name from the colloquial term, *mustang,* often applied to the wild horse. Loosely, the word means "stray." According to Ryden, "Stray horses sighted by the Spaniards were dubbed *mestenos* (belonging to the *mesta,* a Spanish word referring to stock growers)" (H. Ryden, *America's Last Wild Horses* [New York: Dutton, 1970], 46). Dobie also explains: "It [mustang] is an English corruption of *mesteno* or *mestena* (feminine), a word already legalized in Spain when Copernicus asserted the diurnal rotation of the earth. In 1273, the Spanish government authorized the Mesta as an organization of sheep owners. On the long 'walks' between summer and winter ranges, many sheep were lost. They were called *mestenos* (belonging to the Mesta). They were also called *mostrencos* (from *mostrar,* to show, exhibit). The estrayed animal had to be *mostrado* (shown) in public to give the owner a chance to claim it. *Bienes mostrencos* were, in legal terminology, goods lacking a known owner. The organization of sheep owners, the Mesta, claimed all animals of unproved ownership, but the crown, and the

church, seized the mostencos. *Mostengo*, a later form of mostrenco, is as a word nearer to mustang than mesteno, and some etymologists have regarded it as the origin" (J.F. Dobie, *The Mustangs* [Boston: Little, Brown and Company, 1952], 93-94).

6. For a discussion of "Herd Management Area Plans," see the BLM publication, *Our Public Lands* (Washington, D.C.: U.S. Government Printing Office, 1980), 30(1):6.

7. Such proponents have been cautioned by the Wild Horse Advisory Council of the National Academy of Sciences, who have noted: "Some observers believe that the vegetation in the West was vulnerable to the introduction of domestic herbivores because it had experienced little grazing pressure since the late Pleistocene period. These observers consider equids to be particularly disruptive to the ecosystem because they are alien to the region. However, the view may need to be tempered by a knowledge of the paleohistory of equids in North America. The possibility exists that there are vacant niches into which these animals could fit." Excerpt from "Wild and Free-Roaming Horses and Burros," *Final Report of the Committee on Wild and Free-Roaming Horses and Burros*, Document No. PB83-153189, Board on Agriculture and Renewable Resources, National Research Council (Washington, D.C.: National Academy of Sciences Press, 1982), 69-70.

8. From "Wild Horses and Burros," published by the Public Affairs Dept., BLM, P.O. Box 12000, Reno, NV 89520. For more information about wild horses, contact Maxine Shane, public affairs specialist.

2 SOCIAL ORGANIZATION OF THE NATURAL HORSE

1. Preoccupation with this equine rape syndrome represents the argument in Joel Berger's, *Wild Horses of the Great Basin: Social Competition and Population Size* (Chicago: University of Chicago Press, 1986).

2. Some, if not all of this misguided effort to induce sterility in harem mares and monarchs has fortunately been halted by pressure from various animal rights groups. At least one university professor has been exploring one of nature's intended methods of population control—predation.

3. Precipitation figure based on normal annual precipitation (inches) for Winnemucca, Nevada, citing statistics from the National Oceanic and Atmospheric Administration, U.S. Commerce Department, for the period 1951–1980. *The World Almanac and Book of Facts, 1986* (New York: Newspaper Enterprise Association Inc., 1986), 758–759.

3 MOVEMENT OF THE NATURAL HORSE

1. R. H. Smythe, *The Horse: Structure and Movement* (London: J. A. Allen & Co., 1972), 125.

2. Alois Podhajsky, *The Complete Training of Horse and Rider* (New York: Doubleday, 1967), 108.

3. Xenophon, *The Art of Horsemanship*, trans. M. H. Morgan (London: J. A. Allen & Co., 1962), 55–56.

4. Leslie Emery et al., *Horseshoeing Theory and Hoof Care* (Philadephia: Lea & Febiger, 1977), 182.

5. Waldemar Seunig, *Horsemanship* (New York: Doubleday, 1956), 127.

6. Ibid., 259–260.

7. Podhajsky, *Training of Horse and Rider*, 51.

8. Wilhelm Museler, *Riding Logic* (New York: Arco Publishing, 1984), 107.

9. Seunig, *Horsemanship*, 264.

10. Xenophon, *Art of Horsemanship*, 17.

11. Peter C. Goody, *Horse Anatomy* (London: J. A. Allen & Co., 1986), 23.

12. Xenophon, *Art of Horsemanship*, 16.

13. Podhajsky, *Training of Horse and Rider*, 48.

14. Ibid., 48.

15. Ibid., 49.

16. Smythe, *The Horse*, 163.

17. Podhajsky, *Training of Horse and Rider*, 158.

18. Richard L. Watjen, *Dressage Riding* (London: J. A. Allen & Co., 1979), 86. The late Richard Watjen, born in 1891, was trained at the Spanish Riding School in the early part of this century. During World War II, he, like many other accomplished German and Austrian calvary officers—including Alois Podhajsky, Waldemar Suenig, and Hans Handler of the Spanish Riding School—donned the uniform of the Wehrmact (German army) and, thus, became complicit in Germany's quest for world domination during World War II. Because of their involvement in the German army, they were banned from international equestrian competition, including the Olympic Games, during the 1950s.

4 THE NATURAL HORSE AND ITS HOOVES

1. Three sets of specimens were removed by BLM veterinarians from two mares, ages eight and twenty years, and one eight-year-old stallion. These stressed animals, unable to adapt to captivity, had to be destroyed for different reasons. I was able, however, to preserve their hooves in their natural shapes and sizes by means of freeze drying. In March 1988, I exhibited several of these hoof specimens before an audience of the American Farriers Association during their national convention in Lexington, Kentucky. I also collected other specimens from wild horse skeletal remains found in different western Nevada rangelands. These were also typical of natural hoof shape and were used for several of the photographs included in this chapter.

2. Barbara Maxwell, "Wild Horses of the Pryor Mountains," *Your Public Lands* 35 (1) (1985):9–11.

3. See the following for historical accounts suggesting that light-colored hooves are inherently weaker and less durable than black or dark-colored hooves. D. E. Worcester, "Spanish Horses Among the Plains Tribes," *Pacific Historical Review* 14 (1945): 409–417; J. B. Tyrell (ed.), "David Thompson's Narrative of his Explorations in Western America, 1784–1812," *Champlain Soc. Publi.*, No. 12, Toronto; John Ewers, *The Horse in Blackfoot Indian Culture*, Bulletin 159 (Washington, D. C.: Smithsonian Institution, Bureau of American Ethnology, 1955), 218.

4. See Robert Loest, "Separations in the Hoof: A New Approach to Problem Feet," *American Farriers Journal* 10 (4) (July/August 1984): 328–339.

5. What an interesting name for this strange little widget. Xenophon called it "swallow," for its resemblance to the forked tail of that bird. It is called "frog" today because of its closer resemblance in texture and feel to the amphibian that bears its name.

6. Xenophon, *The Art of Horsemanship*, trans. by M. H. Morgan (London: J. A. Allen & Co., 1962), 15.

7. Ibid., 29.

8. I measured all four hooves of approximately thirty horses at Litchfield (30 percent of my sample) and found that data for left and right hooves varied by less than 0.5 centimeters (less than one-quarter inch). Left and right hooves generated results so close as to be mutually indistinguishable.

9. Leslie Emery et al., *Horseshoeing Theory and Hoof Care* (Philadelphia: Lea & Febiger, 1977), 70–73.

10. "Profile: Milton Trout, Farrier: His Work Is Scheduled by Nature," *American Farriers Journal* 14 (2) (Mar/Apr, 1988): 32–33.

11. Emery et al., *Horseshoeing Theory*, 27.

12. For a discussion of horn tubules and their relative strengths at different toe angles, see Ibid., 89.

5 GENERAL CARE OF THE HORSE

1. Xenophon, *The Art of Horsemanship*, trans. by M. H. Morgan (London: J. A. Allen & Co., 1962), 33.

2. Ibid, 28-29.

3. Zarn et al., write the following: "Tyler (1972) reported that coprophagy was common in pony foals up to three or four weeks old. The feces eaten almost always belonged to the foal's mother, but on two occasions a foal was observed eating its own feces. Blakeslee (1974) also reported young foals eating feces, usually their mothers'. Older foals did not eat feces. Hafez (1962) reports that adult domestic horses reject the feces of their own kind but that foals eat a considerable amount of fresh feces of adult horses. They attribute this behavior to the need for proper bacterial flora for the foal's intestines." See Mark Zarn et al., "Wild, Free-Roaming Horses: Status of Present Knowledge," *Technical Note 294*, (U. S. Department of Interior and U. S. Department of Forest Service, March 1977), 45. See also S. Tyler, "The Behavior and Social Organization of New Forest Ponies, *Animal Behavior Monographs*, 5 (2) (1974): 84–196.; J. K. Blakeslee, *Mother-Young Relationships and Related Behavior Among Free-Ranging Appaloosa Horses* (M.S. thesis, Idaho State University, 1974), 113 pp.; E. S. E. Havez et al., "The Behavior of Horses," in *The Behavior of Domestic Animals* (Baltimore, Maryland: Williams and Wilkins, 1962), 370–396.

6 HOOF CARE THE NATURAL WAY

1. Leslie Emery et al., *Horseshoeing Theory and Hoof Care* (Philadelphia: Lea & Febiger, 1977), 232.

2. John Ewers, *The Horse In Blackfeet Indian Culture* (Washington, D. C.: Smithsonian Institution, 1955), 48.

3. Luther Standing Bear, *Land of the Spotted Eagle* (Lincoln: University

of Nebraska Press, 1933), 21.

    4. John Ewers, *The Horse*, 48.

    5. Ibid.

    6. Ibid.

    7. Ibid.

    8. Xenophon, *The Art of Horsemanship*, trans. by M. H. Morgan (London: J. A. Allen & Co., 1962), 28–29.

    9. Emery et al., *Horseshoeing Theory*, 249.

7 A NATURAL WAY TO RIDE

    1. Hans Handler, *The Spanish Riding School* (New York: McGraw-Hill, 1972), 139.

    2. Ibid., 139.

    3. Ibid.

    4. Alois Podhajsky, *The Complete Training of Horse and Rider* (New York: Doubleday, 1967), 53.

    5. Handler, *Spanish Riding School*, 138.

    6. Wilhelm Museler, *Riding Logic* (New York: Arco, 1984), 60.

    7. Podhajsky, *Training of Horse and Rider*, 222.

    8. Handler, *Spanish Riding School*, 152–153.

    9. From Robert Vavra, *Such Is the Real Nature of Horses*, (New York: William Morrow, 1979), 205. "Most horses do not enjoy fighting. Stallions fear violent combat, which can lead to death from shattered jaws or broken legs. Only when there is no other choice will they furiously attack one another with hooves and teeth. The symbolic battles and rituals in which dominance may be decided by posturing, breath testing and flank sniffing, and by mild skirmishes, offer an alternative to battle." In relation to actual training, see also Handler, *Spanish Riding School*, 153.

    10. Podhajsky, *Training of Horse and Rider*, 131.

    11. Handler, *Spanish Riding School*, 150.

    12. Xenophon, *The Art of Horsemanship*, trans. by M. H. Morgan (London: J. A. Allen & Co., 1962), 55–56.

    13. Handler, *Spanish Riding School*, 151.

    14. Ibid., 140. Francois Robichon de la Gueriniere was an eighteenth-century riding master who in 1751, according to Alois Podhajsky, "produced the most revolutionary book on riding of all times," *Ecole de cavalerie contenant la connaissance, l'instrtuction, et la conversation du cheval.* Gueriniere's timeless principles of horsemanship, which are based largely on the natural movements of the horse, are practiced unaltered to this day at the Spanish Riding School.

    15. Ibid.

    16. Ibid.

    17. Ibid.

BIBLIOGRAPHY

American Association of Equine Practioners. *Official Guide for Determining the Age of the Horse*. 1981.

Berger, Joel. *Wild Horses of the Great Basin: Social Competition and Population Size*. Chicago: University of Chicago Press, 1986.

"David Thompson's Narrative of His Explorations in Western America, 1784-1812." *Champlain Soc. Publi.* 12 (1916).

Dobie, J. F. *The Mustangs*. Boston: Little, Brown and Company, 1952.

Emery, Leslie, Jim Miller, and Nyles Van Hoosen. *Horseshoeing Theory and Hoof Care*. Philadelphia: Lea & Febiger, 1977.

Ewers, John. *The Horse in Blackfoot Indian Culture*. Bulletin 159. Washington, D.C.: Smithsonian Institution, Bureau of American Ethnology, 1955.

Food and Agricultural Organization Staff. *Przewalski's Horse and Restoration to Its Natural Habitat in Mongolia*. Lanham, Maryland: UNIPUB, 1987.

Goody, Peter C. *Horse Anatomy*. London: J. A. Allen & Co., 1986.

Handler, Hans. *The Spanish Riding School*. New York: McGraw Hill, 1972.

Loest, Robert. "Separations in the Hoof: A New Approach to Problem Feet." *American Farriers Journal* 10 (4) (July/August 1984).

Maxwell, Barbara. "Wild Horses of the Pryor Mountains." *Your Public Lands* 35 (1). Washington, D.C.: Government Printing Office, 1985.

Museler, Wilhelm. *Riding Logic*. New York: Arco Publishing, 1984.

Podhajsky, Alois. *The Complete Training of Horse and Rider*. New York: Doubleday, 1967.

"Profile: Milton Trout, Farrier—His Work Is Scheduled by Nature." *American Farriers Journal* 14 (2) (March/April 1988).

Ryden, Hope. *America's Last Wild Horses*. New York: Dutton, 1970.

Seunig, Waldemar. *Horsemanship*. New York: Doubleday, 1956.

Smythe, R. H. *The Horse: Structure and Movement*. London: J. A. Allen & Co., 1972.

Standing Bear, Luther. *Land of the Spotted Eagle*. Lincoln: University of Nebraska Press, 1933.

U.S. National Research Council. *Wild and Free-Roaming Horses and Burros*. Report No. BLM—TE-82-001-4700. Washington, D.C.: National

Academy Press, October 1982.

Vavra, Robert. *Such Is the Real Nature of Horses*. New York: William Morrow, 1979.

Watjen, Richard L. *Dressage Riding*. London: J. A. Allen & Co., 1979.

"Wild Horses and Burros: Getting Their Fair Share." *Our Public Lands* 30 (1) Washington, D.C.: U.S. Government Printing Office, 1980.

Worcester, D. E. "Spanish Horses Among the Plains Tribes." *Pacific Historical Review* 14 (1945).

The World Almanac and Book of Facts, 1986. New York: Newspaper Enterprise Association, Inc., 1986.

Xenophon. *The Art of Horsemanship*. M. H. Morgan, trans. London: J. A. Allen & Co., 1962.

Zarn, Mark, Thomas Heller, and Kay Collins. "Wild Free-Roaming Horses: Status of Present Knowledge." *Technical Note 294*. Denver, Colorado: U.S. Department of Interior and U.S. Department of Forest Service, (March 1977).

INDEX

BOOKS AND VIDEOS

ESSENTIAL LEARNING MATERIALS

HORSE OWNERS GUIDE TO NATURAL HOOF CARE

BY JAIME JACKSON

The "Bible" of the natural hoof care movement is now updated (2002), expanded, and made more valuable than ever • Step-by-step instructions for the Natural Trim • For horse owners wanting to do their own hoof work or improve their understanding of natural hoof care • For farriers wanting to transition to natural hoof care • How to make a successful transition from shod to unshod • New Trouble-shooting section • Interviews and narratives • Biographies of Natural Hoof Care Practitioners • Extensive resource section for all the necessities (tools, equipment, videos) to get started • Over 200 illustrations • • 320 pages, perfect bound, soft cover.

29.95

MAKING NATURAL HOOF CARE WORK FOR YOU

BY PETE RAMEY

Pete Ramey is a skilled, full-time natural hoof care practitioner from Georgia. Pete has written his first book about the many horses, both shod and lame, he has brought successfully into barefootedness and soundness since then. Written in down-to-earth language, and chock full of photos and drawings, *Making Natural Hoof Care Work For You* is Pete's unique spin on natural hoof care. A perfect companion to Jaime's HOG, horse owners will find countless bits of useful information in Pete's book to make their hoof care programs more successful • 192 pages, perfect bound, soft cover.

$26.95

FOUNDER: PREVENTION AND CURE THE NATURAL WAY

BY JAIME JACKSON

Founder kills thousands of horses every year, and leaves tens of thousands of others debilitated in its wake. In this startling revelation and guide to the natural, holistic cure and prevention of founder, author and hoof care expert Jaime Jackson brings an entirely new perspective to the treatment table. This may be the most controversial book yet written on the subject . . . and the most useful. 156 pages, soft cover, perfect bound.

$19.95

Founder is a time bomb ticking away in every domestic horse on every continent of this planet. No horse is exempt. It explodes into the horse owner's life like a terrible nightmare. You have two choices: ignore Nature's stern warnings until it's too late. Or get with the program now. – JJ

All prices shown subject to change.

www.star-ridge.com

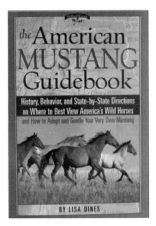

THE AMERICAN MUSTANG GUIDEBOOK

BY LISA DINES

This book is a combination travel guide, gentling and training guide, resource book, natural history, and American history • Detailed state-by-state directions and maps show where to best view America's wild horses in their native pastures • Contact names and addresses of the state BLM offices, a list of wild horse handlers, local and national wild horse organizations • 152 pages, soft cover.

$19.95

I have had many requests from readers to tell them where they can go and see wild horses in their natural habitats. Author Lisa Dines has come to our rescue, providing a very precise guide to locating America's mustangs from coast to coast. Also an excellent resource for adopting a mustang. — JJ

THE LAME HORSE

BY JAMES ROONEY, DVM

Explains anatomy and biomechanics of the horse • Explains why horses "break down" from abuse of their natural capabilities • Hundreds of photos, drawings, and x-rays of pathologies facing horses due to abusive practices • Advocates barefootedness, balanced riding, and natural trimming • De-bunks numerous veterinary myths • 264 pages, soft cover, perfect bound.

$29.95

Most veterinarians today are completely unfamiliar with the burgeoning natural hoof care movement. What they know about it they have learned from their horse owner clients — not their schools or professional symposiums. Help temper this pathetic reality by referring your vet to Dr. Rooney's landmark book above — the first and only book by a U.S. vet who embraces the natural hoof and barefootedness. — JJ

CREATING THE PERFECT HOOF (VIDEO)

WITH JAIME JACKSON

Learn what a "natural trim" is by watching hoof care expert Jaime Jackson in action. Close-up footage gives you the trimming detail horse owners want. Excellent sections on non-violent horse handling, balancing the horse, selection and use of tools, exercises to condition your body, securing the horse's hooves, using the hoof stand, and much more! Includes remarkable close-up shots of wild horse hooves. 2 hrs. 40 min, VHS.

$39.95

I created this video to show you how we do it. All the principles, methodology, tools, etc., that I've laid out in my companion book, Horse Owners Guide, are brought to life here. Short of an actual hands-on clinic, this is the next best thing. And maybe better, since you can refer to it as often as you need to. As I point out in this video, trimming is the easy part of a much bigger picture. And it's all the rest that really makes the trimming so easy. This video spells out the rest of the story. — JJ

www.star-ridge.com

STAR RIDGE VIDEOS AND BULLETINS

ESSENTIAL LEARNING FOR ADVANCED TRIMMING

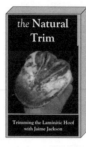

NATURAL TRIM: TRIMMING THE LAMINITIC HOOF
WITH JAIME JACKSON

Learn how to trim laminitic hooves with master trimmer Jaime Jackson. Jaime brings to bear his entire arsenal of information and technique to put laminitic hooves on the road to healing and soundness. Use with companion bulletin. VHS, NTSC, 1 hr. 30 min.
$39.95

NATURAL TRIM: ELIMINATING FLARE, QUARTER CRACKS, AND RUN-UNDER HEELS
WITH JAIME JACKSON

Jaime receives more questions about dealing with wall flare, cracks, and run-under heels then any other facet of trimming. Here's his step-by-step presentation of solutions to these and other aberrations of normal hoof growth. Use with companion bulletin. VHS, NTSC, 1 hr. 30 min.
$39.95

GUIDE TO BOOTING HORSES FOR HOOF CARE PROFESSIONALS (book)
BY JAIME JACKSON

Complete how-to guide for the fitting and use of the Swiss Horse Boot • Meticulous descriptions of every aspect of booting: from fitting & modifying, to quick mounting and easy removal • Illustrations, photographs and diagrams • Resource section for obtaining boots, tools, and equipment. • 192 pgs./softcover
$26.95

GUIDE TO BOOTING HORSES FOR HOOF CARE PROFESSIONALS (video)
BY JAIME JACKSON

Shows how to measure and fit hooves with the Swiss Horse Boot • Action footage shows boots being put on, removed, and used by clients • How to modify boots with inserts, toe slot, heat fitting • Repairs • Sections correspond to chapters in companion book of same name • 2 hrs. • VHS
$39.95

STAR RIDGE BULLETINS

These unique educational bulletins by Jaime Jackson are published as pdf documents to give you the highest quality photos and diagrams. They present the most up-to-date information available on natural horse/hoof care. Shorter bulletins are available via email, longer on CD.

E-MAIL **$7.95**
CD **$12.95**

See our website for current special
for buying all bulletins on one CD

Bulletin No.	Article Title	Format
100	hgc: Hoof Growth Cycle	e-mail
101	Trimming for Natural Toe Angle (T°), Toe Length (TL), and Heel Length (HL)	e-mail
102	Supercoriaitis: Laminitis Redefined	e-mail
103	The Supercoriatic (Laminitis) Pathway	e-mail
104	Trimming The Supercoriatic (Laminitic) Hoof	CD
106	Rules of Rasping: Eliminating Wall Flare, Splits, and Run-Under Heels	CD
107	The Correct Mustang Roll	CD
108	A New Mechanistic Theory: Time and Mass In A 4th-Dimensional Hoof Mechanism	CD
109	The Whole Horse Trim: Finding the Natural Hoof Within	e-mail
110	The Supercorium	CD
111	Does Horseshoeing Cause Hoof Contraction?	e-mail

www.star-ridge.com

BASIC TRIMMER'S KIT

TRIMMING TOOLS

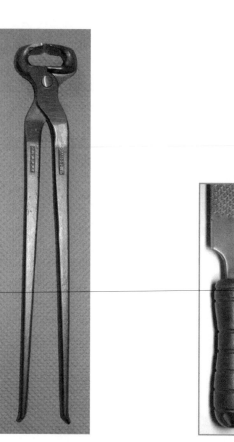

STAR RIDGE HOOF NIPPER

ESSENTIAL TRIMMING TOOL

We added this superior professional hoof nipper last year, which was upgraded by its manufacturer (Cooper Tools). 12 and 15-inch models with beefed-up jaws and sharp cutting blades will get you through the toughest horn, eliminating the need for compound nippers. 12 in. model is suitable for ladies and men with smaller hands.

15 IN. (HIS) $74.95
12 IN. (HERS) $71.95

F. DICK RASP HANDLE

ESSENTIAL TRIMMING TOOL

This is an excellent rasp handle by F. Dick in Germany. It is light, durable, and offers superior grip. It is a screw-on type which adapts excellently to both the "his" and "her" F. Dick rasp sizes.

$5.95

F. DICK HOOF RASP

ESSENTIAL TRIMMING TOOL

I gravitated to this professional level German product for several reasons. It is consistently sharp, and properly cared for will enable a full year's worth of trims for six horses at 4 week intervals. What separates this rasp from others is the layout of the coarse cutting teeth (chisels), which span the entire width of the rasp — which I've not seen on any other professional rasp. This translates to less work for each swipe of the rasp. Offers superb bite and will render a beautiful mustang roll. "His" (large, 14") and "Her's" (small, 12") sizes.

HIS $20.95
HERS $19.95

www.star-ridge.com

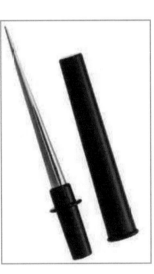

ISTOR HOOF KNIFE SHARPENER

ESSENTIAL TRIMMING TOOL

As sharpeners go, this Istor Sharpener from Switzerland is unparalleled. There are two models, the "Professional" (*above*) and a smaller version, the "Regular." Both work well, one difference being that the Professional model has a protective handle with thumb guard to prevent accidental cuts if you slip. The smaller model is a little easier to work near the crook of the hoof knife. Both are excellent for sharpening other implements (e.g., kitchen knives) and make for wonderful gifts for the non-horsey minded set too.

ISTOR PROFESSIONAL 18.95
ISTOR STANDARD $11.95

BUCK DIAMOND HOOF KNIFE CROOK SHARPENER

ESSENTIAL TRIMMING TOOL

Use this high quality tapered diamond sharpener manufactured by the Buck Knives Company to sharpen the crook (curved portion) of your F. Dick hoof knife.

$16.95

F. DICK HOOF KNIFE

ESSENTIAL TRIMMING TOOL

This is the favored European hoof knife, which sports a handsome Rosewood handle and a super sharp blade made of the finest steel. I've selected this model because the cutting blade is neither too "flat" nor too "curved." I'm particularly concerned about hoof knives with the latter conformation as they facilitate excessive scooping of the hoof's solar dome — a dangerous practice with potentially devastating consequences for the hoof. This is an excellent, highest quality professional knife that can enable you to do a superb natural trim quickly and efficiently.

F. DICK GRIP MASTER $23.95
F. DICK ASCOT $19.95

TRIMMER'S APRON AND HOOF STAND WORK CENTER

ESSENTIAL APPAREL & EQUIPMENT

(above) AANHCP practitioner Richard Drewry of Arkansas puts hoof cradle to work on Star Ridge Hoof Stand.

STAR RIDGE DELUXE TRIMMER'S APRON

This superior leather apron is the one I've used for over 25 years. Double-leather pads to protect your knees. Heavy duty belt and leg straps adjust to fit all sizes, men and women. Right knife pocket. Made in the USA.

$84.95

Adjustable leg straps render good fit for all sizes.

www.star-ridge.com

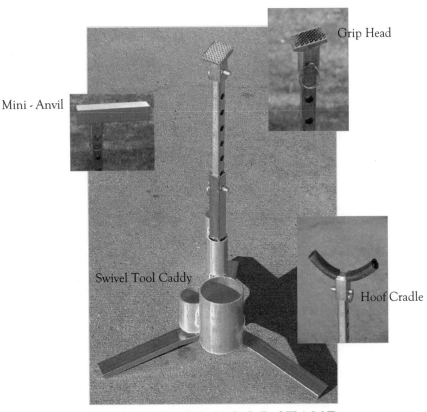

Mini - Anvil

Grip Head

Swivel Tool Caddy

Hoof Cradle

STAR RIDGE HOOF STAND
AND WORK CENTER

Here's the low down on this incredibly important piece of equipment that is indispensable to efficient professional natural hoof care: Zinc-plated, super strong steel core is lightweight for easy positioning under horse • Stand takes all the horse's weight — you concentrate on your work, instead of back or knee pain • Handy aluminum tool caddy swivels into optimal position for accessing your tools • Telescopic shaft is adjustable so stand height can be set for you and your horse's comfort and balance •

Work center breaks down into component parts, including three detachable legs, for compact storage and traveling • Comes with serrated grip head to secure horse's hoof, optional hoof cradle to support hoof and save your back and knees, and optional mini-anvil for modifying horse boots.

HOOF STAND $150.00*
HOOF CRADLE $14.95
MINI ANVIL $19.95

*Note: special shipping charges apply

STAR RIDGE CATALOGUE AND WEBSITE OFFERING NATURAL HOOF CARE SUPPLIES

FULL LINE OF TOOLS AND EQUIPMENT, EDUCATIONAL MATERIALS, HOOF CARE SUPPLIES

come visit our

Star Ridge Internet marketplace

www.star-ridge.com

shop securely on-line 24/7

Star Ridge mail order catalogue available by request and also with any order

Star Ridge Company

PO Box 2181

Harrison, AR 72601

AMERICAN ASSOCIATION OF NATURAL HOOF CARE PRACTITIONERS

SERVING THE WILD HORSE HOOF MODEL

The American Association of Natural Hoof Care Practitioners (AANHCP) was founded on the belief that genuine natural hoof care deserves a systematic approach to training and evidence of competence. The AANHCP Certification Program is the culmination of combined efforts and continuing dedication to this belief. Students are systematically instructed in an intense, hands-on, and stepwise program designed to build technical skills and theoretical knowledge. The clinicians, instructors and examiners of the Association are highly skilled and experienced practitioners who "mentor" each candidate to provide individual guidance while ensuring the successful graduate's competence. All certified graduates enjoy the full recognition and support of AANHCP officers, staff, and membership.

The AANHCP is a 501 (c) (3) non-profit organization, dedicated to the promotion and practice of humane and natural hoof care. The organization embraces fully the wild horse and its exemplary hooves for its natural hoof/horse care model.

The AANHCP motto: *"Cause no harm...respect the healing powers of nature"*

www.aanhcp.org